R. Gupta's®

Economic & Social Issues in India

By
DHRUB KUMAR
B.Com., M.A. (Mass Communication)
M.A. (Human Rights)

Ramesh Publishing House, New Delhi

Published by
O.P. Gupta *for* Ramesh Publishing House

Admin. Office
12-H, New Daryaganj Road, Opp. Officers' Mess,
New Delhi-110002 ① 23261567, 23275224, 23275124

E-mail: info@rameshpublishinghouse.com
Website: www.rameshpublishinghouse.com

Showroom
● Balaji Market, Nai Sarak, Delhi-6 ① 23253720, 23282525
● 4457, Nai Sarak, Delhi-6, ① 23918938

Book Code: R-289

1st Edition: 1804

ISBN: 978-93-87918-01-6

HSN Code: 49011010

Demographic Trends

POPULATION

India in World Population

First results of Census 2011 have been released. India now has a population of 1.21 billion, comprising 624 million males and 587 million females. This is an increase of 181 million people since the Census 2001 which is nearly equivalent to the population of Brazil.

India is a second country in the world after China to cross the one billion mark. It is now estimated that by 2050, India will most likely overtake China and become the most populous country on the earth with 19.4% population living here. The three most populous countries, viz., China, India and USA, together account for four of every ten persons of the world. At present, a little more than one out of every six persons in the world is from India.

Population of Ten Countries

S. No.	Country	Population (in millions)	Decadal change (in %)
1.	China	1,341.0	5.43
2.	India	1,210.2	17.64
3.	U.S.A.	308.7	7.26
4.	Indonesia	237.6	15.05
5.	Brazil	190.7	9.39
6.	Pakistan	184.8	24.78
7.	Bangladesh	164.4	16.76
8.	Nigeria	158.3	26.84
9.	Russian Fed.	140.4	−4.29
10.	Japan	128.1	1.1
	Other Countries	2844.7	15.43
	World	6908.7	12.97

DISTRIBUTION OF POPULATION

It is clear that India has a highly uneven pattern of population distribution. The percentage shares of population of the States and the Union Territories in the country show that Uttar Pradesh has the highest population followed by Maharashtra, Bihar, West Bengal and Andhra Pradesh.

U.P., Maharashtra, Bihar, West Bengal, Andhra Pradesh along with Tamil Nadu, Madhya Pradesh, Rajasthan, Karnataka and Gujarat, together account for about 76 per cent of the total population of the country. On the other hand, share of population is very small in the states like Jammu & Kashmir 1.04%, Arunachal Pradesh (0.11%) and Uttarakhand (0.83%) in spite of these states having fairly large geographical area.

Such an uneven spatial distribution of population in India suggests a close relationship between population and physical, socio-economic and historical factors. As far as the physical factors are concerned, it is clear that climate along with terrain and availability of water largely determine the pattern of the population distribution. Consequently, we observe that the North Indian Plains, deltas and Coastal Plains have higher proportion

India's Population At A Glance : 2011 (Final Data)

S.I. No.	State/UTs	Population	Sex Ratio	Density	Literacy Rate (%)	(%) Decadal Growth Rate (2001-2011)
1.	Jammu & Kashmir	1,25,41,302	889	124	67.2	23.6
2.	Himachal Pradesh	68,64,602	972	123	82.8	12.9
3.	Punjab	2,77,43,338	895	551	75.8	13.9
4.	Chandigarh	10,55,450	818	9258	86.0	17.2
5.	Uttarakhand	1,00,86,292	963	189	78.8	18.8
6.	Haryana	2,53,51,462	879	573	75.6	19.9
7.	Delhi	1,67,87,941	868	11320	86.2	21.2
8.	Rajasthan	6,85,48,437	928	200	66.1	21.3
9.	Uttar Pradesh	19,98,12,341	912	829	67.7	20.2
10.	Bihar	10,40,99,452	918	1106	61.8	25.4
11.	Sikkim	6,10,577	890	86	81.4	12.5
12.	Arunachal Pradesh	13,83,727	938	17	65.4	26.0
13.	Nagaland	19,78,502	931	119	79.6	−0.6
14.	Manipur	25,70,390	992	115	79.2	−18.6
15.	Mizoram	10,97,206	976	52	91.3	23.5
16.	Tripura	36,73,917	960	350	87.2	14.8
17.	Meghalaya	29,66,889	989	132	74.4	27.9
18.	Assam	3,12,05,576	958	398	72.2	17.1
19.	West Bengal	9,12,76,115	950	1028	76.3	13.8
20.	Jharkhand	3,29,88,134	948	414	66.4	22.4
21.	Odisha	4,19,74,218	979	270	72.9	14.0
22.	Chhattisgarh	2,55,45,198	991	189	70.3	22.6
23.	Madhya Pradesh	7,26,26,809	931	236	69.3	20.3
24.	Gujarat	6,04,39,692	919	308	78.0	19.3
25.	Daman & Diu	2,43,247	618	2191	87.1	53.8
26.	Dadra & Nagar Haveli	3,43,709	774	700	76.2	55.9
27.	Maharashtra	11,23,74,333	929	365	82.3	16.0
28.	Andhra Pradesh	8,45,80,777	993	308	67.0	11.6
29.	Karnataka	6,10,95,297	973	319	75.4	15.6
30.	Goa	14,58,545	973	394	88.7	8.2
31.	Lakshadweep	64,473	947	2149	91.8	6.3
32.	Kerala	3,34,06,061	1084	860	94.0	4.9
33.	Tamil Nadu	7,21,47,030	996	555	80.1	15.6
34.	Telangana	3,50,03,674	999	312	66.54	13.58
35.	Puducherry	12,47,953	1037	2547	85.8	28.1
36.	Andaman & Nicobar Islands	3,80,581	876	46	86.6	6.9
	India	**1,21,08,54,977**	**943**	**382**	**73.0**	**17.7**

of population than the interior districts of southern and central Indian States, Himalayas, some of the north eastern and the western states. However, development of irrigation (Rajasthan), availability of mineral and energy resources (Jharkhand) and development of transport network (Peninsular States) have resulted in moderate to high proportion of population in areas which were previously very thinly populated.

Density of Population

The density of population was increased in all states and union territories between 2001 and 2011. Among major states Bihar is the most densely populated state with a population density of 1106 in 2011. West Bengal is now the second highest density populated state pushing Kerala to the third place.

Population Growth : India 1901 to 2011

The population of India, at the turn of the twentieth century, was only around 238.4 million. This has increased by more than four times in a period of one hundred and ten years to reach 1210 million in 2011. Interestingly, the population of India grew by one and half times in the first half of the twentieth century, while in the later half it recorded a phenomenal three-fold increase. Following Table presents the population of India as recorded in each decadal Census since 1901. Some other indicators of growth rate such as decadal growth rate, change in decadal growth, average annual exponential growth rate and progressive growth rate over 1901 during each decade have also been presented in this Table.

Sex Ratio

Sex ratio is defined as the number of females per thousand males. It is 943 as per census 2011. It has been deteriorated over the decades. There has been slight improvement in this ratio during the last decade where it increased from 926 in 1991 to 933 in 2001. Kerala (1084) and Puducherry (1037) are

Population and its growth, India : 1901-2011

Census Years	Population	Decadal growth		Change in decadal growth		Average annual exponential growth rate (per cent)	Progressive growth rate over 1901 (per cent)
		Absolute	Per cent	Absolute	Per cent		
1901	23,83,96,327	-	-	-	-	-	
1911	25,20,93,390	1,36,97,063	5.75	-	-	0.56	5.75
1921	25,13,21,213	–7,72,177	(0.31)	–1,44,69,240	–6.05	–0.03	5.42
1931	27,89,77,238	2,76,56,025	11.00	2,84,28,202	11.31	1.04	17.02
1941	31,86,60,580	3,96,83,342	14.22	1,20,27,317	3.22	1.33	33.67
1951	36,10,88,090	4,24,27,510	13.31	27,44,168	–0.91	1.25	51.47
1961	43,92,34,771	7,81,46,681	21.64	3,57,19,171	8.33	1.96	84.25
1971	54,81,59,652	10,89,24,881	24.80	3,07,78,200	3.16	2.20	129.94
1981	68,33,29,097	13,51,69,445	24.66	2,62,44,564	–0.14	2.22	186.64
1991	84,64,21,039	16,30,91,942	23.87	2,79,22,497	17.12	2.16	255.05
2001	1,02,87,37,436	18,23,16,397	21.54	1,92,24,455	10.54	1.97	331.52
2011	1,21,01,93,422	18,14,55,986	17.64	–8,60,411	–0.47	1.64	407.64

the two states where sex ratio is in favour of females while, Haryana has the lowest sex ratio (879) in India.

Rural-Urban Composition

Of the total 1,210 million persons of the country (2011), 833 millions live in rural areas. It is slightly less than three-fourth (68.8 per cent) of the total population.

Urban Population: About 377 million people live in urban areas (2011). They constitute 31.2 per cent of the total population of the country. The rate of increase in urban population was slow up to 1941 when it was 13.9 per cent of total population from 10.8 per cent in 1901. It jumped to 17.3 per cent in 1951 and 27.8 per cent in 2001. Still India is one of the least urbanised countries in the world. Nearly 45 per cent of world population lives in urban centres. The urban population of India record an eleven-fold increase during the last 100 years.

India is the second most populated country in the world with nearly a fifth of the world's population. According to the

United Nations in July 2016, the population stood at 1,326,801,576.

India is projected to be the world's most populous country by 2022, surpassing the population of China. It is expected to become the first political entity in history to be home to more than 1.5 billion people by 2030, and its population is set to reach 1.7 billion by 2050. Its population growth rate is 1.2%, ranking 94th in the world in 2013. The Indian population reached the billion mark in 1998.

India has more than 50% of its population below the age of 25 and more than 65% below the age of 35. It is expected that, in 2020, the average age of an Indian will be 29 years, compared to 37 for China and 48 for Japan; and, by 2030, India's dependency ratio should be just over 0.4.

India has more than two thousand ethnic groups, and every major religion is represented, as are four major families of languages (Indo-European, Dravidian, Austroasiatic and Sino-Tibetan languages) as well as two language isolates (the Nihali language spoken in parts of Maharashtra and the Burushaski language spoken in parts of Jammu and Kashmir).

The sex ratio is 944 females for 1000 males (2016).

DEMOGRAPHIC TRENDS IN INDIA

India, as it is made clear, is the second most populous country in the world. Its total population crossed the mark of 121.2 crore by March 2011. Its population is currently increasing at the rate of 18.15 million per year. The average annual exponential growth rate of India's population is 1.76% in 2011. The salient demographic features or trends of India's population may be noted below.

1. Growth Rate of Population: The population of India grew at a slow rate prior to 1921. But its population has started growing at a fantastic rate of speed particularly after 1931. The average annual growth rate of India's population was 0.56% in 1911 and it reached the record height of 2.22% in 1981. However, it has come down to 1.9% in 2001 and further to 1.76% in 2011.

2. Uneven Distribution of Population: Population of India is not equally distributed among all the states. On the contrary, we find heavy concentration of people in some states rather than in others. It shows the ten most populous states in the country by rank.

As per 2011 Census, the state of Uttar Pradesh comes first with about 200 million people followed by Maharashtra with 112 million, Bihar with 103 million and so on. It is significant to note that these 10 states account for about 76.34% of the total population of India.

3. Sex Composition: Sex ratio is one of the characteristics of the population. It has an important bearing upon marriage rate, death rate, birth rate and even migration rate. The sex ratio is defined as "the number of females per 1,000 males." In any study of population, analysis of the sex composition or sex ratio plays a vital role.

The major trends in the sex ratio in the country from 1901 onwards are represented. According to the 2001 census figures, there are 933 females per 1000 males in India. This sex ratio recorded a slight increase from 933 in 2001 to 940 in 2011.

There are various reasons for this imbalance in the sex ratio. Factors such as female infanticide, neglect of female infants, early marriage, bad treatment and hard work of women, craving for male children, practice of dowry, dominant patriarchal values, etc. have been instrumental in reducing the number of females in India.

4. Age Composition: As per 2011 Census, the population of children [0-to-6 years] has declined by 5 million over the 2001 Census. In general, the proportion of population below

15 years is showing decline, whereas the proportion of elderly people in the country is increasing. This trend may continue in the time to come. The increase in the elderly population will impose a greater burden on the already outstretched health services in the country.

5. Life Expectancy: Life expectancy or expectation of life at a given age is the average number of years which a person of that age may expect to live, according to the mortality pattern prevalent in that country. Demographers consider it as one of the best indicators of a country's level of development and the overall health status of its population.

As far as India is concerned, in the year 1901, the life expectancy of males and females at birth was found to be 23.63 years and 23.93 years, respectively. These figures have increased respectively to 62.80 years and 63.80 years in 2000.

Trends in life expectancy show that people are living longer, and they have a right to a long life in good health, rather than one of pain and disability. Health policy makers need to recognise this changing demographic pattern, and plan for prevention and control of diseases associated with old age.

6. Density of Population: Density is also a major factor in the study of population. In the Indian context, density is defined as the average number of persons living per square kilometre. The trends of the density of population in the country from 1901 onwards are shown.

The density of population was found to be 77 in 1901 and 324 in 2001and it increased to the record mark of 382 in 2011. Delhi with 11297 persons per sq. km in 2011 is the most densely populated state in India.

Arunachal Pradesh with just 17 persons per sq. km is the least densely populated state. Comparatively, China has a density of population of 135 persons, whereas Canada, Australia and America have 3, 2, and 31 persons respectively.

7. Dependency Ratio: The proportion of persons above 65 years of age and children below 15 years of age are considered to be dependent on the economically productive age group [15 – 64 years]. 'The ratio of the combined age groups 0-14 years plus 65 years and above to the 15 – 65 years age group – is referred to as the total dependency ratio. The dependency ratio reflects the need for a society to provide for their younger and older population groups.

In terms of dependency ratio, we can also speak of young age dependency ratio [0-14 years]; and old age dependency ratio [65 years and more]. These ratios are, however, relatively crude, since they do not take into consideration elderly or young persons who are employed or working age persons who are unemployed. It shows the trends of dependency ratio in India.

8. Literacy Structure: As far as the literacy structure of the country is concerned, in 2011, on an average, around 74.04% people are found to be literate [82.14% males and 65.46% females]. Kerala is a state wherein we find the highest literacy rate, that is 93.91% and Bihar has the lowest one, that is, 63.82%.

Of the total literate people in India in 1991 [846.3 million], 56.7% had less than 3 years education, 23.8% 3-6 years education, 11% 7-1 years education, 6.8% 12-14 years education and 1.7% more than 14 years education. It is evident that we find a very limited number of people with college education. While the literacy rate for males rose from 75.26 to 82.14% marking a rise of 6.9% it increased by 11.8% for females to go from 53.67 to 65.46 per cent.

URBANIZATION IN INDIA

Urbanization and economic development have a strong positive correlation which is indicated by the fact that a country with a high per capita income is also likely to have a high degree of urbanization. The economic advantages provided by urban areas are many. Generally, the industrial, commercial and service sectors tend to concentrate in and around urban areas. These areas provide a larger concentration of material, labour, infrastructure and services related inputs on the one hand and also the market in the form of consumers, on the other. But the situation is different for India.

Urbanization in India: A brief Introduction

According to 2001 census, the urban population of the country was 286.11 million, living in 5161 towns, which constitutes 27.81% of the total country's population. However, the same as per 2011 census has risen to 377.16 million viz. 32.16% of the total country's population and at the same time number of towns has gone up to 7935. The rate of urban growth in the country is very high as compared to developed countries, and the large cities are becoming larger mostly due to continuous migration of population to these cities. India's current urban population exceeds the whole population of the United States, the world's third largest country. By 2050, over half of India's population is expected to be urban dwellers. This creates enormous pressure on existing urban infrastructure.

Over the years, there has been continuous concentration of population in class I towns. On the contrary the concentration of population in medium and small towns either fluctuated or declined. The graduation of number of urban centers from lower population size categories to class I cities has resulted top heavy structure of urban population in India indicating the tendency towards concentration in larger agglomerations. Urban agglomeration is a continuous urban spread constituting a town and its adjoining urban out growths (OGs) or two or more physical contiguous town together and any adjoining urban out growths of such towns. Examples of out growths are railway colonies, university campus, port area, military campus, etc. that may come up near a statutory town or city.

Therefore India's urbanization is often termed as over-urbanization, pseudo-urbanization. The large population size is leading to virtual collapse in the urban services and followed by basic problems in the field of housing, slum, water, infrastructure, quality of life, etc.

Urbanization in India began to accelerate after independence, due to the country's adoption of a mixed economy, which gave rise to the development of the private sector. Urbanisation is taking place at a faster rate in India. Population residing in urban areas in India, according to 1901 census, was 11.4%. This count increased to 28.53% according to 2001 census, and crossing 30% as per 2011 census, standing at 31.16%. According to a survey by UN State of the World Population report in 2007, by 2030, 40.76% of country's population is expected to reside in urban areas. As per World Bank, India, along with China, Indonesia, Nigeria, and the United States, will lead the world's urban population surge by 2050.

Mumbai saw large scale rural-urban migration in the 20th century. Mumbai accommodates 12.5 million people, and is the largest metropolis by population in India, followed by Delhi with 11 million inhabitants. Witnessing the fastest rate of urbanisation in the world, as per 2011 census, Delhi's population rose by 4.1%, Mumbai's by 3.1% and Kolkata's by 2% as per 2011 census compared to 2001 census.

The contribution of the agricultural sector to the GDP of India started to decline and the percentage contribution from secondary sector increased. The period after 1941, withnessed rapid growth of four metropolitan cities in India, which were Kolkata, Delhi, Mumbai, and Chennai. The nation's economy saw a rise due to industrial revolution and the invention of new technologies increased the standard of living of people living in urban areas. The growth of public sector resulted in development of public transport, roads, water supply, electricity, and hence the infrastructure of urban areas.

The global experience has been that as countries develop, rural-to-urban migration accelerates, and decelerates only when the urbanization level is very high – usually well over 50%. In India, however, migration began decelerating when urbanization was below 25%, and the trend continued over three Censuses – 1991, 2001, and 2011.

The Connection between Urbanization and Growth

Global and Indian experiences (across states) show that productivity and growth are strongly correlated with urbanization. Given that urban productivity is much higher than rural, a shift in labour force from rural to urban activities is a key source of growth. International evidence also suggests that allowing existing urban agglomerations to grow may be a more efficient strategy than creating new urban areas.

The theory in favour of urbanization is also quite compelling. There are three economic explanations for the link between urbanization and productivity. First, it deepens local product and labour markets, leading to greater competition and efficiency. Second, it permits more specialization and division of labour, and hence, productivity improvements. Third, it enables greater learning at all levels of workers, and better technology adoption and innovation. Also, urbanization lowers transaction and logistical costs, and permits greater economies of scale and scope, all of which contribute to growth.

Urbanization is also strongly linked to rapid improvements in social indicators, such as health and education, as economies of scale and scope are more pronounced in the supply of these services than even in industry. Health and education indicators are persistently higher in urban areas relative to rural, across and within Indian states.

MIGRATION IN INDIA

Migration is an important feature of human civilization. It reflects, human endeavour to survive in the most testing conditions both natural and man made. Migration in India is in existence historically, but, in the context of Neo Liberal Globalisation assumes special significance, for Trade Unions and Civil Society.

As a consequence of the neo-liberal policies followed by the successive governments, there are serious income disparities, agrarian distress, inadequate employment generation, vast growth of informal economy and the resultant migration from rural areas to urban, urban to urban and backward to comparatively advanced regions in the most appalling conditions. Under the pressure from the International Finance Capital, Governments both Central & Provincial are further de-regulating the labour markets and further enlargement of the informal sector. In the given context Migrant Labour poses a serious threat and challenge to Civil Society in general and Trade Unions in particular.

Causes of Migration

Migration in India is mostly influenced by Social Structures and pattern of development. The development policies by all the governments since Independence have accelerated the process of migration. Uneven development is the main cause of Migration. Added to it, are the disparities, Inter regional and amongst different socio-economic classes. The landless poor who mostly belong to lower castes, indigenous communities and economically backward regions constitute the major portion of Migrants. In the very large Tribal Regions of India intrusion of outsiders, settlements by the outsiders displacing the local tribal people and deforestation also played a major role in Migration.

Indian agriculture became non remunerative, taking the lives of 100,000 peasants during the period from 1996 to 2003, *i.e.,* a suicide of an Indian peasant every 45 minutes. Hence, the rural people from the downtrodden and backward communities and backward regions such as Bihar, Orissa, Uttar Pradesh travel to far distances seeking employment at the lowest rungs in construction of roads, irrigation projects, commercial and residential complexes, in short, building the "Shining" India.

The pull factors of higher wages caused external migration to the middle-east countries by skilled and semi-skilled workers. Migration of professionals such as Engineers, Medical Practitioners, Teachers and Managers to developed countries constitute a small fraction of the total migrants.

Magnitude of Migration

Migration in India is predominantly short distance with around 60% of migrants changing their residences within their district of birth and 20% within their state (province), while the rest move across the state boundaries. The total migrants as per the census of 1971 are 167 million persons, 1981 census 213 millions, 1991 census 232 million and 2001 census 315 millions. As per the census of the year 1991, nearly 20 million people migrated to other states seeking livelihood. Within a decade, the number of inter state migration doubled to 41,166,265 persons as per the census figures of 2001. According to census 2011, about 45 crore (450 million) Indians in India are migrants— now settled in a place different from their previous residence. Most of the migrats are females. It is estimated that, the present strength of inter state migrants is around 80 million persons of which, 40 million are in the construction industry, 20 million as domestic workers, 2 million as sex workers, 5 million as call girls and somewhere from half a million to 12 million in the illegal mines otherwise called as "small scale mines".

It is estimated that at present around five and a half million Indians are working in the oil exporting countries of middle-east and another 2 millions in the developed world.

92% of the domestic workers are women, girls and children and 20% of these females are under 14 years of age, as per a study conducted by an organization called "Social Alert". There is a perceptible phenomenon in this migration, that is, the tremendous increase of women workers migrating either individually or in groups to find work. They are travelling very long distances even for short-term employment, in the absence of any prospect or promise of employment, still they are migrating. This is a disturbing trend, as in the event of not getting employment, they end up as victims of sexual abuse. Even if they get employment, they have to work under inhuman conditions.

2

Gender Issues

Our Constitution gives equal rights to both men and women in every field. Today, women enjoy voting rights, right to inheritance and property. In fact, the Constitution lay down that the government should promote with special care the interests of the weaker sections of the people. Several laws have been passed since independence to promote the interests of women. These laws relate to marriage, inheritance of property, divorce, dowry, etc. In 1976, the Equal Remuneration Act was passed to provide for equal remuneration to men and women for similar work.

Recently, the government has started a scheme for the protection of girl child. The scheme is called *'Ladli'*, in which an amount is set aside at the time of the birth of a girl child which she gets when she completes eighteen years of age. This amount is then used for the education or the marriage of the child. Similarly, there is another scheme called 'Jaccha Baccha scheme'. Under this scheme, the state governments take care of the birth of the child and all expenditure related to medical assistance for the upbringing of the child.

However, in spite of these provisions, we find a lot of discrimination against women.

In India females are discriminated in various fields like health, education and jobs. The girls carry the liability of dowry on their head, and they have to leave their parents home after marriage. Besides, in order to safeguard their old age parents prefer to have male offspring. Many female babies are aborted, abandoned, deliberately neglected and underfed simply as they are girls. This is worst in the state of Rajasthan. But now there is a great change in this direction. In some states like Haryana where girl child ratio is very low, the government has taken out many schemes to promote education of girls. Reservation of jobs for women and even six months maternity leave is provided to them besides many others.

The World Bank Document, "A New Agenda for Women's Health and Nutrition" estimates that in developing countries, 450 million adult women have their development problems due to lack of protein input during their childhood. In many communities, women and girls get less food or poor quality food compared to men and boys. When they are ill, they get less attention or receive some attention only when the disease becomes extremely serious. There is ample evidence at the global level of disparity in health status between men and women and their access to medical services.

In a majority of the countries, literacy rate for women is significantly lower than that for men. In 66 countries, the gap between the male and female literacy rates is estimated to be larger than 10 percentage points and in 40 countries, it is larger than 20 percentage points in the age group of 6-11, which corresponds to primary level education. According to 2011 census, there is a gap of 16.7 per cent between the literacy rate of men and women *i.e.,* men's literacy rate is 82.14 per cent compared to women's literacy rate that stands at 65.46 per cent. About 24.5 per cent (85 million) of the girls in the world are estimated to be out of school compared to 16.4 per cent (60 million) boys.

In most Indian families, a girl child is least welcome although in India women were respected from the early ages. Even though there are growing instances of girls excelling in education, tradition, custom, and social practices place greater value on sons than on daughters, who are often viewed as an economic burden. This attitude of the society also stands in the way of the girl child being able to achieve her full potential. A recent report on the girl child makes the following observations: *"Girls are the world's most squandered gift. They are precious human beings with enormous potential, but across the world, they are generally the last to have their basic needs met and first to have their basic rights denied."*

The need of girls for food clothing, shelter, healthcare, education, nurture, and time to play often goes unmet. Their rights to safety, freedom from harassment and exploitation, as also their rights to grow, develop and blossom, are denied.

Prejudice against the girl child becomes clearer and sharper from the data in sex ratio in the age group 0-6 years. In the Census, 2011 this ratio has been recorded as 914, down from 927 in the Census, 2001. The child sex ratio has steadily declined from 976 in 1961 to 914 in 2011.

Dowry System

The practice of dowry is one of the worst social practices that has affected our culture. In independent India, one of the landmark legislations is the passing of the Dowry Prohibition Act in 1961 by the Government of India. Despite the fact that the practice of both giving as well as accepting dowry is banned by law and such acts are punishable offences, the system is so thoroughly imbedded in our culture that it continues unabated. Whether it is rural or urban India, the blatant violation of this law is rampant. Not only dowry deaths, even most of the acts of domestic violence against women including psychological as well as physical torture are related to matters of dowry. Some of the very basic human rights of women are violated almost every day. Sometimes it is heartening to see some girls stand firm to assert their rights against dowry. But there is an urgent need to strengthen such hands by taking some concrete as well as comprehensive social, economic, political and administrative measures in order to free Indian society of this disease.

Female Infanticide and Female Feticide

Female Feticide is the act of aborting a baby because it is of a female gender. Sex selective abortion is a big problem in India. The number of abortions by medical professionals have increased so much that today it has become a industry even though it is punishable by law.

Female Infanticide is the act of killing a female girl either new-born or within the first few years of life. It could be actively, murdering through suffocation, poisoning etc. Such acts can also be passive, where no interest is taken with regards to feeding or towards her general health in affect total neglect.

The traditions in India are deeply-rooted. The sons are who inherit and perpetuate the surname. And all that it entails, they will take care of their parents when old age takes hold. The sons take responsibility of funeral arrangements as this task is not deemed appropriate for females.

Marriages

The majority of marriages in India are arranged. This practice is legal in India, however, it is forbidden to marry until the ages of 21 years old for men and 18 years old for women. In spite of this fact many marriages are between couples below the age guidelines and they are generally widely celebrated by the families involved. According to UNICEF 56% of cases involving early marriage happen in rural India and a 29% in the urban area. The population's beliefs consider it to be beneficial for the daughter because she will get use to the arrangement easier and adapt quicker into her husband's family.

After the wedding the wife lives with her husband's family. From that moment the only wish is having a boy. Conceiving a male child would gain the recognition of the family and hailed as an achievement for the wife. If she gave birth to a girl, in some cases, the husband's family can blame her resulting in mistreatment which can lead to inflicting physical and psychological damage. They can instruct her to commit suicide because of the strong beliefs which surround female birth.

Education

Since the new law in 2010, the education is free for every child between the age of 6 to 14 years old, however, it is not compulsory; this means the children have the right to education but not the obligation to go. A lot of girls do not go to the school because their parents would rather send their sons who will be the future for them. The girls have to help at home doing housework.

Trafficking, Slavery

Thousands of girls are kidnapped every year in India for trafficking, slavery, prostitution and so on.

Paradoxically there are not enough girls or women in India for getting married; in some states. So as a result of that, a new practice takes place in India; kidnapping of women or girls from other states or countries like Bangladesh or Nepal. The families pay a fortune for a woman or girl who will belong to them forever. The threat received from the family who has purchased the child is even worse than normally; the kidnapped woman does not have any rights.

Other women are convinced working in another state or in the capital would result in a better lifestyle, however, in reality the circumstances they find themselves in are worse and they are often left feeling cheated. They are forced to work from dusk until dawn without a salary and in addition they live in indescribable conditions. As a result some of them are dedicated to prostitution.

India is a country of enormous complexity and its problems are just as complex as the country.

In 2016, India ranked 130 out of 146 in the Gender Inequality Index released by the UNDP. It is evident that a stronger turn in political discourse is required, taking into consideration both public and private spaces. The normalization of intra-household violence is a huge detriment to the welfare of women. Crimes against women have doubled in the period between 1991 and 2011. NFHS data reports that 37 per cent of married women in India have experienced physical or sexual violence by a spouse while 40 per cent have experienced physical, sexual or emotional violence by a spouse. While current policy discourse recommends employment as a form of empowerment for women, data presents a disturbing correlation between female participation in labour force and their exposure to domestic violence. The NFHS-3 reports that women employed at any time in the past 12 months have a much higher prevalence of violence (39-40 per cent) than women who were not employed (29 per cent). The researchers advocate a multi-faceted approach to women's empowerment beyond mere labour force participation, taking into consideration extra-household bargaining power.

Gender inequality extends across various facets of society. Political participation is often perceived as a key factor to rectify this situation. However, gender bias extends to electoral politics and representative governance as well. The relative difference between male and female voters is the key to understanding gender inequality in politics. While the female voter turnout has been steadily increasing, the number of female candidates fielded by parties has not increased. More women contest as independents, which does not provide the cover for extraneous costs otherwise available when they are part of a political party.

Financial Inclusion

In the developing world, women have traditionally been the focus of efforts of financial inclusion. They have proved to be better borrowers (40 per cent of Grameen Bank's clients were women in 1983. By 2000, the number had risen to 90 per cent) – largely attributed to the fact that they are less mobile as compared to men and more susceptible to peer pressure. However, institutions in microfinance are exposed to the trade-off between market growth and social development since having more female clients lead to the inevitable drip-down of social incentives. As an attempt to overcome this hurdle, a larger role can be played by donors with a gender driven agenda, for the financial inclusion sector will drive the idea further.

Gendered contextualisation of products is highly necessary for microfinance institutions (MFIs) – men and women do not ascribe to choices in a similar fashion. Trends emerging from prior research indicates that when health insurance coverage was held under the MFI sector, by both men and women, women benefited from the coverage only so far as they were the holders and not using spousal status (if their husbands were insured). Thus healthcare seeking behaviour becomes an important factor to be considered in insurance coverage under the MFIs.

The JAM trinity – Jan Dhan Yojana, Aadhar, Mobile – can be used to improve financial inclusion from a gender perspective as well. The metrics to consider would be the number of Jan Dhan accounts held by women, percentage of women holding Aadhar cards and access to mobile connectivity for women.

Health

In terms of healthcare focusing on women, the Janani Suraksha Yojana (JSY) and National Health Mission are vital to the policy landscape. The JSY has improved maternal healthcare in India through the emphasis on institutional deliveries. Increase of 22 per cent in deliveries in government hospitals, was mirrored by an 8 per cent decline in childbirth at private hospitals and a 16 per cent decline in childbirth at home. The National Health Mission's ASHA led to greater awareness and education of pregnant women as well as an increase in institutional maternal and neonatal healthcare. Improved infrastructure for maternal and neo-natal has been observed in community hospitals, in addition to the introduction of ambulance services.

A gendered increase in seek care is observed with a large 13 per cent increase in the number of women who report being sick in the last 15 days, driving the overall reportage. Further, an eight per cent decline in rural women seeking private healthcare, has been reported, while a 58 per cent increase in women seeking hospitalization has been reported. Further disaggregated, the data shows a 75.7 per cent increase for rural women seeking healthcare. The overall increase in usage of public hospitals is almost entirely driven by rural women who saw an increase of 24.6 per cent in utilisation of public hospitals over the 10 years (2004-2014). Our results show that the JSY had a significant, positive impact on overall hospitalisation of women in India. It increased the probability of a woman being hospitalised by approximately 1.3 per cent.

The healthcare sector in India has largely focused on maternal healthcare for women. The importance of research on mental health has been ignored in policy discourse. The significant relationship that mental health bears on violence has also been explored in further research. Every fifth suicide in India is that of a housewife (18 per cent overall) – the reportage of suicide deaths has been most consistent among housewives as a category, than other categories. India is the country with the largest rate of female deaths due to 'intentional violence'.

Our work on childhood violence shows that girls are twice more likely to face sexual violence than boys before the age of 18. Larger the population of educated females in the country, lesser is the incidence of childhood violence at home – including lesser violent discipline, physical punishment as well as psychological aggression. Additionally, the lifetime experience of sexual violence by girls is strongly correlated with the adolescent fertility rate in a country. Further, a strong relationship is observed between female experience of sexual violence and female labour force participation within a country. The results show that the higher the labour force participation by women in a country, the higher is the incidence of sexual violence against them. This could be indicative of adverse working conditions within labour markets, and the difficulty of access to labour markets by young women in a country.

Child Labour

Child labour typically means the employment of children in any manual work with or without payment. Child labour is not only limited to India, it happens to be a global phenomenon.

As far as India is concerned, the issue is a vicious one as children in India have historically been helping parents at their farms and other primitive activities. Another concept that needs explanation is the concept of bonded labour which is one of the most common forms of exploitation. Bonded labour means the children are forced to work as employees in lieu of payment of debt by the parents due to exorbitant rates of repayment of interest.

Also associated with the concept of bonded labour is the concept of urban child labour wherein the labourers are the street children who spend most of their childhood on the streets.

UNICEF has categorized child work into three categories:

1. Within the family- Children are engaged in domestic household tasks without pay.

2. Outside the family- Example- commercial shops in restaurants and jobs, prostitution etc.

3. Within the family but outside the home- Example- agricultural labourers, domestic maids, migrant labourers etc.

Child labour is caused by several factors. Some of them include:

1. Poverty: Children who come from poor families may be forced to work to support their siblings and parents or supplement the household income when expenses are more than the parents' earnings. It is a huge problem especially in developing countries where parents are unable to generate income due to the lack of employment opportunities or education. Children can be found employed in mines or hawking in the streets to earn money that is used to provide basic necessities such as food and clothing for the family. Children may also be employed in factories to generate income for the family instead of attending school. Such a practice is a common phenomenon in poverty-stricken regions with large factories set up by international companies.

2. Illiteracy: A society with many educated people understands the importance of going to school and pursuing dreams. Children have the ability and time to become whatever they aspire to be. Illiteracy, on the other hand, makes it difficult for many people to understand the importance of education. Illiterate people view education as a preserve of the privileged in the society. They will therefore not provide support to children so that they can go to school and build solid foundations for future success. The same view of life is seen among illiterate parents who prioritize children contributing to the upkeep of the family over going to school.

3. High cost of education: Quality education is expensive. To many parents who live in abject poverty, priority is given to providing food for the family because education is too expensive to afford especially when there are many children to pay school fees for. Instead of letting children stay at home because there is lack of money to send them to school, parents opt to have them working as unskilled labourers to help support the family. Some parents can also only afford basic education which means that children will be forced to look for work since they cannot pursue their education further.

4. Low Aspiration: It is important for parents and children to understand that they can work hard and make something great of themselves. Low aspirations by parents and children is a major cause of child labour because in such a situation, being employed in a local factory, or selling grocery in the streets is the normal way of life. To these types of children and parents, success only belongs to a certain region or group of people. They do not aspire to become professionals in the society or great entrepreneurs. It is a mindset that forms the very foundation of child labour.

5. Huge demand for unskilled labourers: The demand for unskilled labourers is another cause of child labour. Children are mostly unskilled and provide a cheap source of labour, making them an attractive option for many greedy employers. Child labour, by virtue of being cheap, increases the margin of profits for such entrepreneurs whose only objective is profit maximization even if it comes at the expense of ethics and good business practices. These types of employers can also force children to work under unfavourable conditions through manipulation or blatant threats.

6. Early Marriages: Marrying at an early age is a major contributing factor to overpopulation. Young parents are able to sire a lot of children because they remain fertile for a long time. Having many children with little or no resources to support them leads to child labour. Older children are forced to work in order to help their parents support the family.

Child labour has several negative impacts. Some of them include:

1. Loss of Quality childhood: It is important for human beings to enjoy every stage of their development. A child should play with friends and make memories for a lifetime. Youths should explore life and form strong foundations that would define their adult lives. Child labour, therefore, leads to loss of quality childhood as children will be deprived of the opportunity to enjoy the amazing experiences that come with being young. Children are often encouraged to play because it helps in their growth and development. A child forced to work will miss many of the good things associated with childhood.

2. Health issues: Child labour can also lead to health complications due to undernourishment and poor working conditions. It is highly unlikely that people who employ children also have the moral capacity to ensure that they have good working conditions. Working in places such as mines and badly conditioned factories may result in lifetime health issues for children employed to work in these places. A child assigned physically demanding duties may suffer physical trauma that may scar him or her for life.

3. Illiteracy: Children that are employed do not have the time to go to school. They spend a lot of time in their workstations as the days and years go by. The lack of education and illiteracy makes them individuals with limited opportunities as far as employment is concerned. Education also prepares a person for several challenges in the society and without it, one may turn out to lack the basic skills required to overcome many of life's problems. An individual who has gone to school may be aware of how to approach certain situations in life without resorting to brute force. An illiterate person, on the other hand, considers force to be the only answer to nearly all of the challenges experienced.

4. Mental trauma: It is not a pleasant experience to be kept working as a child while your age-mates are out playing and going to school. Children also lack the ability to shield themselves from most of the challenges that occur in the workplace. Issues such as bullying, sexual exploitation, and unfavourable working hours may result in mental trauma in these children. They will find it hard to forget the past and may become societal misfits because of bad childhood experiences. Child labour may also result in the lack of emotional growth and thus insensitivity.

Solutions

Every child born has the right to have dreams and pursue those dreams. Even though the realization of some of these aspirations may be limited by several challenges, it is still possible to overcome them and achieve the highest levels of success.

There is need to involve various stakeholders to realize this objective. These are some of the ways in which the problem of child labour can be addressed:

1. Awareness: Creating awareness about the illegality of child labour can also help in stemming the practice. Parents should be made aware that sending their children to work has legal ramifications and the law would take its course if they are found to be aiding and abetting this vice. It is the ignorance among many parents and members of the society that makes them participate in child labour practices. Conducting a campaign to create awareness about its harmful effects would eliminate the practice. The government, together with non-governmental organizations and the civil society, can create a strategy to make such an initiative a success.

2. Moral Polishing: Child labour should not be entertained at all. It is legally and morally wrong. Children should not be allowed to provide labour at the expense of getting an education and enjoying their childhood. Factory owners, shopkeepers, and industries among others should not employ children. The society should be educated on the negative impacts of child labour so that it becomes an issue that is frowned upon whenever it occurs. This type of moral polishing would act as a deterrent to people who intend to employ children and use them as a source of cheap labour. Many of the ills that go on in the society do so because people turn a blind eye or fail to consider their moral impacts. With this kind of approach, cases of child labour will greatly fall among our communities.

3. Free education: Free education holds the key to eliminating child labour. Parents that do not have money for school fees can use this as an opportunity to provide their children with education. It has already proved to be a success in many places around the globe and with more effort, the cases of child labour will greatly reduce. Mid-day meals schemes can also be used as a motivating factor for children whose parents can barely afford a meal to learn. Even if they will be attending school because of the free meals, they will still be able to learn and create a good education foundation for themselves.

4. Empowerment of poor people: Poor people are the most affected by child labour. The poor living standards and financial constraints sometimes make them unwilling participants in this vice. Empowering poor people through knowledge and income generating projects would go a long way in reducing cases of child labour. Parental literacy also plays an important role in ensuring that the rights of children are upheld, and minors are not used as a source of labour. Empowering parents with this kind of knowledge can create a positive change in the society and encourage the shunning of child labour practices in communities.

Child Labour Laws in India

The problem of child labour in India had become an issue of concern for one and all post Independence. The drafting committee of the Indian constitution wanted to formulate laws on their own without seeking recommendations from other countries with this regard. Since, India had been under the exploitative regime of the British, it only made sense that the provisions were devised keeping in mind the forms of exploitative labour that India had witnessed under the atrocious regime.

The primitive laws that were formed to prohibit child labour in India were when the Employment of Children Act, 1938 was passed. But this act failed miserably because it failed to address the cause of poverty as it is poverty that drives children into forced labour.

The Indian Parliament time and again has passed Laws and Acts to ensure the protection of children from child labour. The Fundamental Rights enshrined in our Constitution prohibit child labour below the age of 14 years in any factory or mine or engaged in any hazardous employment under Article 24. Apart from this, it is also provided under Article 21-A that State shall provide infrastructure and resources for free and compulsory education for children of the age six upto 14 years.

There exists a set of laws which under the Constitution govern the protection of children from child labour. The Factories Act of 1948 prevents the employment of children below 14 years in any factory. The Mines Act of 1952 prohibits the employment of children below the age of 18 years. The Child Labour (Prohibition and Regulation) Act of 1986 prevents the employment of children below the age of 14 years in life-threatening occupations identified in a list by the law. Further, the Juvenile Justice (Care and Protection) of children Act of 2000 made the employment of children a punishable offence.

Ironically, despite this huge array of laws, there seems to be no improvement in the working conditions of the child labourers and employers also freely flout the provisions of the Act covering the prohibition of child labour.

It needs to be highlighted that the violation of these provisions means a deprivation of the basic human rights and demeaning the childhood of the children. The law also isn't very clear as to how where can the children work. The Acts covers only 10 per cent of the total working children and thus not applicable to the unorganized sector. The Act also exempts the family of the child labourer from its purview if they all are working with the same employee as that of the child. Although the Act prohibits the employment of children in certain hazardous industries and processes, it does not define what constitutes hazardous work. It only provides a list of hazardous occupations.

Role of International Organizations in Fighting Child Labour

The International Programme on the Elimination of Child Labour (IPECL) was launched under the programme of International Labour Organization in 1991 to work towards the elimination of child labour by creating awareness about child labour as a global issue using national platforms. India was among the first nations to sign the MoU with IPECL to help in combating child labour.

National Labour Project (NCLP) is one of the major programmes implemented throughout the country under which seven child labour projects were set up in the year 1988. Rehabilitation is also one of the major policies that have been adopted by the government of India to reduce the incidence of child labour in India.

Unfortunately, the concerned authorities are unable to combat the rising cases of child labour because of varied reasons. They fail to establish the correct age if the child due to the lack of birth proofs and at times fake proofs. Not much is being done on creating the awareness among people. Even if efforts are being made, they cater to a limited population and the endurance among the authorities is not visible. A lot of laxity can be observed during the conduct of awareness programmes. There is still a need to address the issue on global platforms time and again with stringent policy framework in place.

4

Social Justice & Positive Discrimination

Social justice is the idea that all members of society deserve an equal footing in terms of opportunities political rights, and distribution of wealth and privilege so that they can lead fulfilling lives and realize their potential in the community.

Social justice issues are devided into two groups which often overlap. The inter-social treatment issues, such as sexism, racism, ageism, and homophobia, etc; and unequal government policies, such as environmental or tax policies that disadvantage the poor, legal segregation (racism), death penalty. Unequal access to education. Social justice institutions work to provide and expand education, health care, public services, and labour rights, and strive to ensure equitable distribution of wealth and opportunity through progressive taxation and market regulation.

Social justice is ideally justice in terms of the distribution of wealth, opportunities, and privilege within a society.

Social justice implies several sound and eminently desirable concepts enunciated for the good of society in general, and of course, it covers fair play for every section, especially the weaker groups in the population.

The Concept of Social Justice

The term social justice was first used in 1840 by a Sicilian priest, Luigi Taparelli d'Azeglio, and given prominence by Antonio Rosmini Serbati in La Costitutione Civile Secondo la Giustizia Sociale in 1848. It has also enjoyed a significant audience among theorists since John Rawls book. A Theory of Justice has used it as a pseudonym of distributive justice.

The concept of social justice is a revolutionary concept which provides meaning and significance to life and makes the rule of law dynamic. When Indian society seeks to meet the challenge of socio-economic inequality by its legislation and with the assistance of the rule of law, it seeks to achieve economic justice without any violent conflict. The ideal of a welfare state postulates unceasing pursuit of the doctrine of social justice. That is the significance and importance of the concept of social justice in the Indian context of today.

The idea of welfare state is that the claims of social justice must be treated as cardinal and paramount. Social justice is not a blind concept or a preposterous dogma. It seeks to do justice to all the citizen of the state. Democracy, therefore, must not show excess of valour by imposing unnecessary legislative regulations and prohibitions, in the same way as they must not show timidity in attacking the problem of inequality by refusing the past the necessary and reasonable regulatory measures at all. Constant endeavour has to be made to sustain individual freedom and liberty and subject them to reasonable regulation and control as to achieve socio-economic justice. Social justice must be achieved by adopting necessary and reasonable measures. That, shortly stated, is the concept of social justice and its implications. Citizens zealous of their individual freedom and liberty must co-operate with democracy which seeks to regulate freedom and liberty in the interest of social good, but they must be able to resist the imposition of any restraints on individual liberty and freedom which are not rationally and reasonably required in the interests of public good, in a democratic way. It is in the light of these difficult times that the rule of law comes into operation and the judges have to play their role without fear or favour, uninfluenced by any considerations of dogma or isms. The term social justice is a blanket term so as to include both social justice and economic justice.

The Problems of The Poor in India

This vice of social inequality assumes a particularly reprehensible form in relation to the backward classes and communities which are treated as untouchable; and so the problem of social justice is as urgent and important in India as is the problem of economic justice. Equality of opportunity to all the citizens to develop their individual personalities and to participate in the pleasures and happiness of life is the goal of economic justice. The concept of social justice thus takes within its sweep the objectives of removing all inequalities and affording equal opportunities to all citizens in social affairs as well as economic activities. The problem of poverty and unequal distribution of wealth may be confined to the bigger cities and towns in India but the problem accentuated by the vice of social inequality existing in a gross form prevails in all of our villages. For instance, the harijans constitute a large class of landless labourers who are treated as untouchables by the rest of the community, who have no house to live in, generally no clothes to wear, who do not get food to eat & sometimes even decent drinking water is beyond their reach. The poor also have no access to legal assistance. Poor people are vulnerable to injustice. Poverty fosters frustration, ill feeling and a brooding sense of injustice.

Democracy realizes that this problem which concerns a large number of citizens cannot be successfully met unless law is used wisely to restore balance to the economic structure and to remove the causes of economic inequality.

The Constitution of India and Social Justice

The Constitution of India has solemnly promised to all its citizens justices-social, economic and political; liberty of thought expression, belief, faith and worship; equality of status and of opportunity; and to promote among the all fraternity assuring the dignity of the individual and the unity of the nation. The Constitution has attempted to attune the apparently conflicting claims of socio-economic justice and of individual liberty and fundamental rights by putting some relevant provisions.

Article 19 enshrines the fundamental rights of the citizens of this country. The seven sub-clauses of Article 19(1) guarantee the citizens seven different kinds of freedom and recognize them as their fundamental rights. Article 19 considered as a whole furnishes a very satisfactory and rational basis for adjusting the claims of individual rights of freedom and the claims of public good.

Articles 23 and 24 provide for fundamental rights against exploitation. Article 24, in particular, prohibits an employer from employing a child below the age of 14 years in any factory or mine or in any other hazardous employment. Article 31 makes a specific provision in regard to the fundamental right to property and deals with the vexed problem of compulsory acquisition of property.

Article 38 requires that the state should make an effort to promote the welfare of the people by securing and protecting as effectively as it may a social order in which justice social, economic and political shall inform all the institutions of national life. Article 39 clause (a) says that the State shall secure that the operation of the legal system promotes justice, on a basis of equal opportunity, and shall, in particular provide free legal aid, by suitable legislation or schemes, or in any other way, to ensure that opportunities for securing justice are not denied to any citizen by reason of economic or other disabilities.

Article 41 recognizes every citizen's right to work, to education & to public assistance in cases of unemployment, old age, sickness & disablement and in other cases of undeserved want. Article 42 stresses the importance of securing just and humane conditions of work & for maternity relief. Article 43 holds before the working population the ideal of the living wage and Article 46 emphasizes the importance of the promotion of educational and economic interests of schedule castes, schedule tribes and other weaker sections.

The social problem presented by the existence of a very large number of citizens who are treated as untouchables has received the special attention of the Constitution as Article 15 (1) prohibits discrimination on the grounds of religion, race, caste, sex, or place of birth. The state would be entitled to make special provisions for women and children, and for advancement of any social and educationally backward classes of citizens, or for the SC/STs. A similar exception is provided to the principle of equality of opportunity prescribed by Article 16 (1) in as much as Article 16 (4) allows the state to make provision for the resolution of appointments or posts in favour of any backward class of citizens which, in the opinion of the state, is not adequately represented in the services under the state. Article 17 proclaims that untouchability has been abolished and forbids its practice in any form & it provides that the enforcement of untouchability shall be an offence punishable in accordance with law. This is the code of provisions dealing with the problem of achieving the ideal of socio-economic justice in this country which has been prescribed by the Constitution of India.

Positive Discrimination in India

Positive discrimination means treating one person more favourably than another on the ground of that individual caste, race, age, marital status or sexual orientation. While in this situation, the individual's characteristic is being taken into account to benefit that individual, typically because that individual belongs to a group that is often treated unfairly or under-represented in the workforce, this is nevertheless unlawful discrimination.

The term 'positive discrimination' is sometimes used to refer to 'positive measure' or 'special measures'. Special measures aim to foster greater equality by supporting groups of people who face, or have faced, entrenched discrimination so they can have similar access to opportunities as others in the community.

The favours provided by the State to the Scheduled Castes, Scheduled Tribes and Other Backwards Castes can be broadly categorised in three principle kinds as mentioned below :

1. Reservations

2. Financial Assistance

3. Anti-disability Legislation

1. Reservations : Reservation is a compendium form. Reservation epitomises higher educational admissions, State employment and political representations. The reservation of the SCs, STs and OBCs are directed towards constituting a democratic government as the participative government. In a process of administration, they ensure an adequate induction of the backward classes. The objectives of political representations, State employment schemes and higher educational admissions are development and advancement of the tribals and the backward classes.

2. Financial Aid : This is well known that the poverty of SCs, STs and OBCs is an age-old phenomenon. They were not permitted to hold any type of property except commodities such as utensils of low quality and earthen pots. In view of this condition, these SCs, STs and other backward classes are, by and large, a nil-property category. Having known the condition, the financial aid is administered to them by a wide variety of welfare programmes or welfare schemes. The welfare programmes include special loans and financial aid to the family as well as scholarships to the students. These programmes are directed towards the financial upliftment of the targeted categories.

3. Anti-disability Legislation : These kinds of legislation are enacted for the aim of removing the social stigma of untouchability by direct attack or by legislation against the practice of untouchability. It is attached to a category of human beings born to the untouchable parents. It continues to stick to them until such human beings born of untouchable parents die. The aim of this legislation is to eliminate the blot which clings from birth till death.

Untouchability Act 1955, which is now known as the Protection of Civil Rights Act since 1976, is one illustration of the above said legislations. Another instance may be taken of the Temple Entry Enactments passed by the many State legislatures for ensuring an entry into the temples to the untouchable persons who were denied entry due to no fault of theirs.

Evolution of Reservations

From the last decade of nineteenth century to the present a system, which sought to precaution, the interests of backward communities by preferential treatment has remained an integral portion of public policy in our country. Starting with the reservation of jobs in the service under government, reservation has been extended to numerous representative bodies, admissions to educational schools, colleges and universities and ameliorative measures for their economic growth. Hence the evolution of reservation policy may be raced by three facts as follows:

1. Reservation of jobs of the government.

2. Political representation.

3. Economic and educational upliftment.

1. Reservation of jobs of the government : The reservation of jobs in government of our country on caste and community basis has a fairly long history. It was in the second quarter of the nineteenth century that Jyotirao Phule (resident of Poona) raised the demand for adequate representation of members of all castes in the public services. But this was only in 1880s that Shivaji Chattrapati, who was the Maharaja of Kolhapur, took up the reason advocated by Phule. For particular representation, the Maharaja of Kolhapur was instrumental for non-brahmin categories under the Montagu Chelmsford Reforms.

2. Political representation : As a source to emancipate the backward classes of Indian society, political representation from the age old bondage did not find a champion or did not provide recognition in the duration of 19th century. Even the government of India Act, 1909, which conferred the particular protection and privileges on the Mohammedans, did not provide representation to the depressed categories in the bodies of legislative assembly. In 1918-19, the Franchise Committee recognised the claims of depressed categories and favoured nomination.

3. Education and economic uplift : The people belonging to Scheduled Castes obtained their first education in the mission schools. The government schools established by the British Government were open only to the upper categories. By the older of 28th April 1858, the Education Department in our country constituted rules to admit children of SCs in all the institutions of the government. But the government had soon to withdraw this order as the children from higher classes started boycotting their institutions.

Issued Raised

Many issues regarding the reservation problem have been brought up for decision of the government to implement the Mandal Commission recommendations. Among these issues raised the most significant ones are as follows :

1. Does the Mandal Commission assist the backward categories?

2. Should the Government of India do social engineering?

3. Do merit and efficiency suffer?

There are counter arguments and arguments on each of these issues.

1. Does the Mandal Commission assist the backward categories?

Favour : Even though, only 1 per cent of all jobs are created by the centre every year, the scheme is essential because it provides the backwards a sense of being part of governance— and compensates for the generations of discrimination. Besides, it also paves the ground for upward mobility. Opposition to reservations is only an effort of higher castes to preserve the monopoly that they enjoyed over the structure and the system. Backward classes required representation in the administrative machinery. Although Backward Castes make up 52 per cent of the population of the nation their representation in jobs of central government stands at an abysmal 4.69 per cent.

Against : Utilising percentiles of race representation depending upon the report of Mandal Commission is an unmitigated fraud. The most statistical foundations for the pro-Mandal argument are not sustainable. The data is derived from the caste enumeration census of the 1931. He utilised this as his foundation to arrive at his conclusions taking into account population variations as reflected in the population census during 1971 which was not broken down in accordance with race. In the forty years that elapsed between 1931 and 1971 there was no method of knowing which races had moved down or moved up the socioeconomic ladder. His conclusions, hence, are hypothetical projections.

2. Should the Government of India do social engineering?

Favour : To obtain a just and an equal society, the government has the mandate to ruin social discrepancies or differences by engineering a system of balances and checks. The aforesaid Commission has identified categories by many criteria including many matriculates in the community, the percentage living in thatched huts, availability of potable water and practice of child marriage. This is a serious attempt to improve the many backwards who have only 4.69 per cent representation in class I jobs of the central government though they form 52 per cent of the nation.

Against : Reservations for the backwards in central government jobs do not improve the plight of these castes. The selection of an IAS officer from a backward village does not ensure higher rate of literacy, better housing or potable water. Families that have benefited from the job reservations have reduced their living standards as they have not practised family planning. Families that have benefited produce more children and ask for more reservations which leads to a vicious circle. Right now reservations reach only the individual who benefits from the collective backwardness of his race. Even if the argument of under-representation in the government departments was valid at certain point, the reservation of government jobs is a gratituous exercise that ignores reality. Reservations short circuit the State's responsibility to pave the way for overall development. This is a political gimmick aimed at grabbing the support of a vote bank.

3. Do merit and efficiency suffer?

Favour : In Tamil Nadu and Karnataka the administrative structures have demonstrated that our governments may be running well despite of more representations of backward castes. Virtue is not determined by caste. The higher castes dominate the bureaucracy today but the reservation system is still plagued by many evils. Social responsibility demands that jobs must be shared with backward castes despite a little dilution of the merits of the human resource.

Against : It is apparently a right plea by the higher class backwards to increase their count in the strength. If the backwards required more efficient administration in the bureaucracy they must try to remove corruption and apathy. But they only need a bigger portion in the present corrupt system. The advantages of the lowering of standards do not reach the poorest of the poor. The influence of this could be the higher levels of corruption accompanied by added inefficiency in effect. It may not be denied that lowering test scores for entrance examination to medical colleges and engineering institutions and reserving promotion quotas in government services in accordance with castes will squeeze out the meritorious candidates in these educational institutions.

5

Education Sector

The role of education in overall social and economic progress is widely recognized. The right to education has been enshrined as a fundamental right in the Constitution of India, which states that: "the State shall provide free and compulsory education to all children aged six to fourteen years in such a manner as the state may, by law, determine." The literacy rate in India has been constantly rising, improving from 64.8% in the 2001 census to 74.04% in the 2011 census. Both the central and the state governments have been paying increased attention to the need to provide "education for all."

The Indian government has placed lots of emphasis on primary or elementary education. The Right of Children to Free and Compulsory Education Act became operative on April 1, 2010, since which enrolments have increased to become near universal and dropout rates have decreased. Despite this, the provision of quality education with value addition still remains a distant dream. Secondary education covers children aged 14-18, and provides for more than ninety million children. The

SSA has been extended to secondary education in the form of *Rastriya Madhyamik Shiksha Abhiyan*, with special emphasis on the inclusion of disadvantaged sections and profession-based vocational training.

Despite the higher levels of enrolment at all levels of education, actual value addition has been unsatisfying, as revealed by poor learning outcomes. Evidence suggests that learning trajectories for Indian school children are almost flat and are far below the corresponding class levels in other comparable countries. Dropout rates at secondary and higher levels remain high and much higher for socially and economically marginalized groups. The complex nature of the problems of poor quality, inequality and exclusion poses challenges to the Indian education system. In this context, the importance of infrastructure, institutional framework and the governance systems cannot be exaggerated.

Higher education in India is the third largest in the world after China and the United States. By 2030, India will be among the youngest nations and the need for higher education will be even more urgent. Unfortunately, access to education beyond higher secondary schooling in India is a mere 10% among the university-age population, with huge regional and social disparities. The system has many issues of concern at present, such as access, equity, relevance and quality.

Recognising the constraints and need for greater government attention, public spending on education has increased and education expenditure as a percentage of GDP has increased from 3.3% in 2004–05 to over 4% in 2012–13. Education is a subject in the concurrent list, and both central and state governments have their own responsibilities. The central government spending grew at a rate of 25% per year, and the spending incurred by the state governments grew at 19.6% per year during the 11th plan. While about 43% of the total was spent on elementary education, 25% was spent on secondary education and 32% on higher education. For elementary education, the focus remains on the government institutions. The potential for innovative partnerships between the public and the private sectors is explored in secondary education. Gross enrolment at the secondary level in India, though close to the average for all developing countries, remains substantially lower than that of emerging countries like China, Brazil, Indonesia and Thailand. Combined with wide regional and social disparities, it causes considerable concern. Similarly, less than 1/5th of the eligible 120 million students are enrolled in higher education (well below the world average of 26%), and skill acquisition is far less. The "three Es"—expansion, equity and excellence—are to be achieved and the whole system is to be guided by these objectives. Institutions, governance and finance are the major areas in need of revamping and the papers in this volume throw some light on these issues.

There is a broad range of challenges facing the education sector in India. Given the inadequate infrastructure, poor learning outcomes, wide variations across states and social and economic categories, the four main priority areas in our education planning are access, equity, quality and governance, and the papers included in this volume discuss these issues.

Ministry of Human Resource Development has adopted a fresh approach to meet its challenges. It is this approach that will define the thrust areas and ensure that all the goals with the right value system, sensitivity and responsibility are achieved. The various policies and programmes of the ministry have successfully enabled the access to quality, inclusive, affordable and meaningful education to children and the people across the length and breadth of the country.

Mid day Meal Scheme

The Mid Day Meal Scheme covers children of classes I-VIII studying in government local bodies, government aided schools, special training centres (STC) and madarsas/maqtabs supported under Sarva Shikha Abhiyan (SSA). It is the largest school feeding programme in the world, covering 10.03 crore children in 11.50 lakh institutions across the country. Apart from promoting access and retention, the Mid Day Meal Scheme has also contributed to social and gender equity. It has helped in preventing classroom hunger, promoting school participation and fostering social equality and enhancing gender equality.

Norms for Mid Day Meal Scheme

(i) *Calorific Value of Mid Day Meals:* The cooked meal consists of 100 grams of wheat/rice, 20 grams of pulses, 50 grams of vegetables and 5 grams of oil/fat and provides 450 calories of energy and 12 grams of protein at primary stage. For upper primary stage children, it consists of 150 grams of wheat/rice, 30 grams of pulses, 75 grams of vegetables and 7.5 gram of oil/fat and provides 700 calories of energy and 20 grams of proteins. (ii) *Cooking cost under MDM Scheme:* The cooking cost covers the expenditure for pulses, vegetables, cooking oils, condiments, fuel, etc. The cooking cost has been increased by 7 per cent from July, 2016 for 2016-17 which comes out to be ₹ 4.13 per children per day for primary and ₹ 6.18 per child per day for upper primary. The cooking cost is shared between the Centre and the state in the ratio of 60:40 for non-NER states, 100 per cent for UTs and 90:10 for NER states and 3 Himalayan States viz., Himachal Pradesh, Jammu and Kashmir and Uttarakhand.

Sarva Shiksha Abhiyan

The Sarva Shiksha Abhiyan (SSA) is implemented as a centrally sponsored scheme in partnership with state governments for universalizing elementary education across the country. The scheme is implemented from 2010-11 in accordance with the legal framework/provisions of the Right to Children to Free and Compulsory Education (RTE) 2009 which provides for entitlement of all children between the age of 6-14 years for free and compulsory education, attendance and completion of elementary education in a neighbourhood school. The framework for implementation of SSA has been amended to align with the provision of RTE Act, 2009.

The overall goals of SSA include universal access and retention, bridging of gender and social category gaps in education and enhancement of learning levels of children. It provides for a variety of interventions, including opening of new schools, construction of schools and additional classrooms, toilets and drinking water, provisioning for teachers, periodic teacher training and academic resource support, free uniform, textbooks and support for learning achievement. SSA programme has made significant progress in achieving near universal access and equity.

The revised SSA framework for implementation provides a broad outline of approaches and implementation strategies, within which states can frame more detailed guidelines keeping in view their specific social, economic and institutional contexts. The revised SSA framework for implementation is derived from the recommendations of the Committee on Implementation of RTE Act and the Resultant Revamp of SSA, and is intended to demonstrate the harmonization of SSA with the RTE Act. It is also based on child centric assumptions emerging from the National Policy on Education, 1986/92 and the National Curriculum Framework (NCF), 2005.

Impact of SSA and RTE

RTE Act came into force since April 2010. Sarva Shiksha Abhiyaan was started in 2000-01 and the main programme for ensuring universal elementary education, was revised in September 2010 to conform to the RTE mandate. The impact of RTE-SSA may be seen as follows:

Universal Access: 98 per cent habitations have access to primary school and 97 per cent to upper primary school. Since enactment of the Act, 3,67,494 schools have been sanctioned under SSA.

Increased Enrolment: District Information System for Education (DISE) collects annual data as of September of every year on a number of indicators including enrolment across every school in the country. In 2014-15 enrolment in elementary schools was 19.77 crore children as compared to enrolment of 18.79 crore children in 2009-10. The enrolment has been seen increasing over the years at elementary level.

Inclusive Education

The major interventions under SSA for the education of children with special needs (CWSN) are identification, functional and formal assessment, provision of aids and appliances, teacher training, engagement of resource persons exclusively for CWSN, support services and barrier free access. SSA also ensures that every CWSN irrespective of the kind, category and degree of disability, is provided quality inclusive education. The number of children with special needs that have been brought into the fold of education (through enrolment in formal schools, school readiness programme and through home-based education) is 23.18 lakh as per the Unified District Information System for Education (UDISE) 2014-15.

Emphasis on Girl Education

(a) *Kasturba Gandhi Balika Vidyalayas:* Kasturba Gandhi Balika Vidyalayas (KGBVs) have been opened in Educationally Backward Blocks (EBBs) where the female rural literacy is below the national average to provide for residential upper primary schools for girls. 3599 KGBVs are operational in the country enrolling 3.64 lakh girls. The KGBV component of SSA scheme targets girl's education for drop out girl children particularly from low literacy habitations, below poverty line and SC/ST minorities population. (b) *Gender Atlas:* The 'Digital Gender Atlas' for advancing girls education was launched on the occasion of International Women's Day in 2015. This helps to identify and ensure equitable education with a focus on vulnerable girls, including girls with disabilities. The Gender Atlas uses geographical representation and numeric data at state, district and block levels and gives information on key indicators for girls education at primary, upper primary and secondary level for three years. (c) *'Swachh Bharat: Swachh Vidyalaya Initiative:'* The Department launched Swachh Vidyalaya initiative under the rubric of Swachh Bharat Mission with an objective to provide separate toilets for boys and girls in all government schools within a year. Under Swachh Vidyalaya Initiative, 4,17,796 toilets were constructed in 2,61,400 schools in a period of one year, thus ensuring that every single government school now has separate toilet for girls and boys. This includes schools in the most difficult to reach areas in the country such as districts facing Left Wing Extremism in forests, remote mountainous terrain and in crowded slums. The Initiative was made successful in partnership with all State Governments, Central Public Sector Undertakings, and Private Corporates. With this, about 13.58 crore children in 11.08 lakh government schools all over the country now have access to toilet facilities.

New Initiatives

(a) *Rashtriya Aavishkar Abhiyan:* Rashtriya Aavishkar Abhiyan was launched in July 2015, to motivate and encourage children of the age-group 6-18 years, in science, mathematics and technology. The programme framework is on a twin track approach (i) systemic improvements in the school system; (ii) initiatives to encourage science, mathematics through alternative strategies. The strategies of the programme targets, teachers, students, effective classroom transaction, school facilities for science and maths, and community engagement. In 2015-16, an amount of ₹ 124.78 crore and ₹ 108.26 crore have been earmarked under SSA and RMSA respectively. In case of collaborative initiatives with Ministry of Science and Technology and Department of Higher Education, funds would be pooled with their schemes and norms. All state governments/ UTs have also been given a funding of ₹ 5 lakh per district under innovation fund of SSA to undertake innovative activities and build awareness around learning of Science and Mathematics.

(b) *Padhe Bharat Badhe Bharat:* A nationwide sub-programme of Sarva Shiksha Abhiyaan named Padhe Bharat Badhe Bharat (PBBB) was launched in 2014 to ensure quality at the foundational years of schooling *i.e.*, classes I and II. Through this programme it will be ensured that all children are able to read with comprehension as well as basic numeracy skills. The programme envisages dedicated teachers for classes I and II. It centers on capacity building of teachers, organizing separate reading periods in daily school time-table, maintaining a print rich environment, for reading through children's literature in school libraries and reading corners in classes I and II; for tribal children special bridge materials have been prepared in states which have a high tribal population.

6

Health Sector

India has a vast health care system, but there remain many differences in quality between rural and urban areas as well as between public and private health care. Despite this, India is a popular destination for medical tourists, given the relatively low costs and high quality of its private hospitals. International students in India should expect to rely on private hospitals for advanced medical care.

Studying in India offers a number of health challenges that students from developed countries may be unused to, so it is important to know how the health care system in India operates in the event you need it. Health care in India is a vast system and can be much like the rest of the country: full of complexity and paradoxes.

India's Ministry of Health was established with independence from Britain in 1947. The government has made health a priority in its series of five-year plans, each of which determines state spending priorities for the coming five years. The National Health Policy was endorsed by Parliament in 1983. The policy aimed at universal health care coverage by 2000, and the program was updated in 2002.

The health care system in India is primarily administered by the states. India's Constitution tasks each state with providing health care for its people. In order to address lack of medical coverage in rural areas, the national government launched the National Rural Health Mission in 2005. This mission focuses resources on rural areas and poor states which have weak health services in the hope of improving health care in India's poorest regions.

Private and Public

The health care system in India is universal. That being said, there is great discrepancy in the quality and coverage of medical treatment in India. Healthcare between states and rural and urban areas can be vastly different. Rural areas often suffer from physician shortages, and disparities between states mean that residents of the poorest states, like Bihar, often have less access to adequate healthcare than residents of relatively more affluent states. State governments provide healthcare services and health education, while the central government offers administrative and technical services.

Lack of adequate coverage by the health care system in India means that many Indians turn to private healthcare providers, although this is an option generally inaccessible to the poor. To help pay for healthcare costs, insurance is available, often provided by employers, but most Indians lack health insurance, and out-of-pocket costs make up a large portion of the spending on medical treatment in India.

On the other hand private hospitals in India offer world class quality health care at a fraction of the price of hospitals in developed countries. This aspect of health care in India makes it a popular destination for medical tourists. India also is a top destination for medical tourists seeking alternative treatments, such as ayurvedic medicine. India is also a popular destination for students of alternative medicine.

Health Policy

The National Health Policy (NHP) of 2002 guides the strategy adopted by the Government for the health sector. The NHP 2002 evolved from the National Health Policy of 1983. Guidance was provided by the Bhore Committee Report (1946) wherein the main underlying principles for future health development of the country, *inter alia,* included that 'No individual should fail to secure adequate medical care because of inability to pay for it. In view of the complexity of modern medical practice, the health services should provide, when fully developed, all the consultant, laboratory and institutional facilities necessary for proper diagnosis and treatment'.

The National Health Policy, 2002 framework envisages, accelerated achievement of public health goals in the backdrop of the socio-economic circumstances prevailing in the country. Some of the salient aspects of the NHP 2002, *inter alia,* include: making good the deficiencies in availability of health facilities, narrowing the gap between various states, the gap across the rural-urban divide in attainment of health goals and reducing the uneven access to and benefits from the public health system between the better endowed and the more vulnerable sections of society.

Accordingly consistent with the primacy given to equity, a marked emphasis has been provided for expanding and improving the primary health facilities. Emphasis has been laid on the implementation of public health programmes through local self-governments. The need to ensure improved standard of medical education, alleviate the shortage of specialists in Public Health and Family Medicine, need for an improvement in the ratio of nurse visà-vis doctors/beds, the need for basing treatment regimens on a limited number of essential drugs of a generic nature and progressively strengthening the food and drugs administration are among the various aspects emphasized in the policy.

It also envisages setting up of an organized urban primary care structure, a network of decentralized mental health services and upgrading the physical infrastructure of mental health institutions. It visualizes an Information, Education and Communication Policy which maximizes the dissemination of information to those population groups which cannot be effectively approached by using only the mass media and giving priority to school health programmes with an aim at imparting preventive health education apart from providing regular health check-ups and promotion of health seeking behaviour among children.

The Five Year Plan outline the strategy for implementing the policy, bearing in mind the dynamics of a developing economy. Accordingly, the Twelfth Five Year Plan for the health sector envisages transformation of the National Rural Health Mission into a National Health Mission covering both rural and urban areas. It envisages providing public sector primary care facilities in selected low income urban areas, expansion of teaching and training programmes for healthcare professionals, particularly in the public sector institutions, giving greater attention to public health, strengthening the drug and food regulatory mechanism, regulation of medical practice, human resource development, promoting information technology in health and building an appropriate architecture for Universal Health Care. Government has taken a decision to formulate a new health policy in the light of the changes that have taken place in the country's health sector scenario since the formulation of the National Health Policy, 2002. Accordingly, the Draft New National Health Policy, 2015 has been placed in public domain since 2014 for wider stakeholder consultations.

National Health Mission and National Urban Health Mission

The National Health Mission (NHM) has its two submissions, the National Rural Health Mission (NRHM) and the National Urban Health Mission (NUHM). The NHM envisages universal access to equitable, affordable & quality healthcare services that are accountable and responsive to people's needs. The main programmatic components include health system strengthening in rural and urban areas, Reproductive-Maternal-Newborn Child and Adolescent Health (RMNCH+A) and control of Communicable and Non-Communicable Diseases. The framework for implementation of National Health Mission was approved in December, 2013. Under NHM, substantial achievements have been made, the details of which are available in the report. The 7th Common Review Mission (CRM) under NHM was conducted from November 2013 in 14 states/UTs namely Bihar, Jharkhand, Odisha, Uttar Pradesh, Jammu & Kashmir, Himachal Pradesh, Arunachal Pradesh, Meghalaya, Nagaland, Andhra Pradesh, Haryana, Karnataka, Maharashtra, and Gujarat. The CRM observed increased child survival, population stabilization and utilization of health services, though the progress across states was not analogous. The Infant Mortality Rate (IMR), the deaths of children before age 1 per 1000 live-births, has fallen steadily every year, with an all India average of 42. While this is short of the 12th Plan target of 25, some states have made remarkable progress with Goa having an IMR of 10, Kerala 12, Nagaland 18, Manipur 10 and Tamil Nadu 21. The Maternal Mortality Ratio (MMR), which measures the number of women of reproductive age (15 to 49) dying due to maternal causes per 1,00,000 live-births, has come down to 178, though this is far short of the 12th Plan target of 100. Some states have registered significant reduction in MMR with Kerala at 66, Maharashtra at 87 and Tamil Nadu at 90.

There has been a significant improvement in creation of new facilities and infrastructure, though adequate staffing of these facilities by qualified health personnel remains a problem. Availability of drugs has improved at all levels and the robust logistic arrangements for procurement and storage of these drugs are being put in place. An important achievement of NHM has been a considerable reduction in out of pocket expenses from 72 per cent to 60 per cent.

Recently, new initiatives have been launched under NHM. Rashtriya Bal Swasthya Karyakram (RBSK) was launched to provide comprehensive healthcare and improve the quality of life of children through early detection of birth defects, diseases, deficiencies, and development delays including disability. Another initiative, viz., Rashtriya Kishore Swasthya Karyakram (RKSK) was launched to comprehensively address the health needs of the 253 million adolescents, who account for over 21 per cent of the country's population, by bringing in several new dimensions like mental health, nutrition, substance misuse, injuries and violence and non-communicable diseases. The programme has introduced community based interventions through peer educators and is underpinned by collaborations with other ministries and state governments and knowledge partners, coupled with operational research. In addition to these initiatives, the Weekly Iron Folic Acid Supplementation Programme (WIFS) was launched to address adolescent anaemia where under supervised Iron-Folic Acid (IFA) tablets are given to adolescent population between 10-19 years of age in both rural and urban areas throughout the country. NUHM, a sub-mission under the NHM, caters to the healthcare needs of the urban population with the focus on urban poor and is aimed at reducing out of pocket expenses for treatment. NHM is a step towards realizing the objective of Universal Health Coverage in the country.

National Urban Health Mission

National Urban Health Mission (NUHM) seeks to improve the health status of the urban population particularly urban poor and other vulnerable sections by facilitating their access to quality primary healthcare. NUHM would cover all state capitals, district headquarters and other cities/towns with a population of 50,000 and above (as per census 2011) in a phased manner. Cities and towns with population below 50,000 will continue to be covered under NRHM.

ASHA

More than 9.15 lakh Accredited Social Health Activists (ASHAs) are in place across the country and serve as facilitators, mobilizers and providers of community level care. ASHA is the first port of call in the community especially for marginalized sections of the population, with a focus on women and children. Since 2013, when the National Urban Health Mission was launched, ASHAs are being selected in urban areas as well. Several evaluations and successive Common Review Missions show that the ASHA has been a key figure in contributing to the positive outcomes of increases in institutional delivery, immunization, active role in disease control programmes (Malaria, Kala-azar and Lymphatic filariasis, in particular) and improved breastfeeding and nutrition practices. The majority of states have in place an active training and support system for the ASHA to ensure continuing training, on site field mentoring and performance monitoring.

Janani Suraksha Yojana

Janani Suraksha Yojana (JSY) aims to reduce maternal mortality among pregnant women by encouraging them to deliver in government health facilities. Under the scheme, cash assistance is provided to eligible pregnant women for giving birth in a government health facility. Since the inception of NRHM, 8.55 crore women have benefited under this scheme.

Janani Shishu Suraksha Karyakram

Launched on June 01, 2011, JSSK entitles all pregnant women delivering in public health institutions to absolutely free and no expense delivery, including caesarean section. This marks a shift to an entitlement based approach. The free entitlements include free drugs and consumables, free diagnostics, free diet during stay in the health institutions, free provision of blood, free transport from home to health institution, between health institutions in case of referrals and drop back home and exemption from all kinds of user charges. Similar entitlements are available for all sick infants (up to 1 year of age) accessing public health institutions. All states and union territories are implementing this scheme. As per the latest reports received from the states/UTs, 89 per cent pregnant women availed free drugs, 82 per cent free diagnostics, 75 per cent free diet, 49 per cent free home to facility transport and 56.03 per cent free drop back home. For sick infants, 73 per cent sick infants availed free drugs, 40 per cent free diagnostics, 10 per cent sick infants free home to facility transport and 28 per cent free drop back home.

National Urban Health Mission

National Urban Health Mission (NUHM) was put in place as a sub-mission under an overarching National Health Mission (NHM) for providing equitable and quality Primary Health Care (PHC) services to the urban population with special focus on slum and vulnerable sections of the society. NUHM aims to improve the health status of the urban area with more than 50,000 population particularly the poor and other disadvantaged sections by facilitating equitable access to quality healthcare through a revamped primary healthcare systems, targeted outreach services and involvement of the community and the urban local bodies. The Centre-state funding pattern is 75:25 for all the states except northeastern states including Sikkim and other special category states of Jammu and Kashmir, Himachal Pradesh and Uttarakhand, for whom the Centre-state funding pattern is 90:10.

7

Human Development

Human development is a concept within the field of international development. It involves studies of the human condition with its core being the capability approach. The inequality adjusted Human Development Index is used as a way of measuring actual progress in human development by the United Nations. It is an alternative approach to a single focus on economic growth, and focused more on social justice, as a way of understanding progress.

The United Nations Development Programme has defined Human Development as "the process of enlarging people's choices", said choices allowing them to "lead a long and healthy life, to be educated, to enjoy a decent standard of living", as well as "political freedom, other guaranteed human rights and various ingredients of self-respect".

Development concerns expanding the choices people have, to lead lives that they value, and improving the human condition so that people have the chance to lead full lives. Thus, human development is about much more than economic growth, which is only a means of enlarging people's choices. Fundamental to enlarging these choices is building human capabilities – the range of things that people can do or be in life. Capabilities are "the substantive freedoms [a person] enjoys to lead the kind of life [they have] reason to value". Human development disperses the concentration of the distribution of goods and services that underprivileged people need and center its ideas on human decisions. By investing in people, we enable growth and empower people to pursue many different life paths, thus developing human capabilities. The most basic capabilities for human development are: to lead long and healthy lives, to be knowledgeable (*i.e.*, educated), to have access to resources and social services needed for a decent standard of living, and to be able to participate in the life of the community. Without these, many choices are simply not available, and many opportunities in life remain inaccessible.

An abstract illustration of human capability is a bicycle. A bicycle itself is a resource– a mode of transportation. If the person who owns the bicycle is unable to ride it (due to a lack of balance or knowledge), the bicycle is useless to that person as transportation and loses its functioning. If, however, a person both owns a bicycle and has the ability to ride a bicycle, they now have the capability of riding to a friend's house, a local store, or a great number of other places. This capability would (presumably) increase their value of life and expand their choices. A person, therefore, needs both resources and the ability to use them to pursue their capabilities. This is one example of how different resources or skills can contribute to human capability. This way of looking at development, often forgotten in the immediate concern with accumulating commodities and financial wealth, is not new. Philosophers, economists and political leaders have long emphasized human well being as the purpose, or the end, of development. As Aristotle said in ancient Greece, "Wealth is evidently not the good we are seeking, for it is merely useful for the sake of something else."

There is a Human Development Report Office (HDRO) at the United Nations Development Programme (UNDP). The HDRO released the Human Development Report (HDR) recently. India was ranked 131 out of 188 countries. It was ranked behind many smaller countries such as Tunisia, Moldova and slotted in the "Medium Human Development" category which also included countries like Congo and Ghana. Among our neighbours, the Indian rank was closer to that of Pakistan, Bangladesh and Nepal but far behind Sri Lanka (73rd rank). Further, over the years, India's HDI rank has stayed nearly static. Based on these observations, critics have jumped to all sorts of conclusions about Indian living standards and development. However, this is not that straightforward. Before drawing any conclusions, it is important to dig deeper into the specifics of HDI.

HDI essentially is a composite index that integrates three basic dimensions of human development: ability to lead a long and healthy life; ability to acquire knowledge and ability to achieve a decent standard of living. The first dimension is captured by life expectancy at birth. Mean years of schooling and expected years of schooling combined capture the second, while Gross National Income (GNI) per capita (PPP in US$) captures the last dimension. Each dimension is then quantified as an index, calculated as the ratio between (Actual Value - Minimum Value)/(Maximum Value - Minimum Value). Note that the minimum and maximum values are fixed values (boundary limits), same for all the countries. These three indices are then aggregated and their geometric mean is taken as the HDI score for a particular country.

Let us take an example. For the year 2016, the Minimum Life Expectancy was fixed as 20 years and Maximum 85 years. India's life expectancy was 68.3 years. Therefore, the Health Index for India would be computed as (68.3 - 20) / (85 - 20) = 0.743. Using a similar approach, the other two indices -

education and income would be computed. Finally, the HDI score for India would be the geometric mean of all three indices. And this score would determine India's relative rank across several countries. A higher HDI rank should ideally reflect better human development opportunities. Similarly, a year on year increase in HDI rank, would reflect an increase in a country's relative performance.

METHODOLOGY BEFORE AND AROUND HDR 2009

Dimensions	Indicators	Min Value	Max Value
Life Expectancy	Life Expectancy at birth	25 years	85 years
Education / Knowledge	Literate Adult Population (15 years and above)	0%	100%
	Combined Gross Enrolment rates at primary, secondary and tertiary education	0%	100%
Income	Log of GDP/Capita (in PPP US$))	100	40000

Methodology HDR 2016

Dimensions	Indicators	Min Value	Max Value
Life Expectancy	Life Expectancy at birth	20 years	85 years
Education / Knowledge	Mean years of Schooling	0	15 years
	Expected Years of Schooling	0	18 years
Income	Log of GNI per capita (PPP US$)	163	75000

However, there are several issues that complicate this. First, the HDI computation methodology itself keeps changing. As can be seen in the table (above), earlier, Health index was measured by life expectancy at birth; Education index by a combination of adult literacy rate and gross school enrolment rates; and Income index by GDP per capita adjusted for PPP (in US$). Except the health index, methodology for computing the other two indices has now changed significantly. Second, simple arithmetic mean was used to compute HDI scores earlier. Now, geometric mean of each index provides the HDI score. Third, the number of countries for which data is collated also changes year on year. In 2010, there were 169 countries. This number increased to 188 in 2016. Fourth, there have been issues related to timelines of input data. For example, Life expectancy at birth for HDR 2013 corresponded to data for the year 2011. The HDR 2016, on the other hand, used the data for 2015. Especially for the social sectors, there are significant time-lags in data. Finally, and possibly the most serious concerns have been raised over the usage of only three dimensions and giving them equal weights while computing HDI. Experts argue that crucial variables such as political voice, democratic freedom, social connections and relationships, environmental sustainability, and economic/physical security are completely left out. On the other hand, equal weightage to all three indices pulls HDI score of countries like India down. Given the huge population base, India gets consistently low scores on GNI per capita. In fact, on this particular index, India's score was very similar to that of Pakistan and Congo, but less than that of Iraq.

Before reaching conclusions on HDI rankings, the above minutiae must be kept in mind. India is a vibrant democracy and it does offer better development opportunities to its people as compared to many others it lags behind. That said, HDR is still an important reference tool. It contains some useful insights on socio-economic programmes that are working and development areas that need more attention. This can greatly help fine-tune the design of related policies. It is the HDI ranks that should be judged and interpreted with caution. Simple conclusions based on ranks can be misleading. The obsession with HDI should not dilute the focus from other indicators. HDR has data on, nor from the sub-national aspect, captured in State-level HDRs.

Poverty Alleviation

Poverty can be defined as a social phenomenon in which a section of the society is unable to fulfil even its basic necessities of life. When a substantial segment of a society is deprived of the minimum level of living and continues at a bare subsistence level, that society is said to be plagued with mass poverty. The countries of the third world exhibit invariably the existence of mass poverty, although pockets of poverty exist even in the developed countries of Europe and America.

The Planning Commission has now adopted an alternative definition of poverty provided by the "Task force on projections of minimum needs and effective consumption demand". Using the income poverty method, the Task Force has defined the poverty line as the mid point of the monthly per capita expenditure class having a daily calorie intake of 2,400 per person in rural areas and 2,100 in urban areas. On this basis, the cut off points turnout to be ₹ 49 for rural areas and ₹ 57 for urban areas at 1973-74 prices.

POVERTY RATIO AND NUMBER OF POOR IN 2011-12
(Based on Proposed Methodology by Rangarajan Committee)

S. No.	States	RURAL		URBAN		TOTAL	
		Poverty Ratio (%)	No. of Poors (Lakh)	Poverty Ratio (%)	No. of Poors (Lakh)	Poverty Ratio (%)	No. of Poors (Lakh)
1.	Andhra Pradesh	12.7	71.5	15.6	45.7	13.7	117.3
2.	Arunachal Pradesh	39.3	4.3	30.9	1.0	37.4	5.3
3.	Assam	42.0	114.1	34.2	15.4	40.9	129.5
4.	Bihar	40.1	376.8	50.8	61.4	41.3	438.1
5.	Chhattisgarh	49.2	97.9	43.7	26.9	47.9	124.8
6.	Delhi	11.9	0.5	15.7	26.3	15.6	26.7
7.	Goa	1.4	0.1	9.1	0.8	6.3	0.9
8.	Gujarat	31.4	109.8	22.2	58.9	27.4	168.8
9.	Haryana	11.0	18.4	15.3	14.0	12.5	32.4
10.	Himachal Pradesh	11.1	6.9	8.8	0.6	10.9	7.5
11.	Jammu & Kashmir	12.6	11.7	21.6	7.6	15.1	19.3
12.	Jharkhand	45.9	117.0	31.3	25.5	42.4	142.5
13.	Karnataka	19.8	74.8	25.1	60.9	21.9	135.7
14.	Kerala	7.3	12.3	15.3	26.0	11.3	38.3
15.	Madhya Pradesh	45.2	241.4	42.1	86.3	44.3	327.8
16.	Maharashtra	22.5	139.9	17.0	88.4	20.0	228.3
17.	Manipur	34.9	6.7	73.4	6.3	46.7	12.9
18.	Meghalaya	26.3	6.4	16.7	1.0	24.4	7.4
19.	Mizoram	33.7	1.8	21.5	1.2	27.4	3.1
20.	Nagaland	6.1	0.8	32.1	1.9	14.0	2.8
21.	Odisha	47.8	169.0	36.3	26.0	45.9	195.0
22.	Punjab	7.4	12.9	17.6	18.7	11.3	31.6
23.	Rajasthan	21.4	112.0	22.5	39.5	21.7	151.5
24.	Sikkim	20.0	0.9	11.7	0.2	17.8	1.1
25.	Tamil Nadu	24.3	91.1	20.3	72.8	22.4	163.9
26.	Tripura	22.5	6.1	31.3	3.2	24.9	9.3
27.	Uttar Pradesh	38.1	600.9	45.7	208.2	39.8	809.1
28.	Uttarakhand	12.6	8.9	29.5	9.4	17.8	18.4
29.	W. Bengal	30.1	188.6	29.0	86.8	29.7	275.4
30.	Puducherry	5.9	0.2	8.6	0.7	7.7	1.0
31.	Andaman & Nicobar Island	6.6	0.2	4.9	0.1	6.0	0.2
32.	Chandigarh	12.0	0.0	21.5	2.3	21.3	2.3
33.	Dadra & Nagar Haveli	55.2	1.0	15.3	0.3	35.6	1.3
34.	Daman & Diu	0.0	0.0	17.6	0.4	13.7	0.4
35.	Lakshadweep	0.6	0.0	7.9	0.0	6.5	0.0
	All India	**30.9**	**2605.2**	**26.4**	**1024.7**	**29.5**	**3629.9**

TENDULKAR REPORT ON POVERTY

The poverty in India is much more than earlier estimated. The Suresh Tendulkar Committee report submitted to the government, estimates poverty in India at over 37 per cent (2004-05) and not at 28 per cent as calculated earlier. With recent price rise in food items factored, the current level could be even higher.

The Government of India had set up the Tendulkar Committee after facing criticism about under-reporting its official estimates of rural poverty. According to the Committee's estimates, the overall poverty rate comes to be 37.2 per cent and not 27.5 per cent as was estimated in 2004-05. Similarly, poverty in rural India stood at 41.8 per cent and not 28.3 per cent. Urban poverty rate in 2004-05 came to be 25.7% according to the new estimates. States like Odisha, Bihar, Madhya Pradesh, Chhattisgarh and Jharkhand are found to be living under abject poverty.

The Tendulkar Committee has steered away from the calorie norm set in 1973-74, which is the money required to access 2100 calories in urban areas, and 2400 calories in rural areas. Rather the new poverty line has been defined on a wider access to commodity and services like health, sanitation and education. The new all-India average rural poverty line is set at a monthly expenditure ₹ 446.68; the national urban poverty line at ₹ 578.8 a month. Poverty line is now a per capita expenditure of ₹ 12 per day.

The Report also taunts the much hailed theory that 'trickling-down' of growth can reduce poverty over time. This is because despite witnessing annual growth rates of 6-7 per cent, there has been little progress in poverty reduction in the recent years.

POVERTY LINE

Committee	Year	Per capita Expenditure per day (₹)		Per capita Average Monthly Expenditure (₹)		All India Poverty Line (Average Monthly Expenditure per Family of 5)	
		Rural	Urban	Rural	Urban	Rural	Urban
Rangarajan	2011-12	32.4	46.9	972	1407	4760	7035
	2009-10	26.7	39.9	801	1198	4005	5990
Tendulkar	2011-12	27.2	33.3	816	1000	4080	5000
	2009-10	22.4	28.7	673	860	3365	4300

NEW POVERTY LINE

Those spending over ₹ 32 a day in rural areas and ₹ 47 in towns and cities should not be considered poor, an expert panel headed by former RBI governor C. Rangarajan said in a report submitted to the BJP government last week. Based on Suresh Tendulkar Panel's recommendations in 2011-12, the poverty line had been fixed at ₹ 27 in rural areas and ₹ 33 in urban areas, levels at which getting two meals may be difficult.

The panel's recommendation, however, results in an increase in the below poverty line population, which is estimated at 363 million in 2011-12, compared to the 270 million estimate based on the Tendulkar formula—an increase of almost 35%. This means 29.5% of India's population lives below the poverty line as defined by the Rangarajan committee, as against 21.9% according to Tendulkar. For 2009-10, Rangarajan has estimated that the share of BPL group in total population was 38.2%, translating into a decline in poverty ratio by 8.7 percentage points over a two-year period.

The real change is in urban areas where the BPL number is projected to have nearly doubled to 102.5 million based on Rangarajan's estimates, compared to 53 million based on the Tendulkar committee's recommendations. So, based on the new measure, in 2011-12, 26.4% of the people living in urban areas were BPL, compared to 35.1% in 2009-10.

In case of rural areas, the rise is of the order of 20% to 260.5 million, compared to around 217 million based on the Tendulkar formula. Rangarajan's estimates would put the BPL share of total population in rural areas at 30.9%, compared to 39.6% in 2009-10.

Rangarajan panel has suggested to the government that those spending more than ₹ 972 a month in rural areas and ₹ 1,407 a month in urban areas in 2011-12 do not fall under the definition of poverty. Thus, for a family of five, the all-India poverty line in terms of consumption expenditure, as per the Rangarajan committee, would amount to ₹ 4,760 per month in rural areas and ₹ 7,035 per month in urban areas. If calculated on a daily basis, this translates into a per capita expenditure of ₹ 32 per day in rural areas and ₹ 47 per day in urban areas in 2011-12. As per the Tendulkar methodology for 2011-12, the poverty line was ₹ 816 in rural areas and ₹ 1,000 in urban areas, which if calculated on a daily basis come out at ₹ 27 per day in rural areas and ₹ 33 in urban areas. The Tendulkar committee had pegged this at ₹ 4,080 and ₹ 5,000.

CAUSES OF POVERTY

The following are the factors responsible for the problem of poverty in India.

1. **Oppressive Land System:** The landlords exploited their tenants mercilessly.

2. **Over population and its rapid growth:** The population's rapid growth is another significant reason for poverty increase in the nation resulting in a low per capita income.

3. **Low agricultural productivity:** Due to insufficient irrigation, small agricultural holdings, and ignorance of modern agricultural inputs, agricultural productivity is very low in our country.

4. **Underdevelopment:** Because of development of our economy at a slow pace, our national income and per capita income are low.

5. **Inequality:** In the distribution of national income, inequality has been a major cause of mass poverty in India.

6. **Unemployment and underemployment:** Most of the marginal farmers and landless labourers suffer from the disguised unemployment.

STRATEGY TO REMOVE POVERTY

The measures that should be adopted to eradicate poverty in India are as under:

1. **Population control:** Unless there is a control on population, and further wealth generation will be eaten up by a rise in population.

2. **Labour-intensified industries:** Measures should be adopted in the urban areas for using more labour-intensive industries in preference to capital intensive techniques.

3. **Rural industrialisation:** Rural industries with simple technologies and small scale pattern offer much greater opportunities for empolyment.

4. **Provision of common services and social security:** For the provision of free common services such as education, medical and recreation facilities if the State Government spends large amounts on the masses then this step will add to their real consumption and would ameliorate their poverty.

5. **Land reforms:** By imposing of ceiling on land holdings and their effective implementation, large areas of land may be acquired to be distributed among the landless labourers.

6. **Agricultural growth on labour intensive lines:** Reckless mechanization of agriculture which eats up more

employment opportunities than that it creates, must be discouraged.

7. **Rural public works:** To give employment to the rural people, rural public works must be started on an extensive scale.

8. **Acceleration of economic growth:** The greater the economic growth rate, the more the employment opportunities, and the expansion in employment opportunities will assist in removing poverty.

POVERTY ALLEVIATION AND EMPLOYMENT PROGRAMMES

In the early years of planning, it was felt that economic growth would by itself lead to rapid reduction of poverty. When it was seen that this did not happen, a direct assault on poverty through rural development and rural employment programmes was adopted—in the 1970s, with the Fifth Plan. A number of special programmes were set in motion in the 1970s—Small Farmers' Development Agency (SFDA), Marginal Farmers' and Agricultural Labourers' Development Agency (MFAL), Pilot Intensive Rural Employment Project (PIREP), and the Food for Work Programme (FWP).

In 1978-79 came the Integrated Rural Development Programme (IRDP) which was extended to the entire country in the Sixth Plan. The programme was aimed at small and marginal farmers, landless labourers and artisans, and conceived to help create assets for these people. The basic strategy was self-employment of the poor, who could then earn enough to rise above the poverty line. There were other programmes such as the National Rural Employment Programme (NREP), and the Rural Landless Employment Guarantee Programme (RLEGP) which were later merged to form the Jawahar Rozgar Yojana (JRY) in 1989. These were wage employment schemes.

Mahatma Gandhi National Rural Employment Guarantee Act

Evolving the design of the wage employment programmes to more effectively fight poverty, the Centre formulated the Mahatma Gandhi National Rural Employment Guarantee Act (MGNREGA) in 2005. Notified on September 7, 2005, MGNREGA aims at enhancing livelihood security by providing at least one hundred days of guaranteed wage employment in a financial year to every rural household whose adult members volunteer to do unskilled manual work.

During the FY 2012-13, upto 31st December, 2012, the scheme provided employment to around 4.16 crore households through about 70 lakh works with more than 141 crore person days of employment generated at a total expenditure of about ₹ 25000 crore. The average wage rate per day has increased from ₹ 65 in 2006-07 to about ₹ 115 in 2011-12.

Salient features of the Act

- **Right based Framework:** For adult members of a rural household willing to do unskilled manual work.

- **Time bound Guarantee:** 15 days for provision of employment, else unemployment allowance.

- **Guaranteed Employment:** Upto 100 days of guaranteed wage employment in a financial year per household, depending on the actual demand.

- **Labour Intensive Works:** 60:40 wage and material ratio for permissible work at the Gram Panchayat; no contractors/ machinery.

Decentralized Planning:

- Gram Sabhas to recommend works.
- At least 50 per cent of works by Gram Panchayats for execution.

- Principal role of PRIs in planning, monitoring and implementation.
- **Work Site Facilities:** Creche, drinking water, first aid and shade provided at worksites.
- **Women Empowerment:** Priority shall be given to women in such a way that at least one third of the beneficiaries shall be women who have registered and requested for work under this Act.
- **Transparency and Accountability:** Proactive disclosure through Social Audits, Grievance Redressal Mechanism.
- **Funding:** 90 per cent borne by Central Government and 10 per cent by State Government.

Implementation

The Gram Panchayat is the single most important implementation agency for executing works as the Act mandates earmarking a minimum of 50 per cent of the works in terms of costs to be executed by the Gram Panchayat. This statutory minimum, upto hundred per cent of the work may be allotted to the Gram Panchayat (GP) in the annual Shelf of Projects (SoP).

The other Implementing Agencies can be Intermediate and District Panchayats, line departments of the Government, Public Sector Undertakings of the Central and State Governments, cooperative Societies with a majority shareholding by the Central and State Governments, and reputed NGOs having a proven track record of performance. Self-Help Groups may also be considered as possible Implementing Agencies.

Important Instrument to Monitor and Ensure Transparency in Implementation of the Act

In the last six years of implementation of the Act several amendments have been made in the schedules of the MGNREGA to facilitate its implementation. These include amendments to ensure transparency regarding custody of job cards and details to be contained in them, disbursement of wages through banks and post offices, maintenance of records, proactive disclosure of information and processes and procedures to be followed during social audits. As per the amendment in Schedule, notified on 4th May, 2012, 30 New works have been added to enhance livelihood opportunities for the workers. Some of the important initiatives are:

Management Information System (MIS): MGNREGA has one of the most effective ICT enabled public interfaces at http://www.nrega.nic.in. It is fully functional. The architecture of the MIS is constructed on the requirements of the legal process of the Act. All physical and financial performance data are available in public domain.

Social Audits: Social Audits enable the rural communities to monitor and analyze the quality, durability and usefulness of MGNREGA works as well as mobilize awareness and enforcement on their rights. Social Audit is an important tool by which the people can improve and devise strategies to enhance the quality of implementation of MGNREGA. The Ministry has accorded utmost importance to the organization of Social Audits by the Gram Panchayats and issued instructions to the State to make necessary arrangements for the purpose.

District Level Ombudsman: The Ombudsman will be appointed by the State Government on the recommendation of the selection committee. Ombudsmen will be well-known persons from civil society who have experience in the field of public administration, law, academics, social work or management. Ombudsman will be an agency independent of the central or state government. The Ombudsman will receive complaints from MGNREGA workers and others on any matters, consider such complaints and facilitate their disposal in accordance with law.

Transparency in Execution of Works: To maintain transparency and accountability in the execution of works States have been suggested to upload three photographs of the work site, *i.e.*, before start of the work (work site), during execution of work and completed work.

Proactive Disclosure: States have been suggested to proactively disclose the information through Citizen Information Boards, reading out muster rolls information regarding attendance, work done and wage paid.

Payment through Banks and Post Offices: Wages are being paid to the beneficiaries under MGNREGA through post office and savings bank accounts. As of now, more than 9.8 crore savings bank and post office accounts have been opened across the country for distribution of wages under the scheme.

Swarnajayanti Gram Swarozgar Yojana

The Swarnajayanti Gram Swarozgar Yojana (SGSY) was launched with effect from April 1, 1999 to bring the assisted poor families above the poverty line by ensuring appreciable sustained level of income over a period of time.

The programme was a revamp of the erstwhile Integrated Rural Development Programme (IRDP), Development of Women and Children in Rural Areas (DWCRA), Training of Rural Youth for Self-Employment (TRYSEM), Supply of Improved Toolkits to Rural Artisans (SITRA), Ganga Kalyan Yojana (GKY) and Million Wells Scheme (MWS). SGSY was devised keeping in view the positive aspects and deficiencies of the earlier programmes.

The salient features of the SGSY are as follows:

- It aims at establishing a large number of micro-enterprises in the rural areas.

- SGSY is a credit-cum-subsidy programme. However, credit is the critical component in SGSY, subsidy being only a minor and enabling element. Accordingly, SGSY envisages a greater involvement of the banks.

- It seeks to promote multiple credit rather than a one time credit 'injection'.

- Emphasis is to be laid on skill development through well designed training courses.

- SGSY ensures upgradation of the technology in the identified-activity clusters.

- It provides for promotion of marketing of the goods produced by the SGSY *Swarozgaris.* This involves provision of market intelligence and institutional arrangements for the marketing of the goods including exports.

- The programme is implemented by the District Rural Development Agencies (DRDAs) through the panchayat samities.

National Rural Livelihood Mission — Aajeevika

Union government has launched **'National Rural Livelihood Mission'** with the aim to eliminate poverty in rural areas. Mrs. Sonia Gandhi on June 3, 2011 launched this Mission from Banswada District of Rajasthan. Under this mission, Self-Help Groups (SHGs) at the village level is constituted in the form of federation and these SHGs provide beneficial self-employment opportunities to the rural people for ensuring better and stable livelihood. The new mission gives focus on women, scheduled castes/scheduled tribes, minorities and disabled people. The mission proposes to include atleast one woman member of the identified poor family in Self-help Group.

The SGSY is now restructured as the NRLM has been renamed Aajeevika and implemented in mission mode across the country since 2011. The main features of Aajeevika are: (a) One woman member from each identified rural poor household to be brought under the SHG network, (b) Ensuring 50 per cent of the beneficiaries from SC/STs, 15 per cent from minorities, and 3 per cent persons with disability while keeping in view the ultimate target of 100 per cent coverage of BPL families, (c) Training for capacity building and skill development, (d) Ensuring revolving fund and capital subsidy, (e) Financial inclusion, (f) Provision of interest subsidy, (g) Backward and forward linkages, and (h) Promoting innovations.

Indira Awaas Yojana

The objective of IAY is to provide financial assistance for construction/upgradation of houses to BPL rural households belonging to the Scheduled Castes and Scheduled Tribes, freed bonded labourers, non-SC/ST rural households, widows and physically handicapped persons living in the rural areas. The scheme is funded on a cost-sharing basis of 75 : 25 between the Centre and the States. However, in the case of NE States, the funding pattern has recently been revised to 90 : 10.

Construction of an IAY house is the sole responsibility of the beneficiary. Engagement of contractors is prohibited and no specific type, design has been stipulated for an IAY house. However, sanitary latrine and smokeless chullah are required to be constructed alongwith each IAY house. For construction of a sanitary latrine, in addition to financial assistance provided under IAY, the beneficiary can avail of financial assistance as admissible under the Total Sanitation Campaign (TSC).

Jawahar Rozgar Yojana

Prime Minister Rajiv Gandhi announced on 28th April, 1989 the launching of the Jawahar Rozgar Yojana (JRY). All the existing rural wage employment programmes were merged into JRY. This implies that National Rural Employment Programme (NREP) and Rural Landless Employment Guarantee Programme (RLEGP) have been merged so as to be brought under this umbrella programme referred to as Jawahar Rozgar Yojana.

Objectives of JRY

Primary Objective – Generation of gainful employment for the unemployed and under-employed, men and women in rural areas.

Secondary Objectives – JRY had several secondary objectives :

(i) creation of sustained employment by strengthening the rural infrastructure;

(ii) creation of community and social assets;

(iii) creation of assets in favour of the poor for their direct and continuing benefits;

(iv) to produce positive impact on wage levels; and

(v) to bring about over-all improvement in quality of life in rural areas.

Swarna Jayanti Shahri Rozgar Yojana (SJSRY)

The SJSRY came into operation in December 1997 through a restructuring and streamlining of the earlier urban poverty alleviation programmes, the Nehru Rozgar Yojana (NRY), the Urban Basic Services for the Poor (UBSP) and the Prime Minister's Integrated Urban Poverty Alleviation Programme (PMIUPAP). It seeks to provide employment to the urban unemployed or underemployed living below poverty line and educated up to ninth standard through encouraging the setting up of self-employment ventures or provision of wage employment.

It comprises two special schemes: The Urban Self-Employment Programme (USEP) and The Urban Wage Employment Programme (UWEP).

The SJSRY also gives special impetus to empower and uplift the poor women and has launched a special programme, viz., Development of Women and Children in Urban Areas (DWCUA), under which groups of urban poor women setting up self-employment ventures are eligible for subsidy up to 50 per cent of the project cost.

This programme was recast as National Urban Livelihood Mission in 2013-14.

SOCIAL PROTECTION SCHEMES

The poor and the unemployed as they grow older become more and more defenceless, as they are unable to find livelihood or the strength to work. They need public assistance.

National Social Assistance Programme

On August 15, 1995, for the first time a social assistance programme was launched, viz., the National Social Assistance Programme (NSAP).

The basic aim of this programme was to provide social assistance benefit to the rural poor in case of old age, death of primary breadwinner, and for poor women during maternity. It aims at providing them with some dignity and support, thereby ensuring a minimum quality of care and attention from the community. It provides an opportunity for linking the social assistance package to schemes for poverty alleviation and provision of basic needs. A Centrally- sponsored scheme with 100 per cent Central assistance provided to States/UTs, it is implemented through a synergistic partnership with state governments and under the direct supervision of DRDAs in close collaboration with the various PRIs.

At present, NSAP comprises the following schemes:

1. **Indira Gandhi National Old Age Pension Scheme (IGNOAPS)** : Under the scheme, BPL, pensions in the age group of 60-79 years are entitled to a monthly pension of ₹ 200 and BPL persons of age of 80 years and above are entitled to a monthly pension of ₹ 500.

2. **Indira Gandhi National Widows Pension Scheme (IGNWPS)** : BPL widows aged 40-59 years are entitled to a monthly pension of ₹ 200.

3. **Indira Gandhi National Disability Pension Scheme (IGNDPS)** : BPL pensions aged 18-59 years with severe and multiple disabilities are entitled to a monthly pension of ₹ 200.

4. **National Family Benefit Scheme (NFBS):** Under the scheme a BPL household is entitled to lump sum amount of money on the death of the primary breadwinner aged between 18 and 64 years. The amount of assistance is ₹ 10,000.

5. **Annapurna Scheme :** Launched as a Centrally-sponsored scheme, "Annapurna" scheme aims at providing food security to indigent senior citizens who have no income of their own and none to take care of them in the villages. The scheme envisages provision of 10 kg of foodgrains per month, free of cost, to senior citizens who are eligible for old age pension but are at present not receiving it. The gram panchayats identify, prepare and display a list of such persons after giving wide publicity. From 2002-03, the programme has been transferred to the NSAP.

   It aims at providing food security to meet the requirement of those senior citizens who though eligible, have remained uncovered under the NOAPS. The ceiling on the total number of Annapurna beneficiaries will be at least 20 per cent of the persons eligible to receive pension under NOAPS.

Antyodaya Anna Yojana

On December 25, 2000, the prime minister announced the implementation of the Antyodaya Anna Yojana (AAY). The scheme was to provide an estimated one crore 'poorest of the poor' families in the country 25 kg of wheat or rice per month at the highly subsidised rates of ₹ 2 and ₹ 3 per kg respectively. The quantity was enhanced to 35 kg from April 1, 2002.

In June 2003, the government expanded AAY to cover an additional 50 lakh BPL families from amongst the following priority groups: (i) households headed by widows or terminally ill persons or disabled persons or persons aged 60 years or more with no assured means of subsistence or societal support; (ii) widows or terminally ill persons or disabled persons or persons aged 60 years or more or single women or single men with no family or societal support or assured means of subsistence; (iii) all primitive tribal households.

The AAY Scheme has been expanded in subsequent years and presently it is covering 2.50 crore households.

Janashree Bima Yojana

It provides life insurance protection to the rural and urban poor persons below poverty line and marginally above the poverty line. The premium under the scheme was ₹ 200 per annum per member. 50 per cent of the premium, *i.e.,* ₹ 100 was contributed by the member and/or nodal agency/state government and the balance 50 per cent was met by the Social Security Fund. Janashree Bima Yojana has now been merged with the Aam Admi Bima Yojana (AABY) to provide better administration of life insurance cover to the economically backward sections of society. In the event of death (other than by accident) of the member, an amount of ₹ 30,000 is payable. In case of death/total permanent disability due to accident, an amount of ₹ 75,000 is payable. In case of permanent partial disability, due to accident, an amount of ₹ 37,500 is payable.

Aam Admi Bima Yojana (AABY)

Launched on October 2, 2007, insurance to the head of the family of rural landless households in the country will be provided against natural death as well as accidental death and partial/permanent disability. This cover is ₹ 75,000 on death due to accident and permanent disability due to accident, ₹ 37,500 in case of partial permanent disability due to accident and ₹ 30,000 in case of death of a member, prior to terminal date. The premium to be charged under the scheme is ₹ 200 per annum per member, 50 per cent of which is to be contributed by the Central government and remaining by state governments.

Rashtriya Swasthya Bima Yojana

The Rashtriya Swasthya Bima Yojana was formally launched on October 1, 2007. All workers in the unorganised sector who come in the category of Below Poverty Line (BPL) and their families will be covered under the scheme. The scheme also has a provision of smart card to be issued to the beneficiaries to enable cashless transaction for healthcare. Total sum insured would be ₹ 30,000 per family per annum with Government of India contributing 75 per cent of the annual estimated premium while state governments are expected to contribute 25 per cent of the annual premium as well as any additional premium. The cost of smart card would also be borne by Central government.

Atal Pension Yojana

The Government of India is extremely concerned about the old age income security of the working poor and is focussed on encouraging and enabling them to join the National Pension System (NPS). The Finance Minister has announced a new initiative called Atal Pension Yojana (APY) in his Budget Speech for 2015-16. This newly proposed scheme will replace 'Swavalamban Scheme' introduced in 2010-11. The APY will be focussed on all citizens in the unorganised sector, who join the

National Pension System (NPS) administered by the Pension Fund Regulatory and Development Authority (PFRDA) and who are not members of any statutory social security schemes. Under the APY, the subscribers would receive the fixed pension of ₹ 1000 per month, ₹ 2000 per month, ₹ 3000 per month, ₹ 4000 per month, ₹ 5000 per month, at the age of 60 years, depending on their contributions, which itself would vary on the age of joining the APY. The minimum age of joining APY is 18 years and maximum age is 40 years. Therefore, minimum period of contribution by the subscriber under APY would be 20 years or more. The benefit of fixed pension would be guaranteed by the Government.

Atal Innovation Mission

NITI Aayog has constituted an Expert Committee under the Chairmanship of Prof Tarun Khanna, Director, South Asia Institute, Harvard University and Jorge Paulo Lemann Professor, Harvard Business School, USA, to work out the detailed contours of Atal Innovation Mission (AIM) and Self-Employment and Talent Utilisation (SETU). The terms of Reference of the Expert Committee are as under:

1. To review the existing initiatives aimed at promoting innovation and entrepreneurship in India, especially those efforts that result in widespread job growth and the creation of globally competitive enterprises.

2. It will make short and medium-term recommendations for actionable policy initiatives aimed at creating an innovation and entrepreneur friendly ecosystem including such elements as creation of world class innovation hubs and digital SMEs and innovation driven entrepreneurship in such sectors as education and health.

3. To address any other related issues.

National Rural Livelihood Mission—Aajeevika

It is the skill and placement initiative of the Ministry of Rural Development. It is a part of the National Rural Livelihood Mission (NRLM)–the Mission for "Poverty Reduction" is called Aajeevika. It evolved out of the need to diversify incomes of the rural poor and provide them with jobs with regular monthly wages at or above the minimum wages. Under this mission, Self-Help Groups (SHGs) at the village level is constituted in the form of federation and these SHGs provide beneficial self-employment opportunities to the rural people for ensuring better and stable livelihood. The new mission gives focus on women, scheduled caste/scheduled tribes, minorities and disabled people. The mission proposes to include at least one woman member of the identified poor family in Self-Help Group.

The SGSY, now restructured as the NRLM has been renamed Aajeevika and implemented in mission mode across the country since 2011. The main features of Aajeevika are: (a) One woman member from each identified rural poor household to be brought under the SHG network, (b) Ensuring 50 per cent of the beneficiaries from SC/STs, 15 per cent from minorities, and 3 per cent persons with disability while keeping in view the ultimate target of 100 per cent coverage of BPL families (c) Training for capacity building and skill development, (d) Ensuring revolving fund and capital subsidy, (e) Financial inclusion, (f) Provision of interest subsidy, (g) Backward and forward linkages, and (h) Promoting innovations.

Minimum Wages for Unskilled Manual Workers Revised

Government of India revised wages for unskilled manual workers on 23rd March, 2016. The wage rates across the state are as under:

State/UTs	Wage Rate ₹/Day	State/UTs	Wage Rate ₹/Day
1. Andhra Pradesh	194	18. Mizoram	188
2. Arunachal Pradesh	172	19. Nagaland	172
3. Assam	182	20. Odisha	174
4. Bihar	167	21. Punjab	218
5. Chhattisgarh	167	22. Rajasthan	181
6. Gujarat	188	23. Sikkim	172
7. Goa	229	24. Tamil Nadu	203
8. Himachal Pradesh		25. Tripura	172
(a) Non-Scheduled Areas	170	26. Uttar Pradesh	174
(b) Scheduled Areas	213	27. Uttarakhand	174
		28. West Bengal	176
9. Haryana	259	29. Telangana	194
10. Jammu & Kashmir	173	30. Andaman & Nicobar	
11. Jharkhand	167	(a) Andaman	230
12. Karnataka	224	(b) Nicobar	243
13. Kerala	240	31. Dadra & Nagar Haveli	208
14. Madhya Pradesh	167	32. Daman & Diu	192
15. Maharashtra	192	33. Lakshdweep	220
16. Manipur	197	34. Puducherry	203
17. Meghalaya	169	35. Chandigarh	248

Drought-Prone Area Programme (DPAP)

This National Programme was launched in 1973-74 in some selected Drought Prone Areas of the country. The main objective of this plan was to reestablish the environmental balance in these areas by promoting the balanced development of land, water and other natural resources. For this programme, the arrangement of the finance is done by the Centre and the State concerned in the ratio of 75 : 25. Presently 972 blocks of 182 districts in 16 states are covered under the programme. This programme is being carried on by the Rural Development Department.

Along with the urbanisation, the people of the rural areas have a tendency to migrate towards the urban areas. When there is no agricultural work in the villages, the agricultural labourers generally move in large number to the cities in search of job. The number of industrial units are not increasing in the proportion to absorb the increased labour force. The second type of urban unemployment is visible in the form of educated unemployment. Along with the spread of education, the number of educated unemployed is rapidly increasing.

Unemployment and Employment Generation

A person is considered unemployed, if he/she is not working but is either seeking or is available for a work for a relatively longs time throughout the year.

In the NSS survey, all those who were either unemployed or out of labour force but had worked for at least 30 days over the reference year were treated as subsidiary status workers and hence included in labour force. The usual status (US) unemployment rate is generally regarded as the measure of open unemployment during the reference year; the current weekly status (CWS) unemployment, but with reduced reference period of a week. The reference period is one week. A person is considered unemployed if he/she has not worked even for one hour during the week but is seeking or is available for work. The estimates are made in terms of the average number of persons unemployed per week.

TYPES OF UNEMPLOYMENT

(i) **Cyclical Unemployment:** The main cause of cyclical unemployment is the periodic slackness in business activities. This type of unemployment is generally witnessed in the developed countries.

(ii) **Frictional Unemployment:** The temporary unemployment which exists during the period of the transfer of labour from one occupation to another is called frictional unemployment.

(iii) **Structural Unemployment:** Basically, India's unemployment is structural in nature, related to the inadequacy of productive capacity to create enough jobs for all those able and willing to work. Not only is the productive capacity much below the needed capacity, but also it is found increasing at a low rate. This type of unemployment is not a temporary phenomenon in the sense that it will pass of on its own after a lapse of time. It is chronic and is the result of backwardness and low rate of economic development.

(iv) **Disguised Unemployment:** When more people are engaged in a job than actually required, they are called disguisedly unemployed. If a part of labour is withdrawn and the total production remains unchanged, this withdrawn labour is called disguised unemployed labour.

(v) **Seasonal Unemployment:** Generally, seasonal unemployment is confined to the agricultural sector because nature predominates in agriculture. The demand for agricultural labour increases at the time of sowing and harvesting which provides employment for six to eight months and for the remaining period most of the agricultural workers remain unemployed.

The National Sample Survey Organisation (NSSO) uses three concepts of unemployment.

(i) **Usual status or chronic unemployment** (measured in number of persons) refers to persons who remain unemployed for a major part of the year; activity status is determined with reference to a longer period, say a year preceding to the time of survey;

(ii) **Current weekly status unemployment** (measured in number of persons), determines the activity status of a person on an average weekly basis during the survey year. If in the week preceding the survey, the person seeking employment fails to get work for even one hour on any day of the week he/she is considered unemployed. If he/she gets work for an hour or more at any time in that period he/she is considered to be employed. This status includes the chronically unemployed and the intermittently unemployed;

(iii) **Current daily status unemployment** (measured in number of days or person years), considers the activity status of a person each day of the preceding seven days to the survey. A person who works for one hour but less than four hours is considered having worked for half a day. A person working for four hours or more is considered to have been employed for the whole day. The rate is a time rate, unlike the other two which are a person rate.

The Eleventh Five Year Plan has largely used the Current Daily Status (CDS) basis of estimation of employment and unemployment in the country. It has also been observed that the estimates based on daily status is the most inclusive rate of 'unemployment' giving the average level of unemployment on a day during the survey year. It captures the unemployed days of the chronically unemployed, the unemployed days of usually employed who become intermittently unemployed during the reference week and unemployed days of those classified as employed according to the criterion of current weekly status.

TASK FORCE ON EMPLOYMENT OPPORTUNITIES

The Planning Commission constituted a Task Force on Employment Opportunities under the Chairmanship of Dr. Montek Singh Ahluwalia, the then member, Planning Commission to examine the existing employment and unemployment situation in the country and to suggest strategies of employment generation for providing employment opportunities to one crore people on an average.

But the Task Force of the Planning Commission which submitted its Report in 2001 opted to pursue the failed strategy on the employment front even for the next 12 years as given in the projections. The employment projections given in the report reveal that with 6.5 per cent GDP growth, employment will increase from a level of 397 million in 1999-2000 to 468 million in 2012—an increase of 71 million in a period of 12 years, giving an annual average growth of 5.9 million. With 8 per cent GDP growth, employment is expected to increase by 84 million—an annual average of 7 million and with 9 per cent of GDP growth, the employment is expected to grow by 98 million—an annual average of 8.2 million. In other words, the Task Force failed to suggest a strategy with which an annual average growth rate of 10 million jobs can be achieved as specified in its terms of reference. This failure is due to the fact that the Task Force is concentrating on the enlargement of the organised sector employment as the main vehicle of employment generation. However, facts reveal that share of organised sector in employment has plummeted from around 10 per cent in the late 1980s to 7 per cent in the late 1990s. To hope that the organised sector, which accounts for merely 7 per cent of total employment will generate enough employment of the order of 10 million jobs per year over the next 10 years is to live in a fool's paradise.

It would, therefore, be desirable to examine some of the recommendations of the Task Force to understand the logic of our assessment of the recommendations of the Ahluwalia Task Force:

1. It is necessary to encourage private corporate sector to invest in agriculture and related activities by facilitating the creation of organised and corporatised entities like Integrated Agricultural Complexes and Food Parks that would attract commercial investment.

2. Degraded and wasteland can be taken out of the purview of tenancy laws and agro-companies should be allowed to buy, develop, cultivate and sell this land.

3. The active involvement of larger industrial units, including MNCs and cooperatives where possible, in the Food Processing Industries, is essential ... Major national and international food processing companies should be approached to ascertain the nature of the problem which limits their activities at present.

4. A phased process of dereservation of small-scale industries should be completed in the next four years.

5. In the construction sector, the present bias against large construction firms should be removed.

6. Retail trade is characterised by small establishments and modernising retail trade involving large departmental stores is often considered detrimental to the employment objective. The switch to modern retailing will certainly improve the quality of employment in the sector.

7. The road transport sector, at present, is dominated by small operators. This is a sector where considerable economies of scale exist. Emergence of modern and large transport companies will not only improve the efficiency of the sector but will also provide better conditions for workers in this sector and in associated roadside activities like repair services and hotels, etc.

8. Reforms of Labour Laws: India's Labour Laws have evolved in a manner, that has greatly reduced the flexibility available to employers to adjust the labour force in the light of changing economic circumstances. The most important change needed is to abolish the requirement of prior permission of government for retrenchment, layoffs or closure by deleting chapter VB from the Industrial Disputes Act.

The Contract Labour (Regulation and Abolition) Act needs to be suitably amended to allow all peripheral activities to be freely outsourced from specialised firms, even if it means employees of the specialised firms provide the service on the premises of the outsourcing units.

The catalogue of the above recommendations of the Task Force only reveals that most of its recommendations were employment-restricting, rather than employment generating. With this approach, to reach the goal of providing 10 million additional jobs per year as indicated in the terms of reference was well nigh impossible.

Issue of Labour Flexibility

The first issue is that of labour flexibility. The supporters of labour flexibility argue that this helps to stimulate growth. Gerry Rogers of the ILO has examined the issue of security versus performance. The impact of security on levels of employment "is a complex relationship. It is sometimes said that much security is bad for employment – that people with greater security of employment and income put less effort into their work and so are less productive. In other words, greater security reduces output and employment. But in reality the empirical evidence is mixed. High levels of security, for instance, in some public sector enterprises, may make adjustment or innovation difficult, and so adversely affect economic performance. But countries such as Sweden, which have maintained high levels of employment security, or countries such as Netherlands which have ensured high levels of income security, have also performed well in terms of employment. There is no sign that legislation to increase employment security in Chile or Korea in the 1990s had adverse effects on employment. On the contrary, when the Asian financial crisis struck, it could be seen that the mechanisms for security were too weak, and the crisis had unnecessarily large effects on unemployment, incomes and poverty." Thus, to assume that security restricts employment is not the correct assessment. Infact, labour flexibility will give the employers unbridled right of exploitation and trespassing the legitimate rights of workers. There is a need to bring about synergy between the interests of labour and employers so as to promote growth, rather than aggravate dissipation of energy in conflict.

REASONS OF UNEMPLOYMENT

The reasons for unemployment in India can be categorised under three main heads:

   (i) Underdeveloped nature of economy

   (ii) Inadequate employment planning

   (iii) Rapid growth of population.

In the pre-independence period, the British exploited our resources and destroyed indigenous small-scale and cottage industries. The net burden of surplus workers fell on the already overburdened agricultural sector. Even in post-independence phase, due to slow rate of capital formation, the economy was not able to generate sufficient infrastructural facilities which could absorb the people searching for jobs. Employment in agriculture is declining. Also, there has been migration of labour from rural to urban areas.

Sixth Economic Census 2013

According to the Sixth Economic Census 2013, the number of people employed in the country rose by 34.35% to 12.77 crore in eight years to 2013. The employment in urban areas increased by 37.46% to 6.14 crore, while in rural India the growth was 31.59% to 6.62 crore between 2005 and 2013.

The proportion of women in total workforce increased to 25.56% in 2013 from about 20% in 2005. In urban areas, the proportion of female workers was 19.8% compared to 30.9% in rural areas. The economic census does not include those employed in agriculture, public administration, defense and compulsory social security services activities.

Among the states, Maharashtra was on top of the list with maximum number of employees at 1.43 crore, followed by Uttar Pradesh at 1.37 crore, West Bengal at 1.15 crore, Tamil Nadu 1.08 crore and Gujarat at 90.63 lakh. Among the Union Territories, Delhi has the maximum number of employees at 29.84 lakh followed by Chandigarh at 2.38 lakh and Puducherry at 2.17 lakh.

In terms of percentage growth in total employment during the period, number of workers grew at higher rate of 83.29% in Manipur, followed by 78.84% in Assam, 77.14% in Sikkim, 75.26% in Uttar Pradesh and 68.81% in Himachal Pradesh.

Employment till recently did not form an integral part of planning strategy. Suitable labour-intensive techniques have not yet been developed. Poor manpower planning is yet another important cause. There is a mismatch between skills and employment opportunities. The rapid growth of population further adds to the severity of the problem of unemployment. The demand for consumption goods increases and the resources meant for capital formation diminish. Other associated factors are inappropriate technology being used and stunted plan for broadening the resource base.

EMPLOYMENT CHALLENGES FOR THE TWELFTH FIVE YEAR PLAN

Correct estimation of employment and unemployment is essential for proper planning and policy recommendation for a Five Year Plan. Normally there are three approaches (UPSS, CWS and CDS) used in estimating employment/unemployment. Decision on the proper approach to be followed would help in correct estimation and planning. The current employment/ unemployment situation should form the basis for projections for the 12th Plan period. At the same time the estimates of employment/ unemployment should be available at frequent intervals for more effective policy interventions.

One major challenge to be addressed for the 12th Plan period is how to increase the share of formal sector employment opportunities. Movements and transformation of employment from informal sector to formal sector need to be analysed. Incentives have to be given for expanding organized sector employment. Employment interventions already initiated by the Government need to be evaluated. Service sectors like insurance, finance and banking, tourism are going to major generator of employment opportunities. Sector specific strategies need to be adopted to generate employment opportunities. Rigidity in labour laws is often quoted as a major constraint in augmenting organized sector employment. However, the focus should be to promote labour market flexibility without compromising fairness to labour.

When any economy grows, over a period of time the contribution of agriculture sector to GDP should decline while that of manufacturing and services sectors should increase. Concomitant with this the share of employment should also increase in manufacturing and services sector. Unfortunately, for the Indian economy although contribution to GDP from the agriculture has declined sharply (less than 20%), the number of people employed in agriculture continues to be very high.

Although some expansion in employment has taken place in the manufacturing and non-manufacturing sectors, however, a large part of the same falls under informal employment. It is necessary to have urban and rural labour market planning for shifting surplus work force from rural areas. However, option for geographic targeting is limited considering the endowment of different States. Manufacturing sector, however, would have limits in generating new employment as more and more industries adopt capital intensive technologies. Global trends in employment indicate that employment in service sector has increased. Hence, strategies in India must lay emphasis on the service sector for generating more employment.

NSS data shows that female employment has declined both in rural areas and urban areas in recent years. This is a major concern and needs to be addressed during the 12th Plan period. Women workers are the most vulnerable to job losses in case of any global crisis. Unemployment among the educated people is going to be a major issue during the 12th Plan period. India is one of the few countries which have the phenomenon of educated unemployment in large number. The major reason behind this is the dearth of vocational and technical education among youths. Similarly, the issue of promoting employment opportunities for minorities, SC/ST and differently abled people assumes importance. Employment needs and education provided need to be matched.

EMPLOYMENT GENERATION PROGRAMMES IN INDIA

According to a general survey done by the National Sample Survey Organization (NSSO), 58% of total employment exists in rural sector and only 38% in urban sector of our country. As per the estimation by the Rangarajan Panel the number of Below Poverty Line declined to 21.9% of the population in 2011-12 from 29.8% in 2009-10 and 37.2% in 2004-05. As per the Suresh Tendulkar panel's recommendations in 2011-12, the poverty line had been fixed at ₹ 27 spending in rural areas and ₹ 33 in urban areas so total poverty is 21.9% at the national level.

Anti poverty measures and Employment Generating programmes are:

1. **Integrated Rural Development Programme (IRDP):** The Integrated Rural Development Programme (IRDP), which was introduced in 1978-79 and universalized from 2nd October, 1980, aimed at providing assistance to the rural poor in the form of subsidy and bank credit for productive employment opportunities through successive plan periods. On 1st April, 1999, the IRDP and allied programmes were merged into a single programme known as Swarnajayanti Gram Swarozgar Yojana (SGSY). The SGSY emphasizes on organizing the rural poor into self-help groups, capacity-building, planning of activity clusters, infrastructure support, technology, credit and marketing linkages.

2. **Jawahar Rozgar Yojana/Jawahar Gram Samriddhi Yojana:** Under the Wage Employment Programmes, the National Rural Employment Programme (NREP) and Rural Landless Employment Guarantee Programme (RLEGP) were started in Sixth and Seventh Plans. The NREP and RLEGP were merged in April 1989 under Jawahar Rozgar Yojana (JRY). The JRY was meant to generate meaningful employment opportunities for the unemployed and underemployed in rural areas through the creation of economic infrastructure and community and social assets. The JRY was revamped from 1st April, 1999, as Jawahar Gram Samriddhi Yojana (JGSY). It now became a programme for the creation of rural economic infrastructure with employment generation as the secondary objective.

3. **Rural Housing – Indira Awaas Yojana:** The Indira Awaas Yojana (IAY) programme aims at providing free housing to Below Poverty Line (BPL) families in rural areas and main targets would be the households of SC/STs. It was first

merged with the Jawahar Rozgar Yojana (JRY) in 1989 and in 1996 it broke away from JRY into a separate housing scheme for the rural poor.

4. **Food for Work Programme:** The Food for Work Programme was started in 2000-01 as a component of EAS. It was first launched in eight drought-affected states of Chhattisgarh, Gujarat, Himachal Pradesh, Madhya Pradesh, Odisha, Rajasthan, Maharashtra and Uttarakhand. It aims at enhancing food security through wage employment. Food grains are supplied to states free of cost, however, the supply of food grains from the Food Corporation of India (FCI) godowns has been slow.

5. **Sampoorna Gramin Rozgar Yojana (SGRY):** The JGSY, EAS and Food for Work Programme were revamped and merged under the new Sampoorna Gramin Rozgar Yojana (SGRY) Scheme from 1st September, 2001. The main objective of the scheme continues to be the generation of wage employment, creation of durable economic infrastructure in rural areas and provision of food and nutrition security for the poor.

6. **Mahatma Gandhi National Rural Employment Guarantee Act (MGNREGA) 2005:** It was launched on February 2, 2005. The Act provides 100 days assured employment every year to every rural household. One-third of the proposed jobs would be reserved for women. The central government will also establish National Employment Guarantee Funds. Similarly, state governments will establish State Employment Guarantee Funds for implementation of the scheme. Under the programme, if an applicant is not provided employment within 15 days s/he will be entitled to a daily unemployment allowance.

Salient features of MGNREGA are:
   I. Right based framework
   II. Time bound guarantee of employment
   III. Labour intensive work

IV. Women empowerment

V. Transparency and accountability

VI. Adequate funding by central government

7. **National Food for Work Programme:** It was launched on November 14, 2004 in 150 most backward districts of the country. The objective of the programme was to provide additional resources available under Sampoorna Grameen Rojgar Yojna. This was 100% centrally funded programme. Now this programme has been subsumed in the MGNREGA from February 2, 2006.

8. **National Rural Livelihood Mission: Ajeevika (2011):** It is the skill and placement initiative of Ministry of Rural development. It is a part of National Rural Livelihood Mission (NRLM)–the mission for poverty reduction is called Ajeevika (2011).

9. **Pradhan Mantri Kaushal Vikas Yojna:** The cabinet on March 21, 2015 cleared the scheme to provide skill training to 1.4 million youth with an overall outlay of ₹ 1120 crore. This plan is implemented with the help of Ministry of Skill Development and Entrepreneurship through the National Skill Development Corporation. It will focus on fresh entrant to the labour market, especially labour market and class X and XII dropouts.

10. **National Heritage Development and Augmentation Yojna (HRIDAY):** HRIDAY scheme was launched (21 Jan. 2015) to preserve and rejuvenate the rich cultural heritage of the country. This ₹ 500 crore programme was launched by Urban Development Ministry in New Delhi. Initially it is launched in 12 cities: Amritsar, Varanasi, Gaya, Puri, Ajmer, Mathura, Dwarka, Badami, Velankanni, Kanchipuram, Warangal and Amravati. These programmes played/are playing a very crucial role in the development of the all sections of the society so that the concept of holistic development can be ensured in the real sense.

Sustainable Development and Environmental Issues

Sustainable development is a buzz word in natural resources development today. In view of the increase awareness of environmental problems, the accent on sustainable development has grown in recent times, particularly in respect of activities which degrade the environment and affect communities adversely. Mining is one such activity.

Sustainable development, at this time could be the most concern phenomenon. Globally each country together with most developing countries like India and China thinks greatly regarding it, as a result they realise that their future generation should suffer the lack of resources, that is clearly most central to survive. Any country, environmental issues area unit is associated with the amount of its economic development, the supply of natural resources and therefore life style of its populations. In India zoom of population, poverty, urbanization, industrialization and a number of other connected factors area unit is to blame for the speedy degradation of the surroundings. Environmental issues have become serious in several elements of the country, and therefore can't be unnoticed.

The need for equity is starkly reflected in the fact that the emissions per capita in industrialized countries are ten to twelve times those of developing countries. The total emission in the world must decline. We must find a way of solving this problem in a way that does not deprive developing countries of their right to develop.

Economic growth, social development and environment protection are the three pillars of sustainable development. Sustainability has different meanings for different contexts.

Sustainable Development in India encompasses a variety of development schemes in social, cleantech (clean energy, clean water and sustainable agriculture) and human resources segments, having caught the attention of both central and state governments and also public and private sectors. Almost all departments of Government of India are involved in decision making for sustainable development. In fact, India is expected to begin the greening of its national income accounting, making depletion in natural resources wealth a key component in its measurement of gross domestic product (GDP).

India's sustained efforts towards reducing greenhouse gases (GHG) will ensure that the country's per capita emission of GHG will continue to be low until 2030-31, and it is estimated that per capita emission in 2031 will be lower than per capita global emission of GHG in 2005. Even in 2031, India's per capita GHG emissions would stay under four tonnes of CO_2, which is lower than the global per capita emission of 4.22 tonnes of CO_2 in 2005.

In 1972, the then Prime Minister of India, Mrs. Indira Gandhi emphasized, at the UN Conference on Human Environment at Stockholm, that the removal of poverty is an integral part of the goal of an environmental strategy for the world. The concepts of interrelatedness, of a shared planet, of global citizenship, and of 'spaceship earth' cannot be restricted to environmental issues alone. They apply equally to the shared and inter-linked responsibilities of environmental protection and human development.

History has led to vast inequalities, leaving almost three-fourths of the world's people living in less-developed countries and one-fifth below the poverty line. The long-term impact of past industrialization, exploitation and environmental damage cannot be wiped away. It is only right that development in this new century be even more conscious of its long-term impact. The problems are complex and the choices difficult. Our common future can only be achieved with a better understanding of our common concerns and shared responsibilities.

Following are some perspectives and approaches towards achieving a sustainable future:

Poverty Eradication and Sustainable Livelihoods

Poverty and a degraded environment are closely inter-related, especially where people depend for their livelihoods primarily on the natural resource base of their immediate environment. Restoring natural systems and improving natural resource management practices at the grassroot level are central to a strategy to eliminate poverty.

The survival needs of the poor force them to continue to degrade an already degraded environment. Removal of poverty is therefore a prerequisite for the protection of the environment.

Poverty magnifies the problem of hunger and malnutrition. The problem is further compounded by the inequitable access of the poor to the food that is available. It is therefore necessary to strengthen the public distribution system to overcome this inequity.

Diversion of common and marginal lands to 'economically useful purposes' deprives the poor of a resource base which has traditionally met many of their sustenance needs.

Market forces also lead to the elimination of crops that have traditionally been integral to the diet of the poor, thereby threatening food security and nutritional status.

While conventional economic development leads to the elimination of several traditional occupations, the process of sustainable development, guided by the need to protect and conserve the environment, leads to the creation of new jobs and of opportunities for the reorientation of traditional skills to new occupations.

Women, while continuing to perform their traditional domestic roles are increasingly involved in earning livelihoods. In many poor households they are often the principal or the sole breadwinners. A major thrust at the policy level is necessary to ensure equity and justice for them.

Literacy and a basic education are essential for enabling the poor to access the benefits offered by development initiatives and market opportunities. Basic education is therefore a precondition for sustainable development.

A sizeable proportion (about 60 per cent according to some estimates) of the population is not integrated into the market economy. Ensuring the security of their livelihoods is an imperative for sustainable development.

Changing Unsustainable Patterns of Consumption and Production

With increasing purchasing power, wasteful consumption linked to market driven consumerism is stressing the resource base of developing countries further. It is important to counter this through education and public awareness.

In several areas, desirable limits and standards for consumption need to be established and applied through appropriate mechanisms including education, incentives and legislation.

Several traditional practices that are sustainable and environment friendly continue to be a regular part of the lives of people in developing countries. These need to be encouraged rather than replaced by more 'modern' but unsustainable practices and technologies.

Development decisions regarding technology and infrastructure are a major determinant of consumption patterns. It is therefore important to evaluate and make development decisions which structurally lead to a more sustainable society.

Technologies exist through which substantial reduction in consumption of resources is possible. Efforts to identify, evaluate, introduce and use these technologies must be made.

Subsidies often lead to wasteful and unsustainable consumption by distorting the value of a resource. All pricing mechanisms must be evaluated from a sustainable development point of view.

Protecting and Managing the Natural Resource Base of Economic and Social Development

The integration of agriculture with land and water management, and with ecosystem conservation is essential for both environmental sustainability and agricultural production.

An environmental perspective must guide the evaluation of all development projects, recognizing the role of natural resources in local livelihoods. This recognition must be informed by a comprehensive understanding of the perceptions and opinions of local people about their stakes in the resource base.

To ensure the sustainability of the natural resource base, the recognition of all stakeholders in it and their roles in its protection and management are essential.

There is need to establish well-defined and enforceable rights (including customary rights) and security of tenure, and to ensure equal access to land, water and other natural and biological resources. It should be ensured that this applies, in particular, to indigenous communities, women and other disadvantaged groups living in poverty.

Water governance arrangements should protect ecosystems and preserve or restore the ecological integrity of all natural water bodies and their catchments. This will maintain the wide range of ecological services that healthy ecosystems provide and the livelihoods that depend upon them.

Biomass is, and will continue for a long time, to be a major source of fuel and energy, especially for the rural poor. Recognizing this fact, appropriate mechanisms must be evolved to make such consumption of biomass sustainable, through both resource management and the promotion of efficient and minimally polluting technologies, and technologies which will progressively reduce the pressures on biomass, which cause environmental degradation.

The traditional approaches to natural resource management such as sacred groves and ponds, water harvesting and management systems, etc., should be revived by creating institutional mechanisms which recapture the ecological wisdom and the spirit of community management inherent in those systems.

Sustainable Development in a Globalizing World

Globalization as it is taking place today is increasing the divide between the rich and the poor. It has to be steered so that it serves not only commercial interests but also the social needs of development.

Global business thrives on, and therefore encourages and imposes high levels of homogeneity in consumer preferences. On the other hand, for development to be locally appropriate and sustainable, it must be guided by local considerations which lie in cultural diversity and traditions. Therefore, recognition at the policy level, of the significance of diversity, and the need to preserve it, is an important precondition for sustainable development.

In an increasingly globalizing economy, developing countries, for want of the appropriate skills, are often at a disadvantage in negotiating and operating multilateral trade agreements. Regional cooperation for capacity building is therefore necessary to ensure their effective participation in all stages of multilateral trade.

Globalization is driven by a vast, globally spread, human resource engine involving millions of livelihoods. Their security is sometimes threatened by local events causing global distortions (*e.g.*, the impact of the WTC attack on jobs in India or, in a wider context, sanctions against countries not conforming to 'international' prescriptions in human rights or environment related maters). Mechanisms to safeguard trade and livelihoods, especially in developing countries, must be evolved and negotiated to make globalization an effective vehicle of sustainable development.

War and armed conflict are a major threat to sustainable development. It is imperative to evolve effective mechanisms for mediation in such situations and to resolve contentious issues without compromising the larger developmental goals of the conflicting parties.

Health and Sustainable Development

Human health in its broadest sense of physical, mental and spiritual well-being is to a great extent dependent on the access of the citizen to a healthy environment. For a healthy, productive and fulfilling life every individual should have the physical and economic access to a balanced diet, safe drinking water, clean air, sanitation, environmental hygiene, primary healthcare and education.

Access to safe drinking water and a healthy environment should be a fundamental right of every citizen.

Citizens of developing countries continue to be vulnerable to a double burden of diseases. Traditional diseases such as malaria and cholera, caused by unsafe drinking water and lack of environmental hygiene, have not yet been controlled. In addition, people are now falling prey to modern diseases such as cancer and AIDS, and stress-related disorders.

Many of the widespread ailments among the poor in developing countries are occupation-related, and are contracted in the course of work done to fulfil the consumption demands of the affluent, both within the country and outside.

The strong relationship between health and the state of the environment in developing countries is becoming increasingly evident. This calls for greater emphasis on preventive and social medicine, and on research in both occupational health and epidemiology.

Because of the close link, there needs to be greater integration between the ministries of Health and Environment, and effective coordination and cooperation between them.

Basic health and educational facilities in developing countries need to be strengthened. The role of public health services must give preventive healthcare equal emphasis as curative healthcare. People should be empowered through education and awareness to participate in managing preventive healthcare related to environmental sanitation and hygiene.

Most developing countries are repositories of a rich tradition of natural resource-based healthcare. This is under threat, on the one hand from modern mainstream medicine, and on the other from the degradation of the natural resource base. Traditional medicine in combination with modern medicine must be promoted while ensuring conservation of the resource base and effective protection of IPRs of traditional knowledge.

Developing countries should also strive to strengthen the capacity of their healthcare systems to deliver basic health services and to reduce environment-related health risks by sharing health awareness and medical expertise globally.

THE SUSTAINABLE DEVELOPMENT GOALS (SDGs)

In September 2015, the United Nations General Assembly formally adopted the "universal, integrated and transformative" 2030 Agenda for Sustainable Development, a set of 17 Sustainable Development Goals (SDGs). The goals are to be implemented and achieved in every country from the year 2016 to 2030.

Sustainable development, or sustainability, has been described in terms of three spheres, dimensions, domains and pillars, *i.e.,* the environment, the economy and society. The three-sphere framework was initially proposed by the economist René Passet in 1979. It has also been worded as "economic, environmental and social" or "ecology, economy and equity". This has been expanded by some authors to include a fourth pillar of culture, institutions or governance, or alternatively reconfigured as four domains of the social - ecology, economics, politics and culture, thus bringing economics back inside the social, and treating ecology as the intersection of the social and the natural.

Environmental

The ecological stability of human settlements is a part of the relationship between humans and their natural, social and built environments. Also termed as human ecology, this broadens the focus of sustainable development to include the domain of human health. Fundamental human needs such as the availability and quality of air, water, food and shelter are also the ecological foundations for sustainable development; addressing public health risk through investments in ecosystem services can be a powerful and transformative force for sustainable development which, in this sense, extends to all species.

Environmental sustainability concerns the natural environment and how it endures and remains diverse and productive. Since natural resources are derived from the environment, the state of air, water, and the climate are of particular concern. The IPCC Fifth Assessment Report outlines current knowledge about scientific, technical and socio-economic information concerning climate change, and lists options for adaptation and mitigation. Environmental sustainability requires society to design activities to meet human needs while preserving the life support systems of the planet. This, for example, entails using water sustainably, utilizing renewable energy, and sustainable material supplies (*e.g.*, harvesting wood from forests at a rate that maintains the biomass and biodiversity).

An unsustainable situation occurs when natural capital (the sum total of nature's resources) is used up faster than it can be replenished. Sustainability requires that human activity only uses nature's resources at a rate at which they can be replenished naturally. Inherently the concept of sustainable development is intertwined with the concept of carrying capacity. Theoretically, the long-term result of environmental degradation is the inability to sustain human life. Such degradation on a global scale should imply an increase in human death rate until population falls to what the degraded environment can support. If the degradation continues beyond a certain tipping point or critical threshold it would lead to eventual extinction for humanity.

Consumption of non-renewable resources	State of environment	Sustainability
More than nature's ability to replenish	Environmental degradation	Not sustainable
Equal to nature's ability to replenish	Environmental equilibrium economy	Steady state
Less than nature's ability to replenish	Environmental renewal	Environmentally sustainable

Integral elements for a sustainable development are research and innovation activities. A telling example is the European environmental research and innovation policy, which aims at defining and implementing a transformative agendum to green the economy and the society as a whole so to achieve a truly sustainable development. Research and innovation in Europe is financially supported by the programme Horizon 2020, which is also open to participation worldwide. A promising direction towards sustainable development is to design systems that are flexible and reversible.

Pollution of the public resources is really not a different action, it is just a reverse tragedy of the commons, in that instead of taking something out, something is put into the commons. When the costs of polluting the commons are not calculated into the cost of the items consumed, it becomes only natural to pollute, as the cost of pollution is external to the cost of the goods produced and the cost of cleaning the waste before it is discharged exceeds the cost of releasing the waste directly into the commons. So, the only way to solve this problem is by protecting the ecology of the commons by making it, through taxes or fines, more costly to release the waste directly into the commons than would be the cost of cleaning the waste before discharge.

So, one can try to appeal to the ethics of the situation by doing the right thing as an individual, but in the absence of any direct consequences, the individual will tend to do what is best for the person and not what is best for the common good of the public. Once again, this issue needs to be addressed. Because, left unaddressed, the development of the commonly owned property will become impossible to achieve in a sustainable way. So, this topic is central to the understanding of creating a sustainable situation from the management of the public resources that are used for personal use.

Agriculture

Sustainable agriculture consists of environment friendly methods of farming that allow the production of crops or livestock without damage to human or natural systems. It involves preventing adverse effects to soil, water, biodiversity, surrounding or downstream resources—as well as to those working or living on the farm or in neighbouring areas. The concept of sustainable agriculture extends intergenerationally, passing on a conserved or improved natural resource, biotic, and economic base rather than one which has been depleted or polluted. Elements of sustainable agriculture include permaculture, agroforestry, mixed farming, multiple cropping, and crop rotation.

Numerous sustainability standards and certification systems exist, including organic certification, Rainforest Alliance, Fair Trade, UTZ Certified, Bird Friendly, and the Common Code for the Coffee Community (4C).

Energy

Sustainable energy is clean and can be used over a long period of time. Unlike fossil fuels and biofuels that provide the bulk of the world's energy, renewable energy sources like hydroelectric, solar and wind energy produce far less pollution. Solar energy is commonly used on public parking meters, street lights and the roof of buildings. Wind power has expanded quickly, its share of worldwide electricity usage at the end of 2014 was 3.1%. Most of California's fossil fuel infrastructures are sited in or near low-income communities, and have traditionally suffered the most from California's fossil fuel energy system. These communities are historically left out during the decision-making process, and often end up with dirty power plants and other dirty energy projects that poison the air and harm the area. These toxicants are major contributors to health problems in the communities. As renewable energy becomes more common, fossil fuel infrastructures are replaced by renewables, providing better social equity to these communities. Overall, and in the long run, sustainable development in the field of energy is also deemed to contribute to economic sustainability and national security of communities, thus being increasingly encouraged through investment policies.

Technology

One of the core concepts in sustainable development is that technology can be used to assist people meet their developmental needs. Technology to meet these sustainable developmental needs is often referred to as appropriate technology, which is an ideological movement (and its manifestations) originally articulated as intermediate technology by the economist E. F. Schumacher in his influential work, *Small is Beautiful,* and now covers a wide range of technologies. Both Schumacher and many modern-day proponents of appropriate technology also emphasise the technology as people-centred. Today appropriate technology is often developed using open source principles, which have led to open-source appropriate technology (OSAT) and thus many of the plans of the technology can be freely found on the Internet. OSAT has been proposed as a new model of enabling innovation for sustainable development.

Transport

Transportation is a large contributor to greenhouse gas emissions. It is said that one-third of all gases produced are due to transportation. Motorized transport also releases exhaust fumes that contain particulate matter which is hazardous to human health and a contributor to climate change.

Sustainable transport has many social and economic benefits that can accelerate local sustainable development. According to a series of reports by the Low Emission Development Strategies Global Partnership (LEDSGP), sustainable transport can help create jobs, improve commuter safety through investment in bicycle lanes and pedestrian pathways, make access to employment and social opportunities more affordable and efficient. It also offers a practical opportunity to save people's time and household income as well as government budgets, making investment in sustainable transport a 'win-win' opportunity.

Some western countries are making transportation more sustainable in both long-term and short-term implementations. An example is the modifications in available transportation in Freiburg, Germany. The city has implemented extensive methods of public transportation, cycling, and walking, along with large areas where cars are not allowed.

Since many western countries are highly automobile-orientated areas, the main transit that people use is personal vehicles. About 80% of their travel involves cars. Therefore, California, is one of the highest greenhouse gases emitters in the United States. The federal government has to come up with some plans to reduce the total number of vehicle trips in order to lower greenhouse gases emission. Such as:

- Improve public transit through the provision of larger coverage area in order to provide more mobility and accessibility, new technology to provide a more reliable and responsive public transportation network.
- Encourage walking and biking through the provision of wider pedestrian pathway, bike share station in commercial

downtown, locate parking lot far from the shopping centre, limit on street parking, slower traffic lane in downtown area.

- Increase the cost of car ownership and gas taxes through increased parking fees and tolls, encouraging people to drive more fuel efficient vehicles. This can produce a social equity problem, since lower income people usually drive older vehicles with lower fuel efficiency. Government can use the extra revenue collected from taxes and tolls to improve public transportation and benefit poor communities.

Other states and nations have built efforts to translate knowledge in behavioural economics into evidence-based sustainable transportation policies.

Business

The most broadly accepted criterion for corporate sustainability constitutes a firm's efficient use of natural capital. This eco-efficiency is usually calculated as the economic value added by a firm in relation to its aggregated ecological impact. This idea has been popularised by the World Business Council for Sustainable Development (WBCSD) under the following definition: "Eco-efficiency is achieved by the delivery of competitively priced goods and services that satisfy human needs and bring quality of life, while progressively reducing ecological impacts and resource intensity throughout the life-cycle to a level at least in line with the earth's carrying capacity" (DeSimone and Popoff, 1997: 47).

Similar to the eco-efficiency concept but so far less explored is the second criterion for corporate sustainability. Socio-efficiency describes the relation between a firm's value added and its social impact. Whereas, it can be assumed that most corporate impacts on the environment are negative (apart from rare exceptions such as the planting of trees), this is not true for social impacts. These can be either positive (*e.g.*, corporate giving, creation of employment) or negative (*e.g.*, work accidents, mobbing of employees, human rights abuses). Depending on the type of impact socio-efficiency thus either tries to minimise negative social impacts (*i.e.*, accidents per value added) or maximise positive social impacts (*i.e.*, donations per value added) in relation to the value added.

Both eco-efficiency and socio-efficiency are concerned primarily with increasing economic sustainability. In this process they instrumentalise both natural and social capital aiming to benefit from win-win situations. However, as Dyllick and Hockerts point out the business case alone will not be sufficient to realise sustainable development. They point towards eco-effectiveness, socio-effectiveness, sufficiency, and eco-equity as four criteria that need to be met if sustainable development is to be reached.

CASI Global, New York "CSR & Sustainability together lead to sustainable development. CSR as in corporate social responsibility is not what you do with your profits, but is the way you make profits. This means CSR is a part of every department of the company value chain and not a part of HR / independent department. Sustainability as in effects towards Human resources, Environment and Ecology has to be measured within each department of the company."

11

Social Movements

A social movement is a mass movement and a collective attempt of people to bring about a change, or to resist any change. The concept central to any social movement is that people intervene in the process of social change, rather than remaining mere spectators or passive participants in the ebb and flow of life.

Social movements primarily take the form of non-institutionalised collective political action which strive for political and/or social change. While India has witnessed many such movements over the centuries, it is only recently that scholars have begun to study them in depth. Social movements possess a considerable measure of internal order and purposeful orientation. A social movement can be described more or less as a persistent and organised effort on the part of a relatively large group of people to bring about or resist change.

Social movement can be viewed as collective enterprises to establish a new order of life. Social movements are generally seen as phenomena of the modern era and industrised society whether located in the 'First' world or not.

Any social movement involves a group or collectivity, comprising different units, segmented on the basis of personal, structural, or ideological ties.

SOCIO-RELIGIOUS REFORM MOVEMENT

(i) Raja Ram Mohun Roy and Brahmo Samaj: Raja Ram Mohun Roy is looked upon as the first Indian who tried to pull the Indian society out of the medieval age. He initiated new ideas which characterised the early years of the 19th century and gave birth to the Indian Renaissance.

His Social Ideas: Ram Mohun Roy desired to rid Hindu society of all irrational observances and evil customs. He was the first and one of the greatest champions of emancipation of Indian women. In 1822, he published "Modern Encroachments on the Ancient Rights of Females according to the Hindu law of Inheritance." In this pamphlet, on the authority of the ancient *Smriti* writers, he opposed all discriminations and evil practices against women. He opposed polygamy, Kulinism and Sati and came out in support of the inheritance of property by daughters.

His Religious Ideas–Brahmo Samaj: Raja Ram Mohun Roy stood for a rational approach to religion. He was deeply influenced by the monotheism and anti-idolatry of Islam, Suffism, the ethical teachings of Christianity and the liberal and rationalist doctrines of the West. He attacked idol worship as degrading and expounded the conception of "One God of all religions and humanity".

Ram Mohun Roy propagated his ideas through the press. In December 1821 he launched a Bengali weekly, *Sabad Kaumudi* or "The Moon of Intelligence", which was the first Indian newspaper edited, published and managed by Indians. After a year, he began publication of another weekly in Persian– *Mirat-ul-Akhbar* or "The Mirror of Intelligence". Through these newspapers he propagated his political and social ideas.

(ii) Later Offshoots of the Brahmo Samaj, Devendranath Tagore and Tattvabodhini Sabha: After Ram Mohun Roy's death the Brahmo Samaj languished for some time for want of dynamic leadership. Maharshi Dwarkanath Tagore and Pandit Ram Chandra Vidyavagish—one of the earliest disciples of the Raja—managed it for about ten years. Then a true leader was found in Devendranath Tagore (1817-1905), Dwarkanath's eldest son.

Before joining the Brahmo Samaj, and with an idea of investigating the religious truths, Devendranath Tagore organised the Tattvaranjini Sabha at Jorasanko (Calcutta), later renamed as Tattvabodhini Sabha.

(iii) Keshav Chandra Sen and Sangat Sabha: In Devendranath's absence Keshav Chandra Sen joined the Brahmo Samaj in 1857 and a became full-time missionary of the Samaj. Under the combined influence of Devendranath and Keshab Chandra Sen, the Brahmo Samaj entered into a new phase of unusual activity. Young Keshab drew around him a number of earnest enthusiasts, mostly young men with whom he established in 1859 a small society known as Sangat Sabha ('Friendly Association'). Its main objective was to discuss the spiritual and social problems of the day.

(iv) Sadharana Brahmo Samaj: The constitution of the Sadharana Brahmo Samaj, drafted by Anand Mohan Bose, was based on democratic principles and gave equal rights to all members in the management of the Samaj. By this time political consciousness had sprouted and important members of the Samaj like Sivnath Sastri, Anand Mohan Bose, Bipin Chandra Pal, Dwarka Nath Ganguly and Sir Surendra Nath Banerjee, were in the forefront of the movement and contributed immensely to the growth of the spirit of nationalism in India.

(v) Young Bengal Movement: The Young Bengal Movement owed its origin to a most remarkable personality of the 19th century—Henry Louis Vivian Derozio (1809-1831) who came to Calcutta in 1826 and was appointed in the Hindu College as a teacher of English literature and History. Besides this he edited *Hesperus* and *Calcutta Literary Gazette*. He was connected with *India Gazette* as well. Derozio drew round him students of the Hindu College and exercised unprecedented influence over his pupils both in and outside the class. He urged them to live and die for truth—to cultivate and practise all the virtues, shunning vice in every shape. He gave the greatest impetus to free discussion on all subjects—social, moral and religious.

(vi) Prarthana Samaj: As a result of Keshav Chandra Sen's visit to Maharashtra, the Prarthana Samaj ('Prayer Society') was founded in 1867. Its chief architect was Mahadev Govind Ranade (1842-1901), described as "the prophet of cultural renaissance in western India". Its two other prominent leaders were Dr. Atmaram Pandurang and R.G. Bhandarkar. The two main planks of the Samaj were worship and social reform.

(vii) Jyotiba Phule and Satya Shodhak Samaj: Jyotiba Phule, who organised a powerful non-Brahmin movement, was born in 1828 in a Mali family. His education, his personal experiences and association with the Christian missionaries, made him critical of the prevailing Hindu religion and custom. In 1854, he opened a school for the 'untouchables' and started a private orphanage to help widows. Jyoti Phule had a violent dislike of the Brahmin priesthood. He made no distinction between non-Brahmins and untouchables.

(viii) Veda Samaj: Keshav Chandra Sen during his visit to Madras in 1864 persuaded the people to establish the Veda Samaj. The founder of the organisation was the young K. Sridharalu Naidu, who visited Calcutta to study the Brahmo Samaj movement. On his return to Madras, he changed the Veda Samaj into the Brahmo Samaj of Southern India in 1871.

The Veda Samaj accepted the theistic ideals of the Brahmo Samaj, while taking care to remain within the bounds of Hinduism, though Doraiswami Iyengar, a close associate of Sridharalu Naidu, openly talked of abandoning the sacred thread.

(ix) Dayanand Saraswati and Arya Samaj: The movements discussed above had a limited appeal which was confined to particular regions. In North India it was the Arya Samaj founded by Dayanand Saraswati, which attracted a large following.

He translated the Vedas and wrote three books: (a) *Satyartha Prakash* in Hindi, (b) *Veda Bhasya Bhumika*, an introduction to his vedic commentary, and (c) *Veda Bhasya*, a Vedic commentary in Sanskrit on the Yajurveda and major part of the Rigveda.

Social Reforms Programme of the Arya Samaj : The Arya Samaj also proposed a programme of social reforms. It stood, however, for the four-fold Varna system to be determined by merit and not by birth. The Arya Samaj stood for equal rights of man and woman in social and educational matters. The Arya Samaj opposed untouchability, caste discrimination, child marriage and supported widow remarriage and inter-caste marriages. Dayanand Saraswati provided the Arya Samaj with a code of social conduct and moral values.

The Dayanand Anglo-Vedic (D.A.V.) Education Movement: Many reform movements witnessed a decline after the demise of their founders, but the Arya Samaj proved an exception. The death of Dayanand Saraswati, its founder, on October 30, 1883, in Ajmer, enthused the Arya Samaj with new energy to honour the departed teacher. The Lahore unit of the Samaj chalked out a plan to establish an educational institution that would impart the Aryan form of education, free from Christian influences.

(x) Vivekananda and Ramakrishna Mission: The Ramakrishna monastic order and mission was officially established in 1887 (formally registered under Societies' Registration Act in 1909) by Vivekananda, the chief disciple of

Swami Ramakrishna Paramahansa (1836-86) of Dakshineshwar. Ramakrishna Paramhansa, who lived and worshipped at the temple of Dakshineshwar, was a mystic. He was not only the source of inspiration and gentle piety to the common people but a powerful magnet for sophisticated middle class westernised men, who were attracted by his utter-humility, humanity and spiritual integrity.

Ramakrishna's humanism very deeply impressed his chief disciple Narendra Nath Dutta, better known as Swami Vivekananda. The former saw in him the one man destined to propagate his message far and wide.

In 1893, he went to America and attended the World Parliament of Religions at Chicago. The **New York Herald** reported: "after hearing him we feel how foolish it is to send missionaries to this learned nation." He stayed in America lecturing, establishing "Vedanta Societies" and making disciples.

The Thoughts of Vivekananda: Vivekananda was a saint par excellence. He believed in the philosophy of Vedanta, which he applied towards resolving the problems of everyday life. Salvation, he insisted, does not come through the life of a recluse, but by serving God in man. He declared that he would talk of religion only when he succeeded in removing poverty and misery from the country.

Swami Narain Sect: Swami Sahajanand, who founded this sect in Gujarat at the beginning of the 19th century, preached a puritanical ideology both of belief and practice. This sect was a sort of protest against the epicurean and luxurious practices of the Vaishnavism. The sect advocated vegetarianism and advised people to shun liquor and drugs.

The Shuddhi Movement: Traditionally Hinduism does not provide conversion or reconversion. The success of the Christian missionaries in converting the lower and untouchable castes, however, led the militant Arya Samajists to develop their own ritual of conversion. Called Shuddhi, it was employed to purify and readmit those Hindus who had converted to Islam or Christianity. The Shuddhi Sabha, founded for the purpose, conducted individual and group reconversions during the 1880s and early 1890s.

Sarvadeshik Hindu Sabha: To counter the challenge from the Muslim League, founded in 1906, the politically conscious Hindus founded the *Punjab Hindu Conference* in 1909. In 1915, at its annual meeting, this conference renamed itself the *Sarvadeshik Hindu Sabha*, and in 1921, the *Akhil Bharat Hindu Mahasabha*. By the mid-1930s, the Mahasabha, under the leadership of V.D. Savarkar, began to expound a Hindu nationalism opposed both to the secular nationalism of the Indian National Congress and the communal nationalism of the Muslim League.

Radhaswami Movement: This movement was founded in 1861 by Tulsi Ram, of Agra, a banker by profession. Tulsi Ram was also popularly known as Shiv Dayal Saheb or Swamiji Maharaj. The Radhaswamis believe in one Supreme Being, the supremacy of the Guru, a "company of the pious people" (*Satsang*), and simple social life.

Deva Samaj: This sect was founded in 1887 at Lahore by Shiv Narain Agnihotri, and erstwhile follower of Brahmo Samaj. The teachings of the Samaj were compiled in book form in *Deva Shastra*.

Madras Hindu Association: There were two of them: the Madras Hindu Social Reforms Association founded by Veresalingam Pantulu (1848-1939) in 1892, and the Madras Hindu Association founded by Mrs. Annie Besant in 1904. Pantulu's Hindu Association was a social purity movement advocating temperance and combating the devadasi custom.

Satnami Sect: Ghasi Das, the founder of the Satnami sect, hailed from Bilaspur district, Madhya Pradesh. An untouchable belonging to the cobbler caste, he opposed the caste system and taught that all men are equal. He propounded the concept of *Satnam*, a single true god, and urged his followers to abandon idol worship.

The Satya Mahima Dharma: Mukund Das, known as Mahima Gosain, founded the Satya Mahima Dharma in the 1860s, assisted mainly by Govind Baba and Bhima Bhoi. Mahima Gosain preached the existence of one deity—Alakh Param Brahma, an eternal being, who was formless and indescribable.

The Paramahansa Mandali: This acculturative movement was founded by Dadoba Pandurung (1842-82) and Bal Shastri Jambhekar of Maharashtra in 1849. Dadoba in his book *Dharma Vivechan*, outlined seven principles of this new movement.

OTHER SOCIAL MOVEMENTS

Lokahitawadi: Gopal Hari Deshmukh (1823-92), popularly known as "Lokahitawadi", was a product of the Western learning in India. He was a judge and a member of the Governor-General's Council in 1880. As a votary of national self-reliance, he attended the Delhi Durbar in 1876 wearing handspun Khadi.

Servants of India Society: It was founded in 1905 by Gopal Krishna Gokhale to build a dedicated group of people for social service and reforms. In the field of famine relief, union organisation, cooperatives and uplift of tribals and depressed, the society did commendable work.

Rahanumai Mazdayasan Sabha: The western educated progressive Parsis like Dadabhai Naoroji, J.B. Wacha, S.S. Bangali and Naoroji Furdonji founded the Rahanumai Mazdayasan Sabha in 1851. The association had for its object "the regeneration of the social condition of the Parsis and the restoration of the Zoroastrian religion to its pristine purity." *Rast Goftar* (Voice of Truth) was its weekly organ.

ANTI-UNTOUCHABILITY MOVEMENTS

Aravipuram Movement: This movement was launched by Sri Narayana Guru on Shivaratri day of 1888. On that day, Sri Narayana Guru defied the religious restrictions traditionally placed on the Ezhava Community, and consecrated an idol of Shiva at Aravipuram.

Temple Entry Movement: The Aravipuram movement was of far-reaching importance in South India. Inspired by its success, a number of socio-religious reform movements were launched in the South. The Temple Entry Movement is the more prominent among them.

The struggle against the disabilities imposed on the *avarnas* or members of depressed classes in various parts of South India was being waged since the end of the 19th century. In Kerala, leading the struggle were several reformers and intellectuals such as Sri Narayana Guru, N. Kumaran Asan and T.K. Madhavan. In 1924, another beginning was made for opening the doors of the temples for the *avarnas*. After 1924 the anti-untouchability programme became a part of the Gandhian constructive programme, attracting to it a new popularity.

SIKH MOVEMENTS

The Namdhari Movement: The Namdhari movement of the Sikhs was an offshoot of the Kuka movement in Punjab, founded by Balak Singh. Balak Singh's followers saw in him a reincarnation of Guru Govind Singh.

The Singh Sabha: The Namdhari unrest, the activities of the Sanatan Dharmis, the Arya Samajists and Christian conversions had shaken the foundations of the Sikh religion. To strengthen Sikhism, a small group of prominent Sikhs, led by Thakur Singh Sandhawalia and Giani Gian Singh, founded the Singh Sabha of Amritsar on October 1, 1873. The objectives of the Sabha were to restore Sikhism to its pristine purity, to publish historical religious books and periodicals, to propagate knowledge using Punjabi, to return Sikh apostates to their faith and to involve Englishmen in the educational programme of the Sikhs.

Gurdwara Reforms Movement: Before 1920 the Sikh Gurdwaras were governed by the Udasi Sikh *mahants*, who treated the gurdwara offerings, and other income of the gurdwaras as their personal income. The British Government supported these *mahants* as a counterpoise to the rising tide of nationalism among the Sikhs. Matters came to such a pass that the priests of the Golden Temple issued a *hukamnama* (injunction) against the Ghadarites, declaring them renegades, and then honoured General Dyer, the butcher of Jallianwala massacre, with a *saropa*.

LOWER CASTE MOVEMENTS

One of the biggest ills afflicting Indian society was its rigid division along caste lines that separated human beings from each other to the extent that a large section of them were *Achhuts*, literally untouchables, whose touch, and sometimes even whose shadow or voice was believed to pollute caste Hindus.

Nature of Caste Movement: According to the census report of 1931, the depressed classes numbered nearly one-fifth of the total Hindu population. This large numerical strength, combined with the immense disabilities that they faced in the social economic and political fields, made it but natural that they sought to assert themselves.

The lower castes, especially an elite section among them, from the last quarter of the 19th century began to engage in activities designed either to improve their position within the caste system—reformative movements—or to overthrow it altogether—alternative movements. A third type of movement was that of the Congress, especially under Gandhian leadership, which tried to incorporate the agitations, both of the intermediate castes and those of untouchables, into the sphere of the national movement.

Dr. Bhimrao Ramji Ambedkar and his Depressed Classes Movement

The most important challenge to Gandhiji's Harijan Welfare Programme as also to the Communists came from Dr. Bhimrao Ramji Ambedkar, who belonged to the untouchable Mahar caste. His programmes were intended to integrate untouchables into Indian society in modern, not traditional ways, and based on education and exercise of legal and political rights, as well as refusal to perform the demeaning traditional caste duties.

In 1924 Dr. Ambedkar founded the Depressed Classes Institute (*Bahishkrit Hitkarini Sabha*) in Bombay. Three years later (1927), he started a Marathi fortnightly, *Bahishkrit Bharat*, and the same year established the *Samaj Samta Sangh* to propagate the gospel of social equality between caste Hindus and untouchables. Ambedkar also organised the Independent Labour Party on secular lines for protecting the interest of the labouring classes. In December 1927 he led the Mahad Satyagraha to establish the rights of untouchables to draw water from public wells and tanks. He also organised temple entry movements like the Parvati temple satyagraha of 1928 and the Kalasam temple satyagraha of 1930-35. There were similar satyagrahas in Kerala, such as the Vaikom temple road satyagraha of 1924-25 and the Guruvayoor satyagraha of 1930-32.

ISLAMIC REFORM MOVEMENTS

In course of time, a number of religious revivalist and even religious-reform movements were launched by the Muslim reformers. These movements were, however, less powerful than their Hindu counterparts, most of them lacking a national-standing. Some of the more important Muslim reformist movements are described below.

Sir Syed Ahmad Khan and the Aligarh Movement: The Revolt of 1857 is the watershed which divides the pre-modernist fundamentalist movements from the modernist, reformist and even traditional movements of modern times. The Revolt shattered the fabric of Muslim upper classes in North India. The prolonged Muslim confrontation with the British had failed everywhere, from the northwest frontier to Bengal. A change in the entire political outlook was necessary as a recognition of the need for adjustment with the new age of Western domination and Western intellectual outlook.

Ahmadiya Movement: The Ahmadiya movement was founded by Mirza Ghulam Ahmad of Qadiyan (1839-1908) in 1889, who began his work as a defender of Islam against the polemics of the Arya Samaj and the Christian missionaries. In 1889 he claimed to be *masih* (messiah) and *mahdi*, and later also to be an incarnation of the Hindu god Krishna and Jesus returned to earth. The movement was really a heresy well within the bounds of Islam, as Ghulam Ahmad, though he called himself a minor prophet, regarded Muhammad as the true and great Prophet whom he followed.

Deoband Movement: The Islamic Seminary at Deoband was founded in 1867 by two theologians, Muhammad Qasim Nanautavi (1837-80) and Rashid Ahmad Gangohi. The Deoband School of Islamic Theology was a poor man's school and its teachers and students lived frugal lives.

12

Multiculturalism

The term 'multiculturalism', however, has not been used only to describe a culturally diverse society, but also to refer to a kind of policy that aims at protecting cultural diversity. Although multiculturalism is a phenomenon with a long history and there have been countries historically that did adopt multicultural policies, like the Ottoman Empire, the systematic study of multiculturalism in philosophy has only flourished in the late twentieth century, when it began to receive special attention, especially from liberal philosophers. The philosophers who initially dedicated more time to the topic were mainly Canadian, but in the 21st century it is a widespread topic in contemporary political philosophy. Before multiculturalism became a topic in political philosophy, most literature in this area focused on topics related to the fair redistribution of resources; conversely, the topic of multiculturalism in the realm of political philosophy highlights the idea that cultural identities are also normatively relevant and that policies ought to take these identities into consideration.

Multiculturalism describes the existence, acceptance, or promotion of multiple cultural traditions within a single jurisdiction, usually considered in terms of the culture associated with an ethnic group. This can happen when a jurisdiction is created or expanded by amalgamating areas with two or more different cultures or through immigration from different jurisdictions around the world (e.g., Australia, Canada, United States, United Kingdom, and many other countries).

Multicultural ideologies and policies vary widely, ranging from the advocacy of equal respect to the various cultures in a society, to a policy of promoting the maintenance of cultural diversity, to policies in which people of various ethnic and religious groups are addressed by the authorities as defined by the group to which they belong.

Multiculturalism that promotes maintaining the distinctiveness of multiple cultures is often contrasted to other settlement policies such as social integration, cultural assimilation and racial segregation. Multiculturalism has been described as a "salad bowl" and "cultural mosaic".

Two different and seemingly inconsistent strategies have developed through different government policies and strategies. The first focuses on interaction and communication between different cultures; this approach is also often known as interculturalism. The second centers on diversity and cultural uniqueness which can sometimes result in intercultural competition over jobs among other things and may lead to ethnic conflict. Cultural isolation can protect the uniqueness of the local culture of a nation or area and also contribute to global cultural diversity. A common aspect of many policies following the second approach is that they avoid presenting any specific ethnic, religious, or cultural community values as central.

Multiculturalism in India

According to the 1961 Census of India, there are 1652 indigenous languages in the country. The culture of India has been shaped by its long history, unique geography and diverse demography. India's languages, religions, dance, music, architecture and customs differ from place to place within the country, but nevertheless possess a commonality. The culture of India is an amalgamation of these diverse sub-cultures spread all over the Indian subcontinent and traditions that are several millennia old. The Indian caste system describes the social stratification and social restrictions in the Indian subcontinent, in which social classes are defined by thousands of endogamous hereditary groups, often termed jatis or castes.

Religiously, Hindus form the majority, followed by Muslims. The statistics are : Hindu (80.5%), Muslim (13.4%), Christian (2.3%), Sikh (2.1%), Buddhist, Bahá'í, Jain, Jew and Parsi populations. Linguistically, the two main language families in India are Indo-Aryan (a branch of Indo-European) and Dravidian. In India's northeast, people speaking Sino-Tibetan group of languages such as Manipuri (Meitei-lon) recognized by the Indian constitution and Austroasiatic languages are commonly found. India (officially) follows a three-language policy. Hindi (spoken in the form of Hindustani) is the official federal language, English has the federal status of associate/subsidiary official language and each state has its own state official language (in the Hindi sprachraum, this reduces to bilingualism). Further, India does not have any national language. The Republic of India's state boundaries are largely drawn based on linguistic groups; this decision led to the preservation and continuation of local ethno-linguistic sub-cultures, except for the Hindi sprachraum which is itself divided into many states. Thus, most states differ from one another in language, culture, cuisine, clothing, literary style, architecture, music and festivities.

India has encountered religiously motivated violence, such as the Moplah Riots, the Bombay riots, the 1984 anti-Sikh riots, the 2002 Gujarat riots, the 2012 Assam violence, and most recently, the 2013 Muzaffarnagar violence in the state of Uttar Pradesh. This has resulted from traditionally disadvantaged communities in public employment such as the policing of the same locality, apprehension of owners in giving properties for sell or rent and of society in accepting inter-marriages. India has the world's largest population of some non-Indian origin religions, such as Bahá'í Faith and Zoroastrianism.

Multiculturalism in Contemporary India

Multiculturalism concerns have long informed India's history and traditions, constitution and political arrangements. Much of the writings on Indian history, culture and politics are marked by some kind of multicultural concern.

India's record of relative political unity and stability seems remarkable indeed. It is argued that at the heart of the resolution of many ethnic conflicts in India lies a set of multicultural state policies. The Indian constitution as the source of these policies can be said to be a basic multicultural document, in the sense of political and institutional measures for the recognition and accommodation of the country's diversity. In the post-independence period, the major form of political recognition of territorially based ethnic identity of the people has remained statehold within the Indian Federation, although other forms, most notably, sub-statehood, in the form of Regional or tribal district councils, have often served similar purposes for small ethnic communities.

Globalization

Globalization is the process of integrating various economies of the world without creating any hindrances in the free flow of goods and services, technology, capital and even labour or human capital.

Indian Government under its policy of liberalisation introduced the phase of globalization in its economy which aims at unification/association of Indian economy with other economies of the world.

The advocates of globalization, more especially from developed countries, limit the definition of globalization to only three components, *viz.*, unhindered trade flows, capital flows and technology flows. They insist on developing countries to accept their definition of globalization and conduct the debate on globalization within the parameters set by them.

GLOBALIZATION AND ITS IMPACT ON INDIAN ECONOMY

Globalization is the new buzzword that has come to dominate the world since the nineties of the last centuries. It is the most widely debated and discussed phenomenon all over the world. Globalization has opened up new and tremendous opportunities for worldwide developers. It has brought far-reaching implications on India's economic, trade and investment relations with the countries of the world. India's economic achievement over the last two decades has attracted the attention of other regional and global powers for closer cooperation with India. Rapid growth and poverty reduction in China, India, and other countries that were poor 20 years ago, has been a positive aspect of Liberalization, Privatization and Globalization (LPG).

Globalization is the integration of economies, industries, markets, cultures and policy-making around the world. Globalization describes a process by which national and regional economies, societies, and cultures have become integrated through the global network of trade, communication, immigration and transportation. In the paradigm of globalization, state is reduced into a sort of security mechanism to protect its citizens from internal disruption and external threats. State is not supposed to care for social and economic interests of its citizens. The world opinion is divided on what constitutes globalization and whether globalization is good or bad. The fact is that today almost every nation state is forced to become a part of a global economy. Globalization has far-reaching implications on India's economic, trade and investment relations with the countries of the world. India's economic achievement over the last two decades has attracted the attention of other regional and global powers for closer cooperation with India. Henry Kissinger predicted that in the twenty-first century, the international system would be dominated by six major powers: the U.S., Europe, China, Japan, Russia and probably India. Globalization has many meanings depending on the context and on the person who is talking about. Though the precise definition of globalization is still unavailable a few definitions are worth viewing, Guy Brainbant says that the process of globalization not only includes opening up of world trade, development of advanced means of communication, internationalization of financial markets, growing importance of MNC's, population migrations and more generally increased mobility of persons, goods, capital, data and ideas but also infections, diseases and pollution. Ideally, it also contains free intercountry movement of labour. In context to India, this implies opening up the economy to foreign direct investment by providing facilities to foreign companies to invest in different fields of economic activity in India, removing constraints and obstacles to the entry of MNCs in India, allowing Indian companies to enter into foreign collaborations and also encouraging them to set up joint ventures abroad; carrying out massive import liberalization programmes by switching over from quantitative restrictions to tariffs and import duties, therefore globalization has been identified with the policy reforms of 1991 in India.

A lot of work has been done in the past on globalization but its effects on the economic development have not been discussed in detail. Globalization is not a new concept. In the past people used to travel to other places for gaining control on others lands, for finding out the better living style, for finding out the new places and to earn profits by selling in different regions. These activities were carried out even thousands of years before. But it is said that the earliest form of Globalization was started from Greek, Roman, Egyptian, and Babylonian Empires. In the regime of Mongols, the famous Silk Road connected the Central Asia and Europe. Statistics indicates that Globalization is expanding very rapidly world wide. Data gathered from WTO shows that economy of the world is expanding since 1950.

IMPACT OF GLOBALIZATION ON INDUSTRIAL SECTOR

Effects of Globalization on Indian Industry started when the government opened the country's markets to foreign investments in the early 1990s. Globalization of the Indian industry took place in its various sectors such as steel, pharmaceuticals, petroleum, chemical, textile, cement, retail, and BPO. Globalization means the dismantling of trade barriers among the nations and the integration of the nations' economies through financial flow, trade in goods and services, and corporate investments between nations. Globalization has increased across the world in recent years due to the fast progress that has been made in the field of technology especially in communications and transport. The government of India made changes in its economic policy in 1991 by which it allowed direct foreign investments in the country. The benefits of the effects of globalization in the Indian industries are that many foreign companies set up industries in India, especially in the pharmaceuticals, BPO, petroleum, manufacturing, and chemical sectors and this helped to provide employment to many people in the country. This helped reduce the level of unemployment and poverty in the country. Also the benefit of the effects of globalization on Indian industries is that the foreign companies brought in highly advanced technology with them and this helped to make the Indian industry more technologically advanced. The negative effects of globalization on Indian industry are that with the coming of technology the number of labour required decreased and this resulted in many people being removed from their jobs. This happened mainly in the pharmaceuticals, chemical, manufacturing, and cement industries.

IMPACT OF GLOBALIZATION ON AGRICULTURAL SECTOR

Agricultural Sector is the mainstay of the rural Indian economy around which socio-economic privileges and deprivations revolve and any change in its structure is likely to have a corresponding impact on the existing pattern of social equity.

The liberalization of India's economy was adopted by India in 1991. Facing a severe economic crisis, India approached the IMF for a loan, and the IMF granted what is called a 'structural adjustment' loan, which is a loan with certain conditions attached which relate to a structural change in the economy. India's Export and Import in the year 2001-02 were to the extent of 32,572 and 38,362 million respectively. Many Indian companies have started becoming respectable players in the international scene. Agriculture exports account for about 13 to 18% of total annual export of the country. In 2000-01 agricultural products valued at more than US $6 million were exported from the country 23% of which was contributed by the marine products alone. Marine products in recent years have emerged as the single largest contributor to the total agricultural export from the country accounting for over one fifth of the total agricultural exports. Cereals (mostly basmati rice and non-basmati rice), oil seeds, tea and coffee are the other prominent products each of which accounts from nearly 5 to 10% of the country's total agricultural exports.

IMPACT ON FINANCIAL SECTOR

Reforms of the financial sector constitute the most important component of India's programme towards economic liberalization. The recent economic liberalization measures have opened the door to foreign competitors to enter into our domestic market. Innovation has become a must for survival. Financial intermediaries have come out of their traditional approach and they are ready to assume more credit risks. As a consequence, many innovations have taken place in the global financial sectors which have its own impact on the domestic sector also. The emergence of various financial institutions and regulatory bodies has transformed the financial services sector from being a conservative industry to a very dynamic one. In this process this sector is facing a number of challenges. In this changed context, the financial services industry in India has to play a very positive and dynamic role in the years to come by offering many innovative products to suit the varied requirements of the millions of prospective investors spread throughout the country. Reforms of the financial sector constitute the most important component of India's programme towards economic liberalization. Growth in financial services (comprising banking, insurance, real estate and business services), after dipping to 5.6% in 2003-04 bounced back to 8.7% in 2004-05 and 10.9% in 2005-06. The momentum has been maintained with a growth of 11.1% in 2006-07. Because of Globalization, the financial services industry is in a period of transition. Market shifts, competition, and technological developments are ushering in unprecedented changes in the global financial services industry.

IMPACT ON IMPORT AND EXPORT

This era of reforms has also ushered in a remarkable change in the Indian mindset, as it deviates from the traditional values held since Independence in 1947, such as self reliance and socialistic policies of economic development, which mainly due to the inward looking restrictive form of governance, resulted in the isolation, overall backwardness and inefficiency of the economy, amongst a host of other problems. This is despite the fact that India has always had the potential to be on the fast track to prosperity. Now that India is in the process of restructuring her economy, with aspirations of elevating herself from her present desolate position in the world, the need to speed up her economic development is even more imperative. And having witnessed the positive role that Foreign Direct Investment (FDI) has played in the rapid economic growth of most of the Southeast Asian countries and most notably China, India has embarked on an ambitious plan to emulate the successes of her neighbours to the east and is trying to sell herself as a safe and profitable destination for FDI. Globalization has many meanings depending on the context and on the person who is talking about.

IMPACT ON INDIAN LANGUAGES

The impact of British period, and the introduction of English in India, on the linguistic map of this country, are not distinctly visible but have left an impact on the language politics and intra-national communication network of India. The dynamics of language of power is not confined to India alone as well. A similar language lining situation exists in other former colonies. The freedom struggle of India is different from the freedom struggle of other colonies. In all these cases, language was part of the agenda of the struggle. In other words, managing linguistic or cultural diversity is one of the central challenges of our time. The challenges are part of historic process of social change, of struggle for cultural and linguistic freedom, of new frontiers in the advance of human freedom and democracy. The important events that need to be studied are the policy decision of the colonizer and neo-colonizer. The language policy, on the one hand is to be a compromise among the language of the elite (English), the national language (*i.e.,* to be Hindi) and the regional language. This paper highlights some of the important policy decisions taken by an imperialist and neo-colonizer – in the backdrop of globalization and economic liberalization.

EFFECT ON HEALTH SECTORS

It is unbelievable that in India, poor people have to spend a minimum of ₹ 200 for a mere seasonal cold or minor stomach ailments, thanks to the multinational pharmaceutical companies engaged in sky rocketing cost of common medicines under their brand names.

The private sector hospitals will be only very happy to prepare a bill of ₹ 5 lakh to ₹ 10 lakh for heart or kidney operation. The monitoring of health electronically through the internet will worsen the situation further in the years to come. Death will be the easiest option for the poor following the effect of globalization in health sector.

EFFECT ON EMPLOYMENT SECTOR

The employment scenario in India is probably the worst in recent years due to globalization. The restrictions of use of child labour and fair pay to workers have badly affected the traditional industries like cottage, handloom, artisans and carving, carpet, jewellery, ceramic, and glassware, etc., where the specialized skills inherited for generations were passed on to the next generation from the early age of 6 to 7 years. The globalization and trade restrictions under the influence of WTO have virtually killed business in these sectors.

IMPACT ON TRADITIONAL OCCUPATIONS

Globalization process has directly hit the traditional occupations of dalits. It is a well known fact that the dalits have historically specialized in the production of all kinds of artistic tools and equipment for household and agricultural production. But globalization is adversely impacting their traditional occupations now. Their livelihood and specialized occupation is now being replaced by global capitalistic productions. Easy availability of mass production goods from the latest technology based industries at cheap prices has proved to be a big challenge for their traditional occupation (Sunar, 2012). Dalits neither have the capacity to complete with these productions nor do they have an alternative way so far to earn their livelihood. Our traditional artisan culture and technological knowledge are on the verge of ruin. Before the introduction of globalization as we know today, dalits would make a numerous essential equipment like pots, plough, clothes, shoes and other leather products and also all kinds of artistic tools for music and dance. In fact, the smooth functioning of any household was simply impossible without the skill and craft of the dalit communities. We have to keep in mind, due to lack of adequate education and employment the livelihood of the majority of dalits depends on their traditional occupation. So under the changing situation, the government needs to urgently take adequate steps to promote and preserve the unique role of these artisans and for realizing their full potential. Besides financial assistance and proper guidance the government should establish production factories for the traditionally skilled dalit community who can share their experience for producing goods and get employment. Priority should also be given to the local produce and artisans so their traditional occupation can be sustained.

IMPACT ON POVERTY

Poverty is a sum total of all deprivations. The incidence of poverty among the dalits is much higher in comparison with all India average. According to 61st round NSSO (National Sample Survey Organization) data, 22.7 per cent of India's population was poor in 2004-05; the SCs and STs are the most poor with a Head Count Ratio (HCR) of 35 per cent. Despite various poverty alleviation programmes and special strategies for their economic development poverty among the dalits is not reducing in a significant manner. In spite of government statistical jugglery, a large number of Indians still live under the poverty line. The high dependence of casual labour, with relatively low earnings coupled with inadequate exposure of education among dalits induced a high degree of deprivation and poverty among them. In fact increased poverty is an unfolding reality among dalits. Globalization is leading to mass pauperization and rapidly widening socio-economic inequalities. The free market ethos unleashed by reforms has contributed significantly to the price rise. It is clear from the day to day experiences that the price of the primary articles of consumption has increased enormously. All the studies on the economic reforms are unanimous in their conclusion that the reforms have significantly contributed inflation. It is factually true that inflation hits the poorest the hardest. Because most of their earnings are spent on food, shelter and clothing. So any rise in prices has had a direct negative effect on dalits' level of consumption. C.P. Chandrasekhar and Joyati Ghosh (2002) rightly pointed out that "…. the trend in aggregate poverty incidence …… was strongly related to neo-liberal economic policies and consequent macro-economic processes of the 1990s, these policies involved neglect of rural investment and of food security system, resulting in slow agricultural growth, reduced employment opportunities in rural areas, and high food prices. All these would typically be likely to be associated with persistent or even increasing poverty".

IMPACT ON INDIAN LABOUR

The globalization process turns out to have performed a double-edged sword for the Indian labour. In terms of 'current daily status' estimates brought out by the National Sample Survey Organization, there has been a significant deceleration in labour force participation rate to 1.3 per cent per annum during 1993-2000 from 2.4 per cent during 1983-1994. Notwithstanding a higher GDP growth in the latter phase, employment growth declined to 1.1 per cent from 2.7 per cent in the backdrop of decline in employment elasticity to 0.16 from 0.52 over the same period. The sharp deceleration in employment growth has raised fears that economic growth in the 1990s has been a 'jobless' variety. Besides, there is evidence of increasing capital intensity almost in all sectors including small un-organised ones and services particularly in the latter half of the 1990s.

Skilled Labour and Wage Inequalities Yet another healthy trend witnessed in the post-reform period has been the shift in the composition of labour force in favour of the skilled labours, in general, and more significantly in the unorganised sector. The dramatic expansion in software exports has certainly contributed to this development. As a natural consequence, labour productivity indicated faster improvement both in organised and unorganised sectors. While the larger absorption of skilled labours in the unorganised sector vis-à-vis the organised sector might have brought down the wage gap across, the same might have widened within the organised sector itself with deemphasis of wage parity and narrow gap between the lowest and the highest paid employees. For example, over 100 out of about 240 PSUs have reportedly not had any pay revision since 1992 (National Commission on Labour, 2002).

Woman Labour Globalization is found to have led to greater feminisation of the workforce both in the developed and the developing world. The issue has assumed considerable importance in view of the acute gender disparity in the country. Here, however, the signals are not unequivocal with evidence of increased youth unemployment rate among rural females coupled with a reverse tendency among urban females in 1999-00 over 1993-94. Nevertheless, the coincident increase in youth unemployment rate among both rural and urban males points to a possible feminisation of the workforce at least in short duration urban informal activities. Increased flexibility in the labour market may be needed if the country is to engage women in the work force fully and compete better in international markets.

Child Labour Child labour, though undesirable, persists primarily in rural and agricultural activities on account of socio-economic compulsions. One of the positive features of the recent employment growth has been the definite decline in the participation of children aged five to fourteen years in the workforce. One fall-out of the decline in child labour has been the substitution effect, which favours the employability of adult females. While the existing literature often identifies poverty as a major determinant of child labour, evidence across Indian states indicates that the correlation between poverty and child labour is very weak. Therefore, one should possibly go beyond the poverty issues and look at areas such as quality of schooling and spread of primary education.

CONCLUSION

During last decade the volume of world trade has increased and the high and middle income countries have managed to increase their share in world trade. India gained highly from the LPG model as its GDP increased to 9.7% in 2007-2008. In respect of market capitalization, India ranks fourth in the world. But even after globalization, condition of agriculture has not improved. The share of agriculture in the GDP is only 17%. The number of landless families has increased and farmers are still committing suicide. But seeing the positive effects of globalization, it can be said that very soon India will overcome these hurdles too and march strongly on its path of development. The lesson of recent experience is that a country must carefully choose a combination of policies that best enables it to take the opportunity - while avoiding the pitfalls.. India, which is now the fourth largest economy in terms of purchasing power parity, may overtake Japan and become third major economic power within 10 years. To conclude we can say that the modernization that we see around us in our daily life is a contribution of globalization. The critically necessities in this context are the collective and cooperative actions which should be realized by all countries of the world and particularly the developed ones. Globalization has both positive and as well as negative impacts on various sectors of Indian Economy. So globalization has taken us a long way from 1991 which has resultant in the advancement of our country.

Privatization

Privatization is a broad concept and its meaning goes slightly different in different countries. Privatization generally refers to inducing private sector participation in the management and ownership of public sector enterprises.

Privatization in generic terms refers to the process of transfer of ownership, can be of both permanent or long term lease in nature, or once upon a time state-owned or public owned property to individuals or groups that intened to utilize it for private benefits and run the entity with the aim of profit maximization.

The transfer of ownership, property or business from the government to the private sector is termed privatization.

Privatization is considered to bring more efficiency and objectivity to the company, something that a government company is not concerned about. India went for privatization in the historic reforms budget of 1991, also known as 'New Economic Policy or 'LPG Policy'.

Privatization may also describe ownership changes not involving the public/government sector. The first is the purchase of all outstanding share of a public traded company by private investors.

Privatization in India is still at a minimalist level. Privatization by way of sale of public sector enterprises is almost negligible while disinvestment is also existent by way of selling of a portion of shares of the 31 public enterprises. Privatization got tremendous boost by the introduction of new economic policy in 1991 that allowed delicensing, relaxing entry restrictions and equity funding.

The economy of India had undergone significant policy shifts in the beginning of the 1990s. This new model of economic reforms is commonly known as the LPG or Liberalisation, Privatization and Globalisation model. The primary objective of this model was to make the economy of India the fastest developing economy in the globe with capabilities that help it match up with the biggest economies of the world.

The chain of reforms that took place with regards to business, manufacturing, and financial services industries targeted at lifting the economy of the country to a more proficient level. These economic reforms had influenced the overall economic growth of the country in a significant manner.

PRIVATIZATION AND ECONOMIC GROWTH

Privatization, described as the transfer of state owned enterprises (SOEs) to the private owners, has become a common economic policy tool around the globe. The trend toward privatization is a debatable issue. Indeed, the debate between the superiority of the private and public sectors has been going on for the past four to five decades. The discussion initially focused on how the size of public sector measured by the size of government consumption affected economic growth (Rubinson, 1977).

Findings of many studies demonstrated that privatization did not contribute to growth but helped to reduce income inequality, inflation contributed negatively to both economic growth and income equalization. On the other hand, several economists stated that Privatization, a method of reallocating assets and functions from the public sector to the private sector play vital role for economic growth. Recently, privatization has been adopted by many different political systems and has spread to every region of the world. The process of privatization can be a successful way to bring about fundamental structural change by formalizing and establishing property rights, which directly creates strong individual incentives. A free market economy mainly depends on well-defined property rights in which people make individual decisions in their own interests. According to experts, privatization may improve efficiency, provide financial relief, boost wider ownership, and increase the availability of credit for the private sector.

Major causes of privatization are:
- To reduce the burden on Government
- To strengthen competition
- To improve public finances
- To fund infrastructure growth
- Accountability to shareholders
- To reduce unnecessary interference
- More disciplined labour force.

While comparing with public sector, the private sector responds to incentives in the market. On the other hand, public sector often has non-economic goals. The public sector is not highly driven to maximize production and allocate resources effectively, causing the government to run high cost, low-income enterprises. Privatization directly shifts the focus from political goals to economic goals, which leads to development of the market economy (Poole, 1996). The downscaling aspect of privatization is very important since bad government policies and government corruption can play a large, negative role in economic growth (Easterly, 2001). Through privatizing, the role of the government in the economy is condensed, thus there is less chance for the government to negatively impact the economy (Poole, 1996).

Privatization may have a positive impact on a country's economic situation. Privatization should not be used to finance new government expenditures and pay off future debts. Instead, privatization enables countries to pay a portion of their existing debt, thus reducing interest rates and raising the level of investment. By reducing the size of the public sector, the government reduces total expenditure and begins collecting taxes on all the businesses that are now privatized. This process can help bring an end to a vicious cycle of over-borrowing and continuous increase of the national debt (Poole, 1996).

Nations around the world have adopted different methods of privatizing state assets depending on the initial conditions of the country's economy and the economic principles of the political party in charge.

Major method of privatization is the sale of state-owned enterprises to private investors. The state would simply decide which institutions should be privatized and through the use of market mechanism, private investors are able to buy shares of each organization. Advantage of this method of privatization is that it creates badly needed revenues for the state while putting privatized firms in the hands of investors who have the incentives and the means of investing and reformation.

Other method of privatization is called voucher privatization. The government universally distributes vouchers to its eligible citizens, which can be sold to other investors or exchanged for shares in other institutions being privatized. Although this method does not create profits for the state, it does privatize state-owned firms in a short period of time.

Next method of privation is called internal privatization, also known as "employee or management buyout". State-owned enterprises are sold to managers (for an extremely low price) who are already familiar with the particular firm and its structure, but there are minimal revenues created for the state. This method creates some incentives but the incentives are much stronger when firms are sold to strategic investors. Furthermore, new owners often do not have the resources to invest and restructure, which is badly needed in a large percentage of state-owned firms in underdeveloped countries (Stirbock, 2001).

One of the noticeable features of privatization is the improved competitive characteristics it provides to the enterprises which prove to be fruitful for the business as well as the country. Nonetheless, privatization contracts are greatly influenced by merger variables and even global issues and are structured on the basis of manipulation of the government and the private actors along with the administering jurisdiction.

Privatization can be Categorized into Three Parts

- **Delegation:** Government keeps hold of responsibility and private enterprise handles fully or partly the delivery of product and services.

- **Divestment:** Government surrenders the responsibility.

- **Displacement:** The private enterprise expands and gradually displaces the government entity.

Privatization certainly is beneficial for the progress and sustainability of the state-owned enterprises.

Advantages of Privatization

The advantages of privatization can be apparent from both microeconomic and macroeconomic impacts that privatization exerts.

Microeconomic advantages

1. State owned enterprises generally are outdone by the private enterprises competitively. When compared, the latter shows better results in terms of profits and efficiency and productivity. Therefore, privatization can provide the necessary push to the underperforming PSUs.

2. Privatization brings about fundamental structural changes providing momentum in the competitive sectors.

3. Privatization leads to implementation of the global best practices along with management and motivation of the best human talent to foster sustainable competitive advantage and improvised management of resources.

Macroeconomic advantages

1. Privatization has a positive impact on the financial growth of the sector which was previously state dominated by way of decreasing the deficits and debts.

2. The net transfer to the State owned Enterprises is lowered through privatization.

3. It helps in escalating the performance benchmarks of the industry in general.

4. It can initially have an undesirable impact on the employees but progressively in the long term, shall prove advantageous for the growth and prosperity of the employees.

5. Privatized enterprises provide better and quick services to the clients and help in improving the overall infrastructure of the country.

Disadvantages of Privatization

1. Private sector mainly focuses more on profit maximization and less on social objectives dissimilar to public sector that initiates socially viable adjustments in case of emergencies and criticalities.

2. There is lack of clearness in private sector and stakeholders do not get the complete information about the functionality of the enterprise.

3. Privatization has provided the unnecessary support to the corruption and unlawful ways of accomplishments of licenses and business deals amongst the government and private bidders. Lobbying and bribery are the common issues corrupting the practical applicability of privatization.

4. Privatization loses the mission with which the enterprise was established and profit maximization programme encourages malpractices like production of lower quality products, elevating the hidden indirect costs, price escalation, etc.

5. Privatization results in high employee turnover and a lot of investment is required to train staff and even making the existing manpower of PSU abreast with the latest business practices.

6. There can be a conflict of interest amongst stakeholders and the management of the buyer private company and initial resistance to change can impede the performance of the enterprise.

7. Privatization intensifies price inflation in general as privatized enterprises do not get government subsidies after the deal and the burden of this inflation affects the common man.

Analysis of Private Sector with Reference to the Indian Economy

Government of India chose for a mixed economy in which both public and private sectors were permitted to operate. The private sector had to operate within the provisions of the Industries (Development and Regulation) Act 1951 and other relevant legislations. In this framework, the Industrial Policy Resolution

1956 stated, Industrial undertakings in the private sector have necessarily to fit into the framework of the social and economic policy of the State and will subject to control and guideline in terms of the Industries (Development and Regulation) Act and other relevant legislation. The Government of India recognizes that it would be desirable to allow such undertakings to develop with as much freedom as possible, consistent with the targets and objectives of the national plan.

Reports indicated that in spite of speedy progress of the public sector in the period of planning, private sector is the principal sector in the Indian economy.

Since many decades, numerous modern industries have been established in the private sector. Important consumer goods industries were set up in the pre-Independence period itself. Examples include cotton textile industry, sugar industry, paper industry and edible oil industry. These industries were set up in response to the opportunities offered by the market forces. They were highly suitable for private sector since they ensured good returns and required less capital for establishment. Though the engineering industries were not established in the pre-Independence period, yet Tata had initiated in the field of iron and steel industry at Jamshedpur. After Independence, a number of consumer goods industries were set up in the private sector. Presently, India is practically self-reliant in its requirements for consumer goods. According to the 1956 resolution, "industries producing intermediate goods and machines can be set up in the private sector". As a result, chemical industries like paints, varnishes, plastics, etc., and industries manufacturing machine tools, machinery and plants, ferrous and non-ferrous metals, rubber, paper, etc., have been set up in the private sector.

In India, there is a need of privatization of companies to enhance economic status. Though the PSUs have contributed a lot to develop the industrial base of the country, they continue to suffer from a number of inadequacies.

Many PSUs have been incurring and reporting losses on a continual basis. Consequently, a large number of PSUs have already been referred to as loss giving units.

Multiplicity of authorities to whom the PSUs are accountable. Delay in implementation of projects leading to cost escalation and other consequences.

There is ineffective and extensive inefficiency on management.

Many PSUs are over-staffed resulting in lower labour productivity, bad industrial relations.

There are many examples of privatization of companies in India such as

- Lagan Jute Machinery Company Limited (LJMC)
- Videsh Sanchar Nigam Limited (VSNL)
- Hindustan Zinc Limited (HZL)
- Hotel Corporation Limited of India (HCL)
- Bharat Aluminium Company Limited (BALCO)

Privatization in infrastructure sector started with the modification of relevant legislation to permit private enterprises to enter power generation in October 1991. Reforms have been much successful in telecommunications sector. Value added services were opened to private sector in 1992, followed by the enunciation of the National Telecom Policy in 1994-95 which opened up basic telecom services to competition. Foreign equity participation up to 49% was permitted in case of a joint venture between an Indian and a foreign firm.

The Telecom Regulatory Authority of India (TRAI) was established in 1997. In order to separate the service-providing function of publicly owned telecom enterprises and policy-making function, both of which were initially with the Department of Telecommunications, a separate Department of Telecom Services was set up in 1999-2000. The two public sector service providers were corporatised in 2000-01. International long-distance business, which was a public sector monopoly, was opened to unrestricted entry in 2002-03.

In roads sector, there are also infrastructure reforms. Major reform was the creation of a major new source of funding for national, state and rural road construction, called the Central Road Fund (CRF) under the Central Road Fund Act of 2000. The National Highway Development Project funded by the CRF is one of the largest single highway projects in the world. It includes the nearly 6,000 km of Golden Quadrilateral (GQ) connecting the four metropolitan cities of Chennai, Delhi, Kolkata and Mumbai and 7,300 km of North-South and East-West Corridor.

Major impact of Privatization on Indian Economy are as under

It frees the resources for a more productive utilisation.

- Private concerns tend to be profit oriented and transparent in their functioning as private owners are always oriented towards making profits and get rid of sacred cows and hitches in conventional bureaucratic management.

- Since the system becomes more transparent all fundamental corruptions are minimised and owners have a free reign and incentive for profit maximisation so they tend to get rid of all free loaders and vices that are inherent in government functions.

- Gets rid of employment inconsistencies like free loaders or overemployed departments reducing the strain on resources.

- Lessens the government's financial and administrative load.

- Effectively minimises corruption and optimises output and functions.

- Private firms are less tolerant towards capitulation and appendages in government departments and hence tend to right size the human resource potential befitting the organisations' needs and may cause resistance and disgruntled employees who are accustomed to the benefits as government functionaries.

- Permits the private sector to contribute to economic development.

- Development of the general budget resources and diversifying sources of income.

In short, privatization is the process of transfer of ownership, it can be of both permanent and long term lease in nature, of an once upon a time state-owned or public owned property to individuals or groups that intend to utilize it for private benefits and run the entity to generate revenues. Privatization is an overriding process to enhance productivity and competitiveness, as well as attracting foreign direct investment.

Economic Reforms

Indian Economy is passing through a process of crucial change. For the first four decades, we have been pursuing a path in which the public sector was expected to be the engine of growth. However, towards the middle of the seventies, disenchantment with the public sector had started but the voices of protest were feeble and were sporadic and inarticulate. The failure of the public sector to fulfil the role assigned to it resulted in the protest becoming louder and more articulate. Although even in the beginning of eighties, the opening of certain areas hitherto reserved for the public sector was undertaken, but the Government was still hesitant to make a clear statement.

Soon after taking over as Prime Minister in 1985, Rajiv Gandhi outlined the new trends in economic policy of the Government. The recipe suggested by him was: Improvement in productivity, absorption of modern technology and fuller utilisation of capacity must acquire the status of a national campaign. The basic thrust of the New Economic Policy was a greater role for the private sector.

Consequently, the New Economic Policy focused its attention on dismantling the edifice of controls so as to remove unnecessary hurdles in securing licenses, in adjusting output to administered price and in denying industrial licensing to MRTP companies. The Government initiated a number of measures in this regard.

The essence of economic reforms is the dismantling of controls over the economy with the state yielding to market forces. It was in 1991 that a comprehensive economic reforms package was drawn up and attempted to be implemented in India.

The problems of the economy which assumed alarming proportions in 1991: The Gulf War in 1990 sharply accentuated the problems. The economy was already fragile for three reasons: (i) fiscal crisis, (ii) unmanageable BoP, and (iii) high rate of inflation.

The fiscal situation had deteriorated throughout the 1980s due to the growing burden of non-development expenditure. The gross fiscal deficit of the Central government was 8.2 per cent of GDP during the late 1980s as compared to 6.3 per cent during the early 1980s. To fill the gap successive governments indulged in excessive borrowing from internal and external sources leading to mounting internal debt from 35 per cent of GDP in 1980-81 to 53 per cent in 1990-91. This made the burden of servicing the debt onerous. Interest payments which increased from 2 per cent of GDP and 10 per cent of the Centre's expenditure in 1980-81 to 4 per cent and 19 per cent in 1990-91 respectively had eaten up 37 per cent of total revenue collections of the Centre.

The BoP crisis too was neither sudden nor unexpected. The policies followed in the 1970s and 1980s created incentives for import-intensive industrialisation and production while export performance was at best modest. Consequently, the current account deficit doubled from an annual average of $2.3 billion or 1.3 per cent of GDP during the early 1980s to an annual average of $5.5 billion or 2.2 per cent of GDP during the late 1980s. These persistent deficits were financed by borrowing from abroad leading to increase in external debt from $23.8 billion or 14.3 per cent of GDP in 1980-81 to $62.3 billion or 22.8 per cent in 1990-91. Consequently, debt service burden also rose from 7.9 per cent of current account receipts and 14.9 per cent of export earnings in 1980-81 to 21.7 per cent and 29.8 per cent respectively in 1990-91. As a result, foreign exchange revenues dropped to levels which were not enough to finance essential imports even for a fortnight during the Gulf crisis.

The vulnerability of the BoP was accentuated by two other factors: (i) difficulty in rolling over existing short-term debt in the range of $6 billion, and (ii) massive net outflow of $1.3 billion of non-resident Indian deposits in 1991. The last resort resources of using stocks of gold to obtain forex, borrowing from multilateral financial institutions and emergency bilateral assistance from donor countries rescued the country from possible default situation. Instead of taking corrective measures to manage BoP, short-term debt was incurred to finance imports of petroleum and fertilisers while borrowings from international market were used to sustain imports and defence purchases. The rapid pile up of external debts and increased burden of debt servicing eroded international confidence in India's capacity for repayment.

The price situation too came under severe pressure. The rate of inflation in terms of wholesale price index (WPI) climbed from 4.5 per cent in 1985-86 to more than 10 per cent in 1990-91. The consumer price index (CPI) rose by 11.2 per cent per annum during this period. This was attributable to the large deficits which were inevitably associated with a monetisation of budget deficits and an excessive growth of money supply.

RESPONSE TO THE CRISIS

Now, the government had two major goals: (a) restoration of stability in the economy by cutting down the fiscal deficits and bringing stability in the BoP; and (b) to make structural changes or adjustments in the economy; a process of reform which had been going on for the last decade but at an insignificant pace, but now to be taken up on a wider scale and at a pace whose impact would be direct and seen in the long term.

The objectives of the structural reforms were to shift resources from (a) the non-traded goods sector to the traded goods sectors (and within the traded goods sector, from import to export activities); and (b) from the government sector to private sectors. It also sought to improve resource utilisation by (a) increasing the degree of openness of the economy, and (b) changing the structure of incentives intervention to rely more on the market place, dismantle controls to rely more on prices and wind down the public sector. To achieve these ends, (a) trade and foreign investment policies, (b) industrial deregulation and public sector reforms, and (c) financial reforms were enunciated. The main endeavour was to raise the rate of growth of output in the medium term.

GLOBAL REFORM IMPACT

Over the year, since the World Bank and IMF began to get actively involved in development assistance and BoP support, the two institutions have evolved some key programmes under the name of structural adjustments in respect of the World Bank and conditionalities in respect of the IMF.

While IMF's conditionalities impel the countries, which borrow to meet BoP crisis, to manage effective demand better, contain deficits and regulate their economies with market-oriented instruments like tariffs, the World Bank, on its part, has evolved a structural programme to reduce governmental intervention and bring about an atmosphere of competitiveness through the entry of the private sector. Elimination of high budget deficits, cutting down subsidies and abolition of price controls and elimination of regulatory and licensing systems are some other reforms advocated by the World Bank.

The policies of the World Bank and IMF, largely shaped by the western perception of market economy (further endorsed by the collapse of the communist regimes and their economic systems), were forced upon the Latin American and African countries to achieve the ends of globalisation of economy. The end result was disastrous for many of these countries.

It were not just the IMF's conditionalities for imparting assistance that led to the government going in for structural reform in 1991, but the realisation the planning and the controlled approach to India's economic development had failed, and as a consequence of not modifying obsolete features, economic growth was severely distorted and stunted. The reform programme aimed to improve efficiency in resource use and resource allocation, and at creating a macroeconomic environment which facilitates and is conducive to rapid growth.

The key areas of policy reform were

1. deregulation and reliance on market forces in the economy;
2. privatisation/commercialisation of public sector enterprises;
3. measures to stimulate domestic production and broaden the supply base of the economy;
4. adoption of realistic exchange rate policy;
5. trade and payment liberalisation;
6. promotion of industrial diversification;
7. boosting exports and imports; and
8. reform of the banking and finance sector.

SECOND GENERATION REFORMS

The concept of second generation reform was evolved by the IMF to insulate developing countries from marginalisation in the wake of globalisation. The first generation reform is not, by itself, enough either to accelerate social progress sufficiently or to allow countries to complete more successfully in global markets.

The need to eliminate distortions and inefficiency in markets provided the motivation for a first generation of reforms intended to make markets work more efficiently–pricing, exchange rate and interest rate reforms, tax and expenditure reforms and establishment of rudimentary market institutions.

It needs to be reiterated that the two generations exist together, and not one after the other.

1. **Extending Reforms to the States:** The reforms in the Central government need to be extended to the state government level. This is because states are responsible for health, education, agricultural extension and agriculture-related services, irrigation, power distribution, rural, state and district roads, municipal services in urban areas which directly affect the life of the people. The efficiency levels in government system have deteriorated in many states. Administrative reforms designed to improve performance and increase accountability are essential if resources are to be translated into effective development work.

   A serious effort should be made by the states to create an investor-friendly environment and reduce the rigours of the "inspection raj".

2. **Labour Legislation:** An area that has not been touched by reforms so far relates to the reforms in the labour market. India's labour laws deny firms the flexibility needed to operate successfully in the highly competitive markets.

Labour laws should be amended to bring them in line with the practices in other countries. The existing laws only apply to the organised sector which constitutes only 8 per cent of the labour force. Ninety-two per cent of the labour population derives no benefit from these laws. Simultaneously, the laws also need to be amended to ensure a particular level of labour protection and welfare measures the effectiveness of measures relating to social security, occupational health and safety, minimum wages and linkage of wages with productivity and the safeguards and facilities required for women and handicapped persons in employment.

3. **Legal System:** The legal procedures in India are enormously time-consuming. There is a need for reforms at two levels: administrative problems of how courts work and redrafting of fossilised legislations. Reform of our legal system is vital for economic progress as well as social justice.

4. **IPR Regime:** India needs to establish a good intellectual property rights (IPR) regime to open up possibilities of huge rewards for innovation. We also need to create a database of our traditional wealth of knowledge to safeguard it from being pirated by other countries.

5. **Education:** The country needs to expand both quantity and quality of educational services in the country. This requires not only universal and compulsory primary education as a first step but also empowerment of parents and local governments such as panchayats for effective results.

6. **Social Security Nets:** India needs to consolidate various anti-poverty measures into a coherent targeted safety net for the poor. There is also the challenge of fulfilling social obligations towards the huge middle class which has been hit hard with inflation and mass unemployment among the educated.

The increase in life expectancy, the breakdown of the joint family system and the desire for modern medical care have created several problems for the aged. We need to set up a system for old age income security. To meet all these obligations, the government should withdraw from most areas of commercial activity and restrict itself to overall governance and social responsibilities.

7. **Environment Sustainability:** Economic growth along with environmental degradation does not increase social welfare. We need to institute effective policies to preserve and regenerate environmental resources. A combination of economic incentives, liability laws and an awareness campaign can help clean up air and water.

Role of Economic Planning

Economic Planning means the allocation of limited resources among different uses in such a way as to bring about the maximum welfare of the people. Economic planning of two basic elements. One is the determination of objectives and the other is the provision of means for the achievements of the objective. The detailed scheme is called Economic Plan. The planning may either be centralized or decentralized depending upon the national requirements and degree of involvement of different sectors. The centralized planning refers to complete central control over major parts of the economic activities. Some of the decisions are related to investments in different sectors of economy, fixation of price structure, rate of wages and the amount of production of a particular commodity.

ROLE OF ECONOMIC PLANNING

Planning is needed even in a free market economy. Although market forces and the price mechanism would take care of growth and production in general, planning is required to focus on the developmental aspect. Plans need to be concentrated on infrastructure and social sectors and those areas in which private initiative is not easily forthcoming.

A role for planning is also seen in expanding the market, making it work competitive and providing access to both big and small economic agents. This is done through a legislative framework, smoother functioning of stock exchanges and financial intermediaries, removing obstacles in movement of goods and consumer protection. And where the market takes a short-term view, such as in the protection of environment, state intervention is unavoidable.

In a developing economy like ours, in which there is a major problem of poverty, unemployment and rapidly growing population, a lot of people will be left behind in the race for economic prosperity if the state is not involved. There is a need to provide a safety net for deprived sections and to involve them in the development process of the country.

Planning provides a direction to the country—it supervises the nation's progress towards its goals and objectives.

OBJECTIVES OF PLANNING

Planning in India derives its objectives and premises from the Preamble and the Directive Principles of State Policy enshrined in the Constitution. Based on this, the Planning Commission set out the following four objectives of planning.

  (i) to increase production to the maximum possible extent so as to achieve higher level of national and per capita income;

 (ii) to achieve full employment;

(iii) to reduce inequalities of income and wealth;

(iv) to set up a socialist society based on equality and justice and absence of exploitation.

Besides, self-reliance too has been an objective in the long term. Growth with social justice and alleviation of poverty has thus been the primary objectives of Indian planning.

Within this framework, each Five-Year Plan evolves its own short-term objectives taking into account fresh possibilities and existing constraints.

- **Growth:** Economic growth, reflected in a rapid and continuous increase in real national income and per capita income, is an important goal of planning.

- **Social Justice:** One aspect of social dimension is to improve the living standard of the poorest groups in society. The other aspect is the reduction in inequalities in asset distribution.

- **Employment:** The plans have recognized that generation of employment is a crucial factor in the removal of inequalities and raising growth rate.

- **Self-Reliance:** Self-reliance is not to be confused with self-sufficiency, but means, in Jawaharlal Nehru's words, avoiding "economic imperialism" in international trade. Interdependence among countries but not subordination to any is the essence of self-reliance. Self-reliance came to be an objective of planning from the Third Plan onwards, but at that time it was adopted to do away with the need for external aid. The goal was concretised in the Fourth Plan. Then onwards, it has been a part of the aims of planning.

DEVELOPMENT STRATEGY

The common elements of development strategy are as follows.

(a) A comprehensive planning is envisaged which includes policies and programmes for economic development as well as for institutional change and social welfare.

(b) A mixed economy is essentially a planned economy. An integrated developmental programme is to be prepared where the role of the private sector, while not explicitly defined, is expected to fall within national priorities of development.

(c) Priority to the development of the public sector is envisaged, especially in crucial sectors such as defence, telecom, core industries and banking.

(d) Accelerated growth–with emphasis on stepping up the rate of capital formation–is another feature.

(e) Balanced growth for a pattern of development where there is a balance between industry and agriculture, consumer goods and producer goods industry and services sector is emphasised.

(f) There is an emphasis on employment, particularly with the development of the labour-intensive industries, *e.g.*, small-scale and cottage industry.

(g) Accelerated development of the backward regions is emphasised.

(h) Upliftment of the backward classes and social welfare programmes have been given importance.

Thus the major elements in the plan strategy are the size of plans; investment pattern in plan, *i.e.*, resource allocations in different sectors, mobilization of resources through fiscal, monetary and foreign aid measures.

TYPES OF PLANNING

Centralised Planning presumes complete central control over a major part of the economy.

Decentralised Planning is the kind of planning where decision making process is dispersed and the implementation of plans is carried through prices and incentives.

Structural Planning involves changes in socio-economic institutions.

Functional Planning involves no such changes in the socio-economic structure of the society but planning is done within the framework of existing institutions.

Fixed-term Plans: Ordinarily a short-term plan, say of five years, is divided into annual plans, each annual plan beginning from where the preceding plan has left. This way it may be called fixed-term planning.

Rolling Plans: A variant of short-term plans is what has come to be known as 'rolling plans'. Two major aspects of rolling plans are:

(i) In a rolling plan, the central outlay allotment for major sectors within the overall five-year plan targets will be fixed on a yearly basis.

(ii) The five year horizon will be extended each year by changing the select central targets for an additional year.

Indicative Planning provides direction for the growth of the economy by spelling out clear goals and providing help in reaching them.

Imperative Planning is essentially a planning wherein the implementation is provided for, along with its formulation. It not only plans what is desirable but also ensures that the economy shapes itself as per plan requirements.

INITIATION OF PLANNING IN INDIA

- **1930:** When our national leaders came under the influence of socialist philosophy. **M. Visvesvarayya** who was a civil engineer and Dewan of Mysore published his book *"Planned Economy in India".*

- **1938:** *Was the year that witnessed the first attempt to develop a national plan for India when National Planning Committee was set up.* This committee was set up by Subhash Chandra Bose and chaired by Jawaharlal Nehru.

- **1944:** Eight Industrialists of Bombay including Mr. JRD Tata, GD Birla, Purshottamdas Thakurdas, Lala Shriram, Kasturbhai Lalbhai, AD Shroff, Ardeshir Dalal, & John Mathai working together prepared *"A Brief Memorandum Outlining a Plan of Economic Development for India"* which was popularly known as **Bombay Plan.** *This plan envisaged doubling the per capita income in 15 years and tripling the national income during this period.*

- **August 1944:** The British India government set up *"Planning and Development Department"* under the charge of Ardeshir Dalal. But this department was abolished in 1946.

- **October 1946:** A *Planning Advisory Board* was set up by Interim Government to review the plans and future projects and make recommendations upon them.

- **A 10 year People's Plan:** Also came out during that era which was based upon Marxist socialism and drafted by M.N. Roy on behalf of the Indian federation of Lahore.

- Another plan called as *Gandhian Plan* was put forward by Shriman Narayan Aggarwal in 1944 who was principal of Wardha Commercial College. It was a modest kind of plan.

- In 1950 *Sarvodaya Plan* came out which was drafted by Jaiprakash Narayan inspired by Gandhian plan as well as Sarvodaya idea of Vinoba Bhave. Along with agriculture it emphasized small and cottage industries as well. It also suggested the freedom from foreign technology and stressed upon land reforms and decentralized participatory planning.

In March 1950 in pursuance of declared objectives of the Government to promote a rapid rise in the standard of living of the people by efficient exploitation of the resources of the country, increasing production and offering opportunities to all for employment in the service of the community the **Planning**

Commission was set **up by a Resolution of the Government of India.** The Planning Commission was charged with the responsibility of making assessment of all resources of the country, augmenting deficient resources, formulating plans for the most effective and balanced utilization of resources and determining priorities. **Jawaharlal Nehru was the first Chairman of the Planning Commission.**

NITI AAYOG

The National Institution for Transforming India (NITI Aayog) came into existence in 2015 replacing the existing Planning Commission which was established in 1950. The NITI Aayog is the successor to the Planning Commission. The new institution is envisaged to be a catalyst to the developmental process; nurturing an overall enabling environment, through a holistic approach to development going beyond the limited sphere of the public sector and Government of India. This is to be built on the foundation of: an empowered role of states as equal partners in national development; underlying the principle of cooperative federalism. A knowledge hub of internal as well as external resources; serving as repository of good governance best practices, and a think tank offering domain knowledge as well as strategic expertise to all levels of government. A collaborative platform facilitating implementation; by monitoring progress, plugging gaps and bringing together the various ministries at the Centre and in States, in the joint pursuit of developmental goals.

Objectives

The Resolution setting up the NITI Aayog includes the following objectives: To evolve a shared vision of national development priorities, sectors and strategies with the active involvement of States in the light of national objectives. The vision of the NITI Aayog is to provide a framework 'national agenda' for the Prime Minister and the chief ministers to provide impetus: To foster cooperative federalism through structured support initiatives and mechanisms with the states on a continuous basis, recognizing that strong states make a strong nation, to ensure, on areas that are specially referred to it, that the interests of national security are incorporated in economic strategy and policy, to pay special attention to the sections of our society that may be at risk of not benefitting adequately from economic progress, to design strategic and long term policy and programme frameworks and initiatives, and monitor their progress and their efficacy. The lessons learnt through monitoring and feedback will be used for making innovative improvements, including necessary mid course corrections: To create a knowledge, innovation and entrepreneurial support system through a collaborative community of national and international experts, practitioners and other partners, to offer a platform for resolution of inter-sectoral and inter-departmental issues in order to accelerate that implementation of the development agenda, to undertake other activities as may be necessary in order to further the execution of the national development agenda, and the objectives mentioned above.

Composition

The composition of the NITI Aayog is as follows:

(a) Prime Minister of India as the Chairperson.

(b) The Governing Council comprising the Chief Ministers of all the States, Chief Ministers of Union Territories with Legislatures, *viz.*, Delhi and Puducherry and Lt. Governors of other Union Territories.

(c) Regional Council will be formed to address specific issues and contingencies impacting more than one state or a region. These will be formed for a specified tenure. The Regional Councils will be convened by the Prime Minister and will comprise the Chief Ministers of States and Lt. Governors of Union Territories in the region. These will be chaired by the Chairperson of the NITI Aayog or his nominee.

(d) Experts, specialists and practitioners with relevant domain knowledge as special invitees nominated by the Prime Minister.

(e) The full time organizational framework will consist of, in addition to the Prime Minister as Chairperson.

  (i) Vice-Chairperson: To be appointed by the Prime Minister.

  (ii) Members: Full Time.

  (iii) Part-time Members: Maximum of 2, from leading universities, research organizations and other relevant institutions in an ex-officio capacity. Part time members will be on a rotational basis.

  (iv) Ex-officio Members: Maximum of 4 Members of the Union Council of Ministers to be nominated by the Prime Minister.

  (v) Chief Executive Officer: To be appointed by the Prime Minister for a fixed tenure, in the rank of Secretary to the Government of India.

  (vi) Secretariat as deemed necessary.

At present the approved constitution of the NITI Aayog is as under:

Chairperson: Shri Narendra Modi, Prime Minister.

Vice Chairperson: Dr. Arvind Panagariya, in the rank of Cabinet Minister.

Full Time Members:

(a) Dr. Bibek Debroy, in the rank of Minister of State

(b) Dr. V.K. Saraswat, former Secretary; Defence R & D, in the rank of Minister of State

(c) Prof. Ramesh Chand, Former Professor & Head, Institute of Economic Growth, Delhi University; and Professor at Punjab Agricultural University, Ludhiana.

Ex-Office Members:

(a) Shri Raj Nath Singh, Minister of Home Affairs.

(b) Shri Arun Jaitley, Minister of Finance; Minister of Corporate Affairs.

(c) Shri Suresh Prabhu, Minister of Railways.

(d) Shri Radha Mohan Singh, Minister of Agriculture.

Special Invitees:

(a) Shri Nitin Jairam Gadkari, Minister of Road Transport and Highways, and Minister of Shipping.

(b) Shri Thaawar Chand Gehlot, Minister of Social Justice and Empowerment.

(c) Smt. Smriti Zubin Irani, Minister of Textiles.

Working of Governing Council of NITI Aayog

The first meeting of the Governing Council of NITI Aayog was held in 2015 in New Delhi. Its second meeting was held on July 15, 2015 where the Prime Minister reiterated the vision that states should be the focus of all development efforts. In order to work towards a federal structure, based on a two-way flow of priorities and cooperative action, a series of meetings were held in NITI Aayog with groups of States to develop a strategy of working together. This exercise culminated in the conference - 'Role of NITI Aayog: Consultation with the States' - held in November 2015.

The conference advocated the need for gradual shifting of the focus from Planning to Policy, in order to influence the behaviour of both public and private actors. This is important in the light of changed economic circumstances where the major share of investments today flows from the private sector. It was also observed that most states had achieved sizes of economy larger than many countries. As a result, they needed to interact a great deal not only with the Central Government but also with international government and non-governmental bodies.

Major Activities

NITI Aayog as a "Think Tank" of the Government is instrumental in providing a directional and policy dynamics for taking steps in liaison with states while fostering the spirit of cooperative federation. Major activities of NITI Aayog include: Appointments of Vice Chairman, Full Time Members and Chief Executive Officer of NITI Aayog have been made. A National Conference on the Role of NITI Aayog - Consultations with States was organized in New Delhi in November, 2016. A Resource Book on Good Practices in Social Sector Service Delivery was published. Assisted Backward states – Bihar, West Bengal and Odisha by granting Special Assistance of ₹ 1,887.53 crore, ₹ 536.77 crore and ₹ 132.07 crore respectively for their key development areas.

NATIONAL DEVELOPMENT COUNCIL (NDC)

The working of the Planning Commission has led to setting up of another extra-constitutional and extra-legal body, *viz.*, the National Development Council. NDC considers the proposals formulated for plans at all important stages and accepts them. Consider the social and economic policy and its effect on national development and ensure fullest development of rural and backward areas of the nation. This Council was formed in 1952, as an adjunct to the planning commission, by a cabinet secretariat resolution to associate the states in the formulation of the plans. The functions of the council are to strengthen and mobilize the efforts and resources of the nation in support of the plans, to promote common policies in all vital spheres and to ensure the balanced and rapid development of all parts of the country.

The sitting Prime Minister is the chairman of the NDC. Since the middle of 1967, all members of the Union Cabinet and the Administrators of the Union Territories have been members of this council. NDC had not much importance in Nehru Era but got importance after 1990. *Similarly decentralization also got importance after 73rd and 74th Constitutional Amendments which made decentralization a constitutional imperative.*

PLAN HOLIDAY

After Independence, a strategy of medium-term planning of Five Year Period was adopted to achieve economic progress. But due to certain emergencies, the five year plans could not be continuously implemented and there had been a time-gap between two consecutive medium-term plans for one reason or the other. This gap is called as *'Plan Holiday'.*

After the Third Five Year Plan, the Fourth Plan could not be initiated due to war, severe drought, devaluation of Indian currency and other economic reasons. This caused a Plan Holiday of three years (1966-1969) in initiating Fourth Plan. But to continue the economic progress with long-term objectives and perspectives, three annual plans were implemented which were subsequently incorporated in the *'Fourth Five Year Plan'.* Similarly, there was a Plan Holiday of two years (1990-91 and 1991-92) between Seventh and Eighth plans, the reasons being political instability, severe resources shortage and some other economic exigencies. The Eighth Plan was from 1992 to 1997. However, during Plan Holiday, annual Plans were implemented to continue the process of economic development.

PERFORMANCE DURING PLANS

First Plan

Keeping in view the large-scale import of foodgrains in 1951 and inflationary pressures on the economy, the First Plan

(1951-56) accorded the highest priority to agriculture including irrigation and power projects. About 44.6 per cent of the total outlay of ₹ 2,069 crore in the public sector (later raised to ₹ 2,378 crore) was allocated for this purpose. The Plan aimed at increasing the rate of investment from five to about seven per cent of the national income.

Second Plan

The Second Five-Year Plan (1956-57 to 1960-61) sought to promote a pattern of development, which would ultimately lead to the establishment of a socialistic pattern of society in India. Its main aims were (i) an increase of 25 per cent in the national income; (ii) rapid industrialisation with particular emphasis on the development of basic and heavy industries; (iii) large expansion of employment opportunities; and (iv) reduction of inequalities in income and wealth and a more even distribution of economic power. The Plan aimed at increasing the rate of investment from about seven per cent of the national income to 11 per cent by 1960-61. It laid emphasis on industrialisation, increased production of iron and steel, heavy chemicals including nitrogenous fertilizers and development of heavy engineering and machine building industry.

Third Plan

The Third Plan (1961-62 to 1965-66) aimed at securing a marked advance towards self-sustaining growth. Its immediate objectives were to: (i) secure an increase in the national income of over five per cent per annum and at the same time ensure a pattern of investment which could sustain this rate of growth in the subsequent plan periods; (ii) achieve self-sufficiency in foodgrains and increase agricultural production to meet the requirements of industry and exports; (iii) expand basic industries like steel, chemicals, fuel and power and establish machine building capacity so that the requirements of further industrialisation could be met within a period of about 10 years mainly from the country's own resources; (iv) fully utilise the manpower resources of the country and ensure a substantial expansion in employment opportunities; and (v) establish progressively greater equality of opportunity and bring about reduction in disparities of income and wealth and a more even distribution of economic power. The Plan aimed at increasing the national income by about 30 per cent from ₹ 14,500 crore in 1960-61 to about ₹ 19,000 crore by 1965-66 (at 1960-61 prices) and per capita income by about 17 per cent from ₹ 330 to ₹ 386 over the same period.

Annual Plans

The situation created by the Indo-Pakistan conflict in 1965, two successive years of severe drought, devaluation of the currency, general rise in prices and erosion of resources available for Plan purposes delayed the finalisation of the Fourth Five Year Plan. Instead, between 1966 and 1969, three Annual Plans were formulated within the framework of the draft outline of the Fourth Plan.

Fourth Plan

The Fourth Plan (1969-74) aimed at accelerating the tempo of development of reducing fluctuations in agricultural production as well as the impact of uncertainties of foreign aid. It sought to raise the standard of living through programmes designed to promote equality and social justice. The Plan laid particular emphasis on improving the conditions of the less privileged and weaker sections especially through provision of employment and education. Efforts were directed towards reduction of concentration of wealth, income and economic power to promote equity.

The Plan aimed at increasing the net domestic product (at 1968-69 factor cost) from ₹ 29,071 crore in 1969-70 to ₹ 38,306 crore in 1973-74. The average annual compound rate of growth envisaged was 5.7 per cent.

Fifth Plan

The Fifth Plan (1974-79) was formulated against the backdrop of severe inflationary pressures. The major objectives of the Plan were to achieve self-reliance and adopt measures for raising the consumption standard of people living below the poverty line. This Plan also gave high priority to bring inflation under control and to achieve stability in the economic situation. It targeted an annual growth rate of 5.5 per cent in the national income. Four Annual Plans pertaining to the Fifth Plan period were completed. It was subsequently decided to end the Fifth Plan period with the close of the Annual Plan 1978-79.

Sixth Plan

Removal of poverty was the foremost objective of the Sixth Plan (1980-85). The strategy adopted was to move simultaneously towards strengthening the infrastructure for both agriculture and industry. Stress was laid on tackling interrelated problems through a systematic approach with greater management, efficiency and intensive monitoring in all sectors and active involvement of people in formulating specific schemes of development at the local level and securing their speedy and effective implementation.

The actual expenditure in the Sixth Plan stood at ₹ 1,09,291.7 crore (current price) as against the envisaged total public sector outlay of ₹ 97,500 crore (1979-80 prices) accounting for a 12 per cent increase in nominal terms. The average annual growth rate targeted for the Plan was 5.2 per cent.

Seventh Plan

The Seventh Plan (1985-90) emphasised policies and programmes, which aimed at growth in foodgrains production, increased employment opportunities and productivity within the framework of basic tenets of planning, *viz.*, growth, modernisation, self-reliance and social justice. Foodgrains production during the seventh Plan grew by 3.23 per cent as compared to a long-term growth rate of 2.68 per cent between 1967-68 and 1988-89 and the growth rate of 2.55 per cent in the eighties due to overall favourable weather conditions, implementation of various thrust programmes and concerted efforts of the Government and the farmers. To reduce unemployment and consequently, the incidence of poverty, special programmes like Jawahar Rozgar Yojana were launched in addition to the existing programmes. Due recognition was accorded to the role, small-scale and food processing industries could play in this regard. The total expenditure during the Seventh Plan stood at ₹ 2,18,729.62 crore (current prices) as against the envisaged total public sector outlay of ₹ 1,80,000 crore, resulting in a 21.52 per cent increase in nominal terms. During this Plan period, the Gross Domestic Product (GDP) grew at an average rate of 5.8 per cent exceeding the targeted growth rate by 0.8 per cent.

Eighth Plan

The Eighth Five-Year Plan (1992-97) was launched immediately after the initiation of structural adjustment policies and macro stabilisation policies, which were necessiated by the worsening Balance of Payments position and the position of inflation during 1990-91. The various structural adjustment policies were introduced gradually so that the economy could be pushed to a higher growth path and improve its strength and thus prevent a crisis in Balance of Payments and inflation in the future. The Eighth Plan took note of some of these policy changes, which were to come about due to these reforms. The Plan aimed at an average annual growth rate of 5.6 per cent and an average industrial growth rate of about 7.5 per cent. These targets were planned to be achieved with relative price stability and substantial improvement in the country's Balance of Payments.

Some of the salient features of economic performance during the Eighth Five Year Plan indicate, among other things, (a) a faster economic growth, (b) a faster growth of the manufacturing sector and agriculture and allied sectors, (c) significant growth rates in exports and imports, improvement in trade and current account deficit, and a significant reduction in the Central Government's fiscal deficit. However, a shortfall in expenditure in the Central sector due to inadequate mobilisation of internal and extra budgetary resources by the PSUs and various departments was witnessed. In the States sector, the reason for the shortfall was lack of mobilisation of adequate resources due to deterioration in the balance of current revenues, erosion in the contribution of state electricity boards and state road transport corporations, negative opening balance, mounting non-plan expenditure and shortfalls in the collection of small savings, etc.

The total expenditure during the entire Eighth Plan stood at ₹ 4,95,669 crore [by taking 1996-97 (RE) as actual], at current prices as against envisaged total public sector outlay of ₹ 4,34,100 crore (1991-92 prices) resulting in a 14.2 per cent increase in nominal terms. The Eighth Plan envisaged an annual average growth rate of 5.6 per cent. Against this an average annual growth rate of 6.8 per cent was achieved during this plan period.

Ninth Plan

The Ninth Plan (1997-2002) was launched in the fiftieth year of India's Independence. The Plan aimed at achieving a targeted GDP growth rate of seven per cent per annum and there was emphasis on the seven identified *Basic Minimum Services* (BMS) with additional Central Assistance earmarked for these services with a view to obtain a complete coverage of the population in a time-bound manner. These included provision of safe drinking water, availability of primary health service facilities, universalisation of primary education, public housing assistance to shelter less poor families, nutritional support to children, connectivity of all villages and habitations and streamlining of the public distribution system with a focus on poor. The Plan also aimed at pursuing a policy of fiscal consolidation, whereby the focus was on sharp reduction in the revenue deficit of the Government, including the Centre, States and PSUs through a combination of improved revenue collection and control of inessential expenditures, particularly with regard to subsidies through recovery of user charges and decentralisation of plannings implementation through greater reliance on States and Panchayati Raj Institutions.

The Specific objectives of the Ninth Plan included: (i) priority to agriculture and rural development with a view to generate adequate productive employment and eradication of poverty; (ii) accelerating the growth rate of the economy with stable prices; (iii) ensuring food and nutritional security for all, particularly vulnerable sections of society; (iv) providing the basic minimum services of safe drinking water, primary health care facilities, universal primary education, shelter and connectivity to all in a time-bound manner; (v) containing the growth rate of population; (vi) ensuring mobilisation and participation of people at all levels (vii) empowerment of women and socially disadvantaged groups such as Schedule Castes, Scheduled Tribes and Other Backward Classes and Minorities as agents of socio-economic change and development; (viii) promoting and developing people's participatory institutions like Panchayati Raj institutions, cooperatives and self-help groups; and (ix) strengthening efforts to build self-reliance.

GROWTH PERFORMANCE IN THE FIVE-YEAR PLANS

(per cent per annum)

Sl. No.	Plan	Target	Actual
1.	First Plan (1951-56)	2.1	3.60
2.	Second Plan (1956-61)	4.5	4.21
3.	Third Plan (1961-66)	5.6	2.72
4.	Fourth Plan (1969-74)	5.7	2.05
5.	Fifth Plan (1974-79)	4.4	4.83
6.	Sixth Plan (1980-85)	5.2	5.54
7.	Seventh Plan (1985-90)	5.0	6.02
8.	Eighth Plan (1992-97)	5.6	6.68
9.	Ninth Plan (1997-2002)	6.5	5.50
10.	Tenth Plan (2002-2007)	8.0	7.7
11.	Eleventh Plan (2007-2012)	8.1	7.9
12.	Twelfth Plan (2012-2017)	8	----

The Ninth Plan envisaged an average target growth rate of 6.5 per cent per annum in GDP as against the growth rate of 7 per cent approved earlier in the Approach Paper. The scaling down of the target was necessitated by the changes in the national as well as global economic situation in the first two years of the Ninth Plan. Against this, the achievement in the growth-rate on an average was to be 5.5 per cent per annum.

Tenth Five-Year Plan

Since economic growth was not the only objective, the Plan aimed at harnessing the benefits of growth to improve the quality of life of the people by setting the following key targets: Reduction in the poverty ratio from 26 per cent to 21 per cent, by 2007; Decadal Population Growth to reduce 21.3 per cent in 1991-2001 to 16.2 per cent in 2001-11; Growth in gainful employment, at least, to keep pace with addition to the labour force; All children to be in school by 2003 and all children to complete five years of schooling by 2007; Reducing gender gaps in literacy and wage rates by 50 per cent; Literacy rate to increase from 65 per cent in 1999-2000, to 75 per cent in 2007; providing potable drinking water to all villages; infant mortality rate to be reduced from 72 in 1999-2000 to 45 in 2007; Maternal mortality ratio be reduced from four in 1999-2000, to two in 2007; Increase in Forest/Tree cover from 19 per cent in 1999-2000, to 25 per cent in 2007; and Cleaning of major polluted river stretches.

The Tenth Plan had a number of new features, that include, among others, the following:

First, the Plan recognised the rapid growth in the labour force. At the then rates of growth and labour intensity in production, India faced the possibility of rising unemployment, which could lead to social unrest. The Tenth Plan therefore aimed at creating 50 million job opportunities during the period, by placing Special emphasis on employment intensive sectors of agriculture, irrigation, agro-forestry, small and medium enterprises, information and communication technology and other services.

Secondly, the Plan addressed the issue of poverty and the unacceptably low levels of social indicators: Although these have been the objectives in the tenth Plan there were specific monitorable targets, which needed to be attained along with the growth target.

Thirdly, since national targets do not necessarily translate into balanced regional development and the potential and constraints of each State differ vastly, the Tenth Plan had adopted a differential development strategy. For the first time a statewise growth and other monitorable targets had been worked out in consultation with the States to focus better on their own development plans.

Another feature of this Plan was the recognition that Governance is perhaps one of the most important factors for ensuring that the Plan was realised, as envisaged. The Plan had laid down a list of reforms in this connection.

Finally, considering the market-oriented economy, the Tenth Plan had dwelt at length on the policies that would be necessary and the design of key institutions. The Tenth Plan not only included a carefully crafted medium-term macro-economic policy stance, both for the Centre and the States, but also laid out the policy and institutional reforms that were required for each sector.

Governance is perhaps one of the most important factors for ensuring that the plan is realised, as envisaged. Some steps required in this direction were: Improved people's participation, especially through strengthening Panchayat Raj Institutions and urban local bodies; involvement of civil society, especially voluntary organisations, as partners in development; enactment of the Right to Information Act; Civil Service reforms for improving transparency, accountability and efficiency; security of tenure, a more equitable system of rewards and punishments; Right sizing both size and role of Government; Revenue and judicial reforms and using information technology for good governance.

Eleventh Five-year Plan (2007-2012)

The Eleventh Five Year Plan (2007-12) which was approved by the National Development Council on 19 December, 2007 provides a comprehensive strategy for inclusive development building on the growing strength of the economy, while also addressing weaknesses that have surfaced. It sets a target for 9 per cent growth in the five year period, which later declined to 8.1 per cent. It also covers 26 other major indices of performance relating to poverty, health, education, women and children, infrastructure, and environment and sets monitorable targets in each of these.

This plan outlines the new priories for the public sector. These relate to reviving dynamism in agriculture and building the necessary supportive infrastructure in rural areas, expanding access to health and education, especially in rural areas, undertaking programmes for improving living conditions for the weaker section and for improving their access to economic opportunity. It also includes a major thrust for infrastructure development in general, which is a critical constraint on our development.

The plan adopts multi-pronged approach towards improvement in agriculture. It provides a major expansion in the programmes of irrigation and water management. As a step towards food security, the National Food Security Mission aims at increasing cereal and pulses production by 20 million tons over a five year period.

There is a massive thrust in this Plan on access to education and health. In education the Plan will spend more than double of what was spent in the tenth plan. In health, the Plan aims at providing improved broad based healthcare in rural areas through the National Rural Health Mission. The Rashtriya Swashya Bima Yojana will provide the much needed insurance cover against illness to the population below the poverty line.

The Plan emphasizes the need for energy conservation, increasing energy efficiency, and development of renewable source of energy.

An important aspect of the Eleventh Plan is that most of the public sector programmes are in the areas that are normally in the domain of the State Governments and where implementation depends upon the active involvement of local level bodies including the Panchayati Raj Institutions. More than any other Plan, this Plan places a much greater reliance upon the involvement of the Panchayati Raj Institutions.

Inclusive Growth in 11th Plan

There are wide income differentials between more developed and relatively poor states which the planning process has not succeeded in overcoming. It is a matter of concern.

There are other disparities besides per capita income. States vary widely in poverty levels, physical quality of life, industrial development, agricultural growth, per capita electricity consumption and proportion of urban population in total population.

The Tenth Plan was the first to mention state-specific targets for growth. The Eleventh Plan continues this initiative of working out the gross state domestic product (GSDP) target for states.

Differences in GSDP and growth rates are summary economic indicators of disparities, wide variations exist in health, education and infrastructure indicators. Backward areas lack even basic amenities. Livelihood options are also limited with agriculture not giving enough returns and industry being practically non-existent in these regions. As the Plan document points out, a large part of the disparities are probably due to historical reasons, differences in initial conditions and natural resource endowments. However, there is no clear pattern that seems to be applicable to all cases.

What is more, it is those areas that are rich in natural resources that continue to lag behind. This has encouraged the Naxalite movement as well as demands for dividing up these states. "Redressing regional disparities is not only goal in itself but is essential for maintaining the integrated social and economic fabric of the country without which the country may be faced with a situation of discontent, anarchy and breakdown of law and order.

Resource flows from the Centre to the states have to be dovetailed to help balanced development. The system of division of powers envisages the Union government getting the most productive sources of revenue, even as the states, and now PRIs, shoulder the major responsibility for delivery of social services. In the circumstances, the Central government needs to ensure that the overall flows of resources from the Centre to the states is such that the relatively backward states are enabled to achieve a level of service delivery at par with the more advanced states. Transfers under the planning process from Centre to states is one means to ensure resources for states. Another significant volume of transfers is through the constitutional mechanism of the finance commissions. The Twelfth Finance Commission (TFC) has used the following criteria and weights for transfer of Central taxes to the states. These have been applied uniformly across all states, both in the Special Category and others.

12th Five Year Plan (2012-17)

The Twelfth Plan fully recognizes that the objective of development is broad-based improvement in the economic and social conditions of our people. However, rapid growth of GDP is an essential requirement for achieving this objective.

The Approach Paper to the Twelfth Plan, had set a target of 9 per cent average growth of GDP over the Plan period (2012 to 2017). That was before the Euro-zone crisis in that year triggered a sharp downturn in global economic prospects, and also before the extent of the slowdown in the domestic economy was known. Twelfth Plan envisaged that the current slowdown in GDP growth can be reversed through strong corrective action, including especially an expansion in investment with a corresponding increase in savings to keep inflationary pressures under control. However, while our full growth potential remains around 9 per cent, acceleration to this level can only occur in a phased manner, especially since the global economy is expected to remain weak for the first half of the Plan period.

Inclusiveness as Poverty Reduction

The poverty estimates for 2011-12 was computed following the extant Tendulkar methodology and this was released in July 2013. The poverty ratio for 2011-12 was estimated as 21.9 at all India level, with 25.7 per cent in rural areas and 13.7 per cent in urban. The Task Force on Elimination of Poverty in India in its report has inter alia, stated that "a consensus in favour of either the Tendulkar or a higher poverty line did not emerge. Therefore, the Task Force has concluded that the matter be considered in greater depth by the country's top experts on poverty before a final decision is made. Accordingly, it is recommended that an expert committee be set up to arrive at an informed decision on the level at which the poverty line should be set".

MAJOR INITIATIVES

Appraisal Document of Twelfth Plan

As a follow up of the decisions taken in the first meeting of the Governing Council the exercise of appraisal of the Twelfth Five Year Plan (2012-17) was undertaken. The appraisal broadly covered physical and financial targets vis-à-vis achievements for the first four financial years of the Plan (2012-16) and the financial targets (Budget Estimates) for the terminal year (2016-17) of the Plan. Breaking away from the past, the Appraisal document is based on the following nine broad themes: (i) economy and policies; (ii) macroeconomic factors; (iii) employment and skill development; (iv) governance; (v) human resource development; (vi) physical infrastructure; (vii) environmental sustainability; (viii) agriculture and rural transformation, and (ix) urban transformation.

The Twelfth Five Year Plan envisaged three scenarios termed as "strong inclusive growth", "insufficient action" and "policy logjam", pegging the average annual GDP growth rate under these at 8 per cent, 6 to 6.5 per cent, and 5 to 5.5 per cent, respectively. The performance in 2012-13 and 2013-14, in line with the projections based on the old GDP series, may be reasonably concluded as below the "policy logjam" scenario. In the later years, the economy recovered. The Appraisal of 12th Plan has provided an opportunity for incorporating the shared vision of national development and important initiatives taking by the Government.

The current financial year (2016-17) is the terminal year of the Twelfth Plan, NITI Aayog has initiated consultations with Union ministries, state governments, experts in the domain and academia, to formulate strategies and draw action plans with differing time horizons.

Atal Innovation Mission

The Government has set up Atal Innovation Mission (AIM) in NITI Aayog with a view to promote a culture of innovation and entrepreneurship in the country. The key initiatives identified under the Mission include; (i) setting up of Atal Tinkering Laboratories (ATLs) in schools for fostering curiosity, creativity and imaginations in young minds, and inculcate skills such as design mindset, computational thinking, adaptive learning, physical computing, etc. The Mission will provide one time grant-in-aid of ₹ 10 lakh towards establishment of ATLs in the first year and another grant of ₹ 10 lakh over a period of five years. During 2016-17, the Mission has selected 257 schools covering 31 states/UTs for this, (ii) setting up Atal Incubation Centres (AICs) for creating high class incubation facilities across India with suitable physical infrastructure in terms of capital equipment and operating facilities, coupled with the availability of sectoral experts for mentoring the start-ups, (iii) providing scale up support to Established Incubation Centres (EICs) in different parts of the country for upgrading their capacity. In addition the Mission will also launch Atal Grand Challenge (AGC) awards for developing novel disruptive technologies/solutions to stubborn socio-economic problems of the country that are ultra-low cost, low maintenance, durable and customised to the local conditions of the country.

Pradhan Mantri Krishi Sinchai Yojana

Pradhan Mantri Krishi Sinchai Yojana (PMKSY), conceived in 2015 is an umbrella scheme for coverage of more and more area under assured irrigation as early as possible. Its major components are (i) Accelerated Irrigation Benefits Programme (AIBP) for major and medium irrigation including National projects; (ii) *Har Khet Ko Pani* which includes command area development and water management (CAD&WM) works, surface minor irrigation, irrigation through groundwater and repair, renovation and restoration (RRR) of water bodies; (iii) per drop more crop for promotion of micro irrigation; and (iv) watershed development for rain water harvesting, effective management of the run-off water, prevention of soil erosion, regeneration of natural vegetation and recharging of the ground water table.

Under AIBP component of PMKSY, 99 projects were prioritized for implementation which will provide additional irrigation coverage over 76 lakh hectare. Out of the 99 prioritized projects, 23 are targeted for completion during 2016-17, 31 projects during 2017-18 and the remaining 45 by December, 2019. All the 99 projects being taken up under AIBP would include CAD&WM works in order to ensure that the irrigation potential created gets utilized without any time lag. Under *Har Khet Ko Pani* (CAD&WM) component priority is for implementation of projects to fully utilize the irrigation potential, which has been created by implementing major, medium and minor irrigation projects in the country.

Soil Health Card

An outlay of ₹ 568.54 crore to assess the soil fertility status in respect of 1,400 lakh land holdings at 2 year interval was initiated. The states will be provided funds for strengthening of the soil testing labs, analysis of soil samples and distribution of the Soil Health Card. This would be a continuous and dynamic exercise to be carried out periodically.

Agri-Tech Infrastructure Fund

Promotion of National Agricultural Market through Agri-Tech Infrastructure Fund (ATIF) with an outlay of ₹ 200 crore for 2015-16 to 2017-18 was formulated. ATIF is aimed at implementation of agricultural marketing reforms by initiating appropriate e-market platforms in states with a view to move towards a national market. It would also increase the farmers' access to markets through warehouse based sales and thus obviate the need to transport the produce to the mandi.

Public Financial Management System

Public Financial Management System (PFMS), earlier known as Central Plan Schemes Monitoring System (CPSMS), is a Central Sector Scheme of NITI Aayog started in April, 2008. It aims at establishing a suitable online Management Information System (MIS) and Decision Support System (DSS) for fund management of the Schemes of the Government of India. The system is envisaged to track the fund disbursement from Government of India under Schemes and ultimately report utilization under these Schemes at different levels of implementation in States/ UTs on a real time basis. PFMS through its interface with banking networks, facilitates end-to-end beneficiary management and electronic payment system to the bank accounts/Aadhar linked bank accounts of the beneficiaries and provides an online-real time MIS to various stakeholders.

In December 2013, a total plan outlay of ₹ 1,080 crore for roll out of PFMS over a period of 4 years (2013-14 to 2016-17) during the 12th Five Year Plan was approved. A four tier dedicated organizational structure has been approved comprising Project Implementation Committee, Central Project Monitoring Unit (CPMU), State Project Monitoring Units (SPMUs) in all the states and District Project Monitoring Units (DPMUs).

PFMS has been fully implemented at Central level in all 98 ministries/departments. Sanction generation, bill generation and transfer of funds of Plan Schemes are through PFMS only.

Complete MIS of sanctions, releases and allocations from Centre to states/UTs, implementing agencies and other recipients is available on PFMS.

The application is integrated with COMPACT and e-Lekha, the core accounting applications and e-payment gateway of CGA, thereby linking the financial and accounting data for comprehensive MIS and DSS. It has developed an interface with Core Banking Solution (CBS) of 103 banks, including India Post, thereby bank balances/float and transactions details of implementing agencies receiving grants from Government is available on a real-time basis.

For monitoring the funds devolved to Consolidated Fund of states (and UTs with legislature) and obtaining real time expenditure information for schemes for which funds are transferred from the Central ministries, an interface for sharing data with state treasuries and state AGs has also been developed in PFMS. Since 2015, it has been transferred to Department of Expenditure.

Housing for All

Housing for All has been proclaimed as a priority by the Government of India. Housing for All has two components: Housing for All (Rural) known as Pradhan Mantri Awaas Yojana (Gramin) implemented by Ministry of Rural Development and Housing for All (Urban) known as Pradhan Mantri Awaas Yojana (Urban) implemented by Ministry of Housing and Poverty Alleviation. To achieve the goal of Housing for All 2022, nearly 3 crore houses are to be built in rural areas and about 2 crore houses in the urban areas in the next 7 years.

Swachh Bharat Mission

The Swachh Bharat Mission (SBM) a joint mission of the Ministry of Urban Development and the Ministry of Drinking Water and Sanitation, emanates from the vision of the Government. Swachh Bharat Mission (SBM) was launched on October 2, 2014, with a target to make the country clean by October 2, 2019.

Smart Cities Mission

Smart Cities Mission (CSM), a Centrally Sponsored Scheme was launched in June 2015 as part of Urban Rejuvenation Mission for the development of 100 smart cities. The objective of the Mission is to promote cities that provide core infrastructure and give a decent quality of life to its citizens, a clean and sustainable environment and application of 'Smart' Solutions. The core infrastructure elements in a Smart City include (i) adequate water supply, (ii) assured electricity supply (iii) sanitation, including solid waste management (iv) efficient urban mobility and public transport (v) affordable housing, especially for the poor (vi) robust IT connectivity and digitalization (vii) good governance, especially e-Governance and citizen participation (viii) sustainable environment (ix) safety and security of citizens, particularly women, children and the elderly, and (x) health and education. The SCM outlay is to be ₹ 48,000 crore (Central Share) over five years @ ₹ 100 per smart city per year. During 2015-16 ₹ 1,475.38 crore have been released by the Centre. Budget allocation in BE 2016-17 for the Mission is ₹ 3,205 crore.

Smart City selection is through a nation-wide 2 stage challenge process. In August 2015, Centre selected 98 potential smart cities in Stage 1 of the challenge. 20 Smart Cities were selected in Stage 2 January 2016, *viz.*, Bhubaneswar, Pune, Jaipur, Surat, Kochi, Ahmedabad, Jabalpur, Visakhapatnam, Solapur, Davanagere, Indore, New Delhi Municipal Corporation, Coimbatore, Kakinada, Belagavi, Udaipur, Guwahati, Chennai, Ludhiana and Bhopal. In 2016-17, 40 more cities are to be selected. Accordingly, 13 fast track cities selected in May, 2016 namely, Lucknow, Warangal, Dharmashala, Chandigarh, Raipur, New Town Kolkata, Bhagalpur, Panaji, Port Blair, Imphal, Ranchi, Agartala and Faridabad. Another 27 more smart cities selected in September, 2016 viz., Amritsar, Kalyan-Dombivili, Ujjain, Tirupati, Nagpur, Mangaluru, Vellore, Thane, Gwalior, Agra, Nashik, Rourkela, Kanpur, Madurai, Tumakuru, Kota, Thanjavur,

Namachi, Jalandhar, Shivamogga, Salem, Ajmer, Varanasi, Kohima, Hubbali-Dharwad, Aurangabad, Vadodara. So far, 60 smart cities have been selected.

Additional Central Assistance for Left Wing Extremism Affected Districts

The Government initiated the scheme Integrated Action Plan (IAP) for selected tribal backward districts in 2010 in 60 districts which was subsequently extended to 82 districts of nine states *viz.*, Andhra Pradesh, Bihar, Chhattisgarh, Jharkhand, Madhya Pradesh, Maharashtra, Odisha, Uttar Pradesh and West Bengal. This scheme was in operation up to March, 2013. In 2013-14, it was decided to continue the financial assistance to 88 districts including 82 districts covered under IAP through the scheme "Additional Central Assistance (ACA) for Left Wing Extremism (LWE) Affected Districts" for the remaining years of the Twelfth Plan. Under the scheme, each district has been allocated ₹ 30 crore per year for 2013-14 and 2014-15.

Backward Regions Grant Fund

The State Component of Backward Regions Grant Fund (BRGF) comprising the Special Plan for KBK districts of Odisha, special Plan for Bihar and West Bengal was being implemented by the erstwhile Planning Commission to address the issues of regional imbalances in development processes. During 2015-16, ₹ 132.07 crore under Special Plan for KBK districts of Odisha, ₹ 1,887.53 crore under Special Plan for Bihar and ₹ 836.77 crore for West Bengal was released as One Time Assistance.

Rural Development

Nearly 70 per cent of India's population is rural, 25 per cent of which lives in poverty. NITI Aayog oversees the Government's mega schemes which seek to ensure that benefits of growth reach rural India, and empower its inhabitants to rise above the poverty line. The schemes - the Mahatma Gandhi National Rural

Employment Guarantee Act (MGNREGA), the Indira Awaas Yojana (IAY) now renamed as Pradhan Mantri Awaas Yojana (PMAY-G), the National Rural Livelihoods Mission (NRLM) now renamed as Deendayal Antyodaya Yojana (DAY) and the National Social Assistance Programme (NSAP) - are implemented by the Ministry of Rural Development (MoRD). The Aayog also monitors the progress of rural drinking water and sanitation schemes of the Ministry of Drinking Water and Sanitation (MDWS).

The Plan and non-Plan provisions of the various schemes during 2016-17 are MGNREGA ₹ 38,500 crore, PMAY-'G' ₹ 5,000 crore, DAY ₹ 3,000 and NSAP ₹ 9,500 crore.

MGNREGA is a demand driven programme and the allocation made for it may vary according to the demand for the year end. Under it, by October 31, 2016, on expenditure of ₹ 38,190.23 crore have been incurred.

Saansad Adarsh Gram Yojana

Saansad Adarsh Gram Yojana (SAGY), a new initiative in rural development, was launched in 2014 with the objective that these Adarsh Grams (Model Villages) serve as the "nucleus of health, cleanliness, greenery and cordiality" within the village community. The scheme's Guidelines call upon Members of Parliament (MPs) to make one village of their choice in their constituency a Model Village by 2016, and another two villages by 2019. Unlike other Schemes, the SAGY does not look at the beneficiaries as receivers and the Government as the doer. Taking development to the doorstep of villages, the scheme aims to empower the villagers to make choices and provide them with opportunities to exercise these choices.

The Adarsh Gram will have a population of three to five thousand in plain areas and 1,000 to 3,000 in hilly, tribal and difficult areas. The Member of Parliament would be free to identify any village for the scheme, other than his own or that of his/her spouse. The scheme would utilize in a convergent manner resources available from existing schemes like IAY, PMGSY, MGNREGS, RKVY, NRLM, National Health Mission (NHM), Sarva Shiksha Abhiyan (SSA), Backward Regions Grant Fund (BRGF), Member of Parliament Local Area Development Scheme (MPLADS), schemes of MLAs and CSR funds, and no additional funding will be required. There will be evaluation mid-term and post project by competent independent agencies.

RURBAN Mission

The Government launched the Dr. Shayma Prasad Mukherji RURBAN Mission in 2014 to deliver integrated project based infrastructure in the rural areas. The RURBAN Mission aims at providing basic amenities in rural areas and check migration from there to cities. The scheme envisages development of economic activities and skill development and helping rural areas get efficient civic infrastructure and associate services. The preferred mode of delivery would be through PPPs, while using various scheme funds. The Mission will be linked with e-governance and achieve targets in a time bound manner. Best practices of cooperatives, NGOs and other sectors can also be dovetailed into the scheme. The scheme has an allocation of ₹ 300 crore during 2015-16 and the same amount has been allocated for mission in 2016-17.

Road Map for Poverty Elimination

Subsequent to the decision taken in the first meeting of the Governing Council of NITI Aayog, a Task Force on Elimination of Poverty in India was constituted in 2015. The background paper addressed two different aspects of the debate around poverty – how to measure, and how to combat poverty. The paper notes that the measurement of poverty, conventionally done through a poverty line, is used in India only for tracking the incidence of poverty across time and space. The other potential uses of a poverty line—identifying who the poor are, and allocation of anti-poverty expenditure across states—are fulfilled through other means. The paper also examines the question of the level at which the poverty line should be set. It recommends further deliberation informed by the idea that the objective behind an official poverty line is to track progress in combating extreme poverty and not identification of the poor for purposes of distribution of government benefits. On combating poverty, the paper recommends a two-pronged strategy – facilitating rapid and sustained employment intensive economic growth, and making anti-poverty programmes more effective.

Challenges

1. *Enhancing the Capacity for Growth:* Today, India can sustain a GDP growth of 8 per cent a year. Increasing this to 9 or 10 per cent will need more mobilization of investment resources; better allocation of these resources through more efficient capital markets; higher investment in infrastructure through both public and PPP routes; and more efficient use of public resources.

2. *Enhancing Skills and Faster Generation of Employment:* It is believed that India's economic growth is not generating enough jobs or livelihood opportunities. At the same time, many sectors face manpower shortages. To address both, we need to improve our education and training systems; create efficient and accessible labour markets for all skill categories; and encourage the faster growth of small and micro-enterprises.

3. *Managing the Environment:* Environmental and ecological degradation has serious global and local implications, especially for the most vulnerable citizens of our country. How can we encourage responsible behaviour, without compromising on our developmental need?

4. *Technology and Innovation:* Technological and organizational innovation is the key to higher productivity and competitiveness. How can we encourage and

incentivize innovation and their diffusion in academia and government as well as in enterprises of all sizes.

5. *Accelerated Development of Transport Infrastructure:* Our inadequate transport infrastructure results in lower efficiency and productivity; higher transaction costs; and insufficient access to our large national market. How can we create an efficient and widespread multi-modal transport network.

6. *Rural Transformation and Sustained Growth of Agriculture:* Rural India suffers from poor infrastructure and inadequate amenities. Low agricultural growth perpetuates food and nutritional insecurities, which also reduces rural incomes. How can we encourage and support our villages in improving their living and livelihood conditions in innovative ways?

7. *Improved Access to Quality Education:* Educational and training facilities have been increasing rapidly. However, access, affordability, and quality remain serious concerns. Employability is also an issue. How can we improve the quality and the utility of our education, while ensuring equity and affordability?

8. *Better Preventive and Curative Healthcare:* India's health indicators are not improving as fast as other socio-economic indicators. Good healthcare is perceived to be either unavailable or unaffordable. How can we improve healthcare conditions, both curative and preventive, especially relating to women and children?

IN THE AGE OF GLOBALISATION

Free market fundamentalists portray planning as antithetical to market reforms. They believe that the market mechanism is sufficient to coordinate all agencies involved in development and other economic activities. They also think that if the market fails to control the activities of various agencies, the government can never succeed in doing so either.

There is also a feeling that the initiative for determining development priorities is *de facto* with the finance departments rather than the planning departments. Hence, it is budgets, not plans, that determine development priorities.

However, in a country like India, which needs large development expenditure spread over many areas and years, plans are needed to allocate and coordinate this expenditure. What is more, planning as a function can never go out of style. It is not just government, everyone needs to plan to a lesser or greater extent. Corporate planning is required in the private sector as much as in the public sector.

Planning gives a government the chance to play its role effectively so that market forces may be channelised to achieve national objectives. The government has to play a decisive role in the social sector, science and technology and infrastructure development.

If properly framed and used, planning may prove to be:

(a) an instrument of economic management to ensure that macro-economic and sectoral strategies are translated into programmes and projects;

(b) an aid to financial management by making it possible to balance commitments with responses and facilitate preparation of annual budgets;

(c) a mechanism for greater accountability, since it requires governments to declare their future investment plans;

(d) a means of strengthening the project cycle by providing a framework in which the preparation, implementation and monitoring of projects can take place;

(e) a frame for coordination of external assistance helping to maximise inflows and channel external resources to priority areas.

CHAPTER

17

Economic Development and National Income

Economic growth and development can mean an economy that becomes advanced, larger, diverse, profitable and can expand into new regions.

When the Britishers left, India was economically backward. The self-sufficient village economy based on cottage industries and old handicrafts items were losing demand because of the introduction of industrial products. With the decline of handicraft industries the traditional economic base of Indian society was in a bad shape. On the other hand, there was insufficiency in the field of industrial society as well. As a result majority population in our country remain undeveloped and poverty-stricken.

Economic development means economic growth along with desired changes in the distribution of national income and other technical and institutional changes. Economic growth means continuous increase in total volume of production over a long period. Economic growth is defined in positive terms. It is measured by the sustained increase in real, national or per capita income of a nation over time. Economic growth is usually measured in terms of an increase in real GNP or GDP over time or an increase in income per head over time. Growth is desirable as it enables a society to consume more goods and services. But per head GNP does not, by itself, constitute or measure welfare or success in development. This is because per capita income does not give any information about income distribution.

Economic growth and development is highly important for improvement in the quality of life of the people of any country. Growth means positive change in the level of production and services by a country over a certain period of time. The most widely used measure of economic growth is the real rate of growth in a country's total output of goods and services indicated by gross product adjusted for inflation or real GDP. National per capita income and consumption per capita are also used for measuring growth.

Rates of economic growth and development are closely related. An increasing economic growth implies positive economic development.

Basic Characteristics of Indian Economy as Developing Economy

India ranks second in the world in terms of population and is the largest democratic country. India has adopted a New Population Policy in 1990-91 which accelerated economic growth rate faster.

Basic characteristics are as follows:

1. **Pre-dominance of Agriculture:** Agriculture is the main sector of Indian economy which is in total contrast to the economic structure of a developed economy. More than 70% of the total population is engaged in agricultural activities while the picture is absolutely different in

advanced countries. Unemployment, poverty, low productivity, lack of irrigation facility are the main problems of agriculture.

2. **High Population:** Population is a major factor influencing the nature of a country's economy. Over population creates complex economic problems. India is the second largest populated country in the world having population of 238 million in 2001 and 1138 million in 2011. It means 17.64% population has been increased since 2001 to 2011. The population pressure is the result of two forces, *i.e.*, high birth rate and lower death rate. As per 2011 census, India's birth rate was 23 and death rate was 7. High population rate is the main problem that India has been facing since 50 years.

3. **Underutilized Natural Resources:** It has been stated that India is a rich country inhabited by poor people. It means that the country possesses abundant stock of natural resources but the problem is that these resources are not fully utilized for the production of material goods and services.

4. **Low Human Development Index:** In the developed countries, people are getting 3600 calories through food but Indians are not getting even 2400 calories through food. It is a great drawback relating to total intake. India's literacy rate is 76% but we can say 24% people are still illiterate. India's life expectancy is 64 at live birth and developed countries life expectancy is more than 80.

5. **Lack of Infrastructure Facility:** Infrastructure is divided into two parts as follows:

   (A) *Physical infrastructure:* Which refers to road, electricity, banking, transportation, communication, insurance, energy, etc. Physical infrastructure is related to development process and it is closely linked with GDP.

(B) *Social infrastructure:* Which refers to education, health, housing, drinking water and sanitation. Social infrastructure is related to human resource development and it is not directly or indirectly related to GDP.

6. **Capital Deficiency:** Capital deficiency affects economy as well as social factors, India suffers from deep rooted shortage of capital. The level of savings is very low and capital formation rate is also low. Capital deficiency is very low because the population rate rises at a rapid rate.

7. **Wide Spread Unemployment:** Unemployment in India is a direct outcome of the rapidly increasing population. More people need more jobs but the underdeveloped economy of India can not accommodate them.

8. **Technological Backwardness:** It is another feature of Indian economy. India is less advanced in technology as compared to developed countries. As a result developed countries are better in production than India. India is facing backward and outdated technology.

9. **Poor Economic Organization:** Economic organization is an important and pushing factor for the economic institutions working in India, however it is not developed enough. Banking systems are not developed well in rural areas, in recent years capital and money markets are not much developed in India. Industrial banks and financial institutions are not very common in India. In this point of view India has lack of structural economic organization set up.

10. **Low Per Capita Income:** Due to large size of population, India is facing the problem of low per capita income. According to the 2011 census, India's population is 121 crore. According to World Development Report, India's per capita income was $3620. It is a very low per capita income as compared to developed countries.

11. **Economic Backwardness:** India is a developing country and has been facing the problem of unemployment, poverty, low per capita income, lack of technology, high growth rate of population, low labor efficiency, economic ignorance, social and religious problem factors, immobility, limited developed occupation and trade, caste system, corruption at every stage, thus reflecting India as economically back ward country.

12. **Poverty:** Majority of people in India have low levels of income and poverty is mostly reflected in low level income people. Lack of educational and health facilities, poor hygienic living conditions, criminal environment, lack of infrastructural facilities affect poverty. Moreover, rural as well as urban areas relate poverty. According to the Indian Planning Commission, there were 29% people below poverty line in 2009-10. Thus it is a huge challenge to reduce poverty.

NATIONAL INCOME

National Income is the total value of all final goods and servies produced by the country in certain year. The growth of National Income helps to know the progress of the country.

According to the National Income Committee, "A national income estimate measures the volume of commodities and services turned out during a given period, counted without duplication". Thus, a total of national income measures the flow of goods and services in an economy. National income is a flow and not a stock. As contrasted with national wealth which measures the stock of commodities held by the nationals of a country at a point of time, national income measures the productive power of an economy in a given period to turn out goods and services for the satisfaction of human wants.

National Income Estimates in India

During colonial age no attempts were made by the government to estimate the national income in a systematic manner. Some individual attempts were, however, made in this direction on the basis of scanty data, reliability of which was doubtful.

Dadabhai Naoroji was the first to produce the statistical estimate of average per capita income. In 1873, he calculated that for the year 1867-68, the total national income of British India was ₹ 3,400 million for a population of 170 million or ₹ 20 per head. Other individual efforts also were made to estimate the national income, notable among them are William Digby (1899); Findlay Shirras (1911, 1922 and 1931); Shah and Khambatta (1921); V.K.R.V. Rao (1925-29 and 1931-32) and R.C. Desai (1931-40). However, the credit for the first scientific estimate of national income during 1931-32 goes to Prof. V.K.R.V. Rao.

After Independence, in view of the country's choice of planned development, the importance of the estimates of national income and its various components was recognised. Accordingly, the National Income Committee was appointed in 1949, with P. C. Mahalanobis as the Chairman, and D.R. Gadgil and V.K.R.V. Rao as members. The Committee was entrusted with the task of preparing a report on the national income and related estimates, suggesting measures for improving the quality of the available data, and for the collection of further essential statistics and recommending ways and means for promoting research in the field of national income.

After the publication of the Report of the National Income Committee, the task of national income estimation was entrusted to the Central Statistical Organisation (CSO). In the beginning, the CSO followed the same method of national income estimation as the National Income Committee had used.

Methods of Calculating National Income

Three methods are usually adopted to calculate national income.

1. **Product Method:** S. Kuznets gave a new name to this method, *i.e.*, product service method. In this method net value of final goods and services produced in a country during a year is obtained and the total obtained value is called total final product. This represents Gross Domestic Product (GDP). Net income earned in foreign boundaries by nationals is added and depreciation is subtracted from GDP.

2. **Income Method:** In this method, a total of net incomes earned by working people in different sectors and commercial enterprises is obtained. According to Dr. Bowley and Robertson, incomes of both categories of people— paying taxes and not paying taxes are added to obtain national income. For adopting this method, sometimes a group of people from various income groups is selected and on the basis of their income national income of the country is estimated. In a broad sense, by income method national income is obtained by adding receipts as total rent, total wages, total interest and total profit.

   Symbolically:
   National Income = Total Rent + Total Wages
   + Total Interest + Total Profit.

3. **Consumption Method:** It is also called expenditure method. Income is either spent on consumption or saved. Hence national income is the addition of total consumption and total savings. For using this method, we need data related to income and savings of the consumers.

   Generally reliable data of saving and consumption are not easily available. Therefore, expenditure method is generally not used for estimating national income.

In India a combination of production method and income method is used for estimating national income.

RELATED TERMS

Gross domestic product (GDP) is a measure of the total flow of goods and services produced by the economy over a specified time period, normally a year. Outputs of goods and services are valued at market price and their values aggregated to obtain the GDP. The value of all intermediate goods (goods used to produce another goods, *e.g.*, flour for bread) is excluded and only the value of the goods (capital) or changes in stocks are included. Intermediate goods are not considered because their values are implicitly included in the prices of the final goods. The word 'gross' indicates that no deduction is made for the 'wear and tear' of the land, buildings and machinery used in the production. The income arising from investments and possessions owned abroad is not included, and only the value of the flow of goods and services produced in the country is estimated in GDP.

When deduction is made for the 'wear and tear' of capital, or what is known as depreciation or capital consumption, from the GDP, we get the **net domestic product (NDP)**.

When we add to the GDP the net earning from abroad, *i.e.*, the income accruing to domestic residents from investments abroad minus the income earned in the domestic market accruing to foreigners abroad, we get the **gross national product (GNP).** When such net earnings are added to the NDP we have the **net national product (NNP).** The NNP at factor cost is the **national income (NI)** of the country.

Summing up the related aggregates of national income.

Gross Domestic Product (at market prices) = GDP at factor cost + net indirect taxes.

Net National Product (at market prices) = GNP at market prices − consumption of fixed capital (depreciation).

Net National Product (at Factor cost) = NNP at market prices − net indirect taxes = National Income.

Per capita income is derived by dividing the total national income of country by its total population:

$$\text{Per Capita Income} = \frac{\text{National Income}}{\text{Population}}$$

An increase in national income in real terms does not necessarily mean an increase in the per capita income. It rather depends on the rate of population growth.

The GDP or GNP/NNP/per capita income in a particular year may be measured in the current prices in that year. This is GDP/GNP/NNP/per capita income at current prices. If measured in the prices of a selected past year which may be assumed to have remained unchanged, it is GDP/GNP/NNP per capita income at constant prices. At constant prices, the national income is called 'real', as the inflationary impact on economic growth is offset.

National income figures give picture of the economy of a nation. They also provide the respective contributions of the different sectors of economy, and details of changes in savings, investment and consumption. NI figures help in

(i) providing governments with some idea of the success of their policies;

(ii) giving some indications of the overall standard of living and average real income per capita;

(iii) providing a standard of comparison of economic performance over the years; and

(iv) helping to provide a comparison of economic progress with other countries.

CAUSES OF INCOME INEQUALITIES

There are glaring income inequalities in India. In fact, these income inequalities have tended to increase in recent years.

In India, there are two basic causes of income inequalities: (i) the existing economic system based on the institution of private property, and (ii) the law of inheritance. At a very high level of national income per capita, these factors may not result in mass poverty but in a country like India where national income per capita is very low, they inevitably lead to denial of basic necessities to a very large section of population.

Private Ownership of Property

India has a mixed capitalist economy. In this economic system people enjoy a right to property. Therefore, not only land, buildings, automobiles, etc., are owned by individuals, but the means of production like factories, buses, farm land, mines etc., are also possessed by private companies and persons. Broadly, people in the country are divided into two main classes. In the first category, we may include all those who own means of production and other property. Their main source of income is their property. In the second category, we may include rest of the people. Since these persons have no property, they rely on their labour power for their subsistence. Except some professionals belonging to this class, all other people falling in this category are poor.

Inheritance Law

According to India's inheritance law, property of the father is inherited by his children and hence sons and daughters of industrialists, traders, big farmers, transporters and other wealthy persons automatically get resources whereby they easily manage large incomes. In contrast, children of workers rarely inherit any property. Even the lucky ones who inherit some property are not so lucky as the children of wealthy persons. Therefore, the law of inheritance is one such institution in the country, which besides accentuating income inequalities also provides legitimacy to them.

Other Causes

Inflation and the price rise

Since the mid-1950s prices have been rising continuously eroding the real income of the working class, while the industrialists, traders, and farmers with large marketable surplus have benefited a great deal from this inflationary process. In India, very little has been done to offset this redistributive effect of inflation, and as a result it has greatly accentuated income inequalities.

The role of the government

Though the State is often proclaimed as a 'precurser' and 'initiator' of economic change in India, the fact is that the State investment essentially plays a supportive role to private investment (especially the large and capital-intensive enterprises). This is due to the fact that the State depends for its support on the same social forces which own the wealth of the country and supply the technicians, administrators and the dominant political groups. In such an environment, the government merely guards the status quo and adopts policies which, on balance, are designed to perpetuate the hegemony of the propertied classes and those allied to them. Even the public expenditure policies in the field of social welfare, *i.e.*, health, education, social security and public housing help the better off people more than they help the wretched poor belonging to the lowest income groups.

Problems of Measurement of National Income in a Developing Economy

Complete and reliable information relating to the numerous ways and methods of estimating national income are not available due to the following problems in an underdeveloped economy.

1. Non-availability of data
2. Illiteracy
3. Non-market transactions
4. Lack of occupational specialisation
5. Non-monetised sectors

1. **Non-availability of data:** Correct and adequate production and cost data are not available in an underdeveloped nation. Such type of data relate to construction workers, small enterprises, activities of petty shopkeepers, animal husbandry, fisheries, forestry, crops *etc.* For estimating national income through the income method, data on unearned incomes and on persons engaged in employment in the services sector are not available. Beside, data on investment and consumption expenditures of the urban and rural population are missing for the estimation of national income through the expenditure method. Moreover, there is no machinery in such nations for the collection of data.

2. **Illiteracy:** In a developing economy, the majority of persons is illiterate and they do not maintain any accounts about the production and sales of their own products. Under these circumstances, the estimates of production and earned incomes are only guesses.

3. **Non-market transactions:** The persons residing in rural regions in underdeveloped economy are able to avoid expenses by building their own huts, implements, tools, garments and other essential goods. In the same way, the persons residing in urban areas having kitchen gardens produce items which they consume themselves. All such production activities do not enter the market transactions and hence are not included in the national income estimates.

4. **Lack of occupational specialisation:** In a developing economy, there is the deficiency of occupational specialisation which makes the national income calculations via the product method. Moreover, the farmers and rural masses are engaged in supplementary occupations like poultry, dairying, cloth making *etc* in an underdeveloped country or in developing economy. But income from such productive activities is excluded from the national net income estimates.

5. **Non-monetised sectors:** There are large non-monetised sectors in an underdeveloped nation. It is the subsistence sector in rural regions in which a large portion of production is partly exchanged for other commodities and is partly kept for personal consumption. Such production and consumption may not be incorporated in national income.

Importance of National Income Analysis

There is significance of data of national income for economy of any country. These days the national income data are regarded as accounts of the economy which are called as social accounts. These refer to net national income and net national expenditure which ultimately become equal to each other. Social accounts teach us how the aggregates of national income output and product result from the income of different individual transactions of international trade and outputs of industries. Their main elements and constituents are related to each other. On the basis of social accounts, the national income data have following importance:

1. **In National policies:** The data of national income are the basis of national policies such as employment policy because these figures enable us to know the direction in which the industrial output, investment and saving *etc* should be channelised so that proper measures may be adopted to bring economy on the right path.

2. **In economic planning:** The national data are very significant in economic planning period. It is necessary that the data pertaining to a nation's gross income, consumption, saving, output, consumption for economic planning from numerous means *etc* must be available. Planning is impossible without data of any economy. Similarly, economists propounded short run as well as long run economic models or long run investment models in which these are very much utilised.

3. **In research:** The national income data are used by the students of economics. These students use the data related to investments, employment consumption, savings and incomes of any country which are obtained from social accounts.

4. **Basis of per capita income:** These data are important for a nation's per capita income which reflects the economic welfare of the nation. When the economic welfare is higher, it is propounded that per capita income is also higher and when the economic welfare is lower, there would be lower per capita income.

5. **In income distribution:** The distribution of income may be calculated by the national income data. From the data pertaining to interests, wages, profits and interests, we know of the disparities in the incomes of many groups of the society. So, the regional distribution of income is revealed. It is only on the basis of these that the government may adopt measures to remove the inequalities in income distribution and to restore regional equilibrium with a view to removing these regional or personal disparities and, taking the decisions to levy more taxes and increase public expenditure.

6. **Interrelationship among different concepts of national income:** Concept of national income may be demonstrated in terms of interrelationship equation.

18

Banking and Monetary Policy

Monetary policy refers to the policy of the central bank with regard to the use of monetary instruments under its control to achieve the goals specified in the Act.

The Reserve Bank of India (RBI) is vested with the responsibility of conducting monetary policy. This responsibility is explicitly mandated under the Reserve Bank of India Act, 1934.

RESERVE BANK OF INDIA (RBI)

The Reserve Bank of India is the apex financial institution of the country which is entrusted with the task of controlling, supervising, promoting, developing and planning the financial system. RBI is the queen bee of the Indian financial system which influences the commercial banks' management in more than one way. The RBI influences the management of commercial banks through its various policies, directions and regulations. Its role in banking is quite unique. In fact, the RBI performs the four basic functions of management, viz., planning, organizing, directing and controlling in laying a strong foundation for the functioning of commercial banks.

RBI possesses special status in our country. It is the authority to regulate and control monetary system of our country. It controls money market and the entire banking system of our country.

The origins of the Reserve Bank of India can be traced to 1926, when the Royal Commission on Indian Currency and Finance – also known as the Hilton-Young Commission – recommended the creation of a central bank for India to separate the control of currency and credit from the Government and to augment banking facilities throughout the country. The Reserve Bank of India Act of 1934 established the Reserve Bank and set in motion a series of actions culminating in the start of operations in 1935. Since then, the Reserve Bank's role and functions have undergone numerous changes, as the nature of the Indian economy and financial sector changed.

Origins of the Reserve Bank of India

- **1926:** The Royal Commission on Indian Currency and Finance recommended creation of a central bank for India.

- **1927:** A bill to give effect to the above recommendation was introduced in the Legislative Assembly, but was later withdrawn due to lack of agreement among various sections of people.

- **1933:** The White Paper on Indian Constitutional Reforms recommended the creation of a Reserve Bank. A fresh bill was introduced in the Legislative Assembly.

- **1934:** The Bill was passed and received the Governor General's assent.

- **1935:** The Reserve Bank commenced operations as India's central bank on April 1 as a private shareholders' bank with a paid up capital of rupees five crore (rupees fifty million).

- **1942:** The Reserve Bank ceased to be the currency issuing authority of Burma (now Myanmar).
- **1947:** The Reserve Bank stopped acting as a banker to the Government of Burma.
- **1948:** The Reserve Bank stopped rendering central banking services to Pakistan.
- **1949:** The Government of India nationalised the Reserve Bank under the Reserve Bank (Transfer of Public Ownership) Act, 1948.

Starting as a private shareholders' bank, the Reserve Bank was nationalised in 1949. It then assumed the responsibility to meet the aspirations of a newly independent country and its people. The Reserve Bank's nationalisation aimed at achieving coordination between the policies of the government and those of the central bank.

The Preamble to the Reserve Bank of India Act, 1934 (the Act), under which it was constituted, specifies its objective as "to regulate the issue of Bank notes and the keeping of reserves with a view to securing monetary stability in India and generally to operate the currency and credit system of the country to its advantage".

The objectives outlined in the Preamble hold good even after 75 years. As evident from the multifaceted functions that the Reserve Bank performs today, its role and priorities have, in the span of 75 years, changed in tandem with changing national priorities and global developments. Essentially, the Reserve Bank has demonstrated dynamism and flexibility to meet the requirements of an evolving economy.

A core function of the Reserve Bank in the last 75 years has been the formulation and implementation of monetary policy with the objectives of maintaining price stability and ensuring adequate flow of credit to productive sectors of the economy. To these was added, in more recent times, the goal of maintaining financial stability. The objective of maintaining financial stability has spanned its role from external account management to oversight of banks and non-banking financial institutions as also of money, government securities and foreign exchange markets.

The Reserve Bank designs and implements the regulatory policy framework for banking and non-banking financial institutions with the aim of providing people access to the banking system, protecting depositors' interest, and maintaining the overall health of the financial system. Its function of regulating the commercial banking sector, which emerged with the enactment of the Banking Regulation Act, 1949, has over time, expanded to cover other entities. Thus, amendments to the Banking Regulation Act, 1949 brought cooperative banks and regional rural banks under the Reserve Bank's jurisdiction, while amendments to the Reserve Bank of India Act saw development finance institutions, non-banking financial companies and primary dealers coming under its regulation, as these entities became important players in the financial system and markets.

Objectives of RBI

Prior to the establishment of the Reserve Bank, the Indian financial system was totally inadequate on account of the inherent weakness of the dual control of currency by the Central Government and of credit by the Imperial Bank of India.

The Preamble to the Reserve Bank of India Act, 1934 spells out the objectives of the Reserve Bank as: "to regulate the issue of Bank notes and the keeping of reserves with a view to securing monetary stability in India and generally to operate the currency and credit system of the country to its advantage."

The important objectives are:

1. **To Act as Monetary Authority:** Formulates implements and monitors the monetary policy to maintain price stability and ensuring adequate flow of credit to productive sectors.

2. **To Regulate and Supervise the Financial System of the Country:** It prescribes broad parameters of banking operations within which the country's banking and financial system functions. It helps to maintain public confidence in the system, protect depositors' interest and provide cost-effective banking services to the public.

3. **To Manage the Exchange Control:** Manages the Foreign Exchange Management Act, 1999 to facilitate external trade and payment and promote orderly development and maintenance of foreign exchange market in India.

4. **To Issue Currency:** Issues and exchanges or destroys currency and coins not fit for circulation to give the public adequate quantity of supplies of currency notes and coins and in good quality.

5. **To Undertake Developmental Role:** RBI performs a wide range of promotional functions to support national objectives.

6. **To Undertake Related Functions by Acting as:**
   - *Banker to the Government:* performs merchant banking function for the central and the state governments; also acts as their banker.
   - *Banker to banks:* maintains banking accounts of all scheduled banks.
   - Owner and operator of the depository (SGL-Subsidiary General Ledger account) and exchange (NDS).

Functions of RBI

RBI performs various traditional banking function as well as promotional and developmental measures to meet the dynamic requirements of the country. Main functions of RBI can be broadly classified into three. These are:

  I. Monetary functions or Central banking functions which includes

A. Issue of currency notes

B. Acting as banker to the Government

C. Serving as banker of other banks

D. Controlling credit

E. Controlling foreign exchange operations

II. Supervisory functions

III. Promotional and Developmental functions.

The Goal(s) of Monetary Policy

The primary objective of monetary policy is to maintain price stability while keeping in mind the objective of growth. Price stability is a necessary precondition to sustainable growth.

In May 2016, the Reserve Bank of India (RBI) Act, 1934 was amended to provide a statutory basis for the implementation of the flexible inflation targeting framework.

The amended RBI Act also provides for the inflation target to be set by the Government of India, in consultation with the Reserve Bank, once in every five years. Accordingly, the Central Government has notified in the Official Gazette 4 per cent Consumer Price Index (CPI) inflation as the target for the period from August 5, 2016 to March 31, 2021 with the upper tolerance limit of 6 per cent and the lower tolerance limit of 2 per cent.

The Central Government notified the following as factors that constitute failure to achieve the inflation target: (a) the average inflation is more than the upper tolerance level of the inflation target for any three consecutive quarters; or (b) the average inflation is less than the lower tolerance level for any three consecutive quarters.

Prior to the amendment in the RBI Act in May 2016, the flexible inflation targeting framework was governed by an Agreement on Monetary Policy Framework between the Government and the Reserve Bank of India on February 20, 2015.

Repo and Reverse Repo Rate

Repo is a transaction wherein securities are sold by the RBI and simultaneously repurchased at a fixed price. This fixed price is determined in context to an interest rate called the repo rate. The transaction is relevant for banks; when they need funds from the RBI, the central bank repurchases the securities. The higher the repo rate, more costly are the funds for banks and hence, the higher will be the rate that banks pass on to customers. A high rate signals that access to money is expensive for banks; lesser credit will flow into the system and that helps bring down liquidity in the economy. The reverse is the reverse repo rate, which banks use to park excess money with RBI.

Cash Reserve Ratio (CRR)

This is the percentage of a bank's total deposit that need to be kept as cash with the RBI. The central bank can change the ratio to a limit. A high percentage means banks have less to lend, which curbs liquidity; a low CRR does the opposite. The RBI can reduce or raise CRR to tighten or ease liquidity as the situation demands.

Open Market Operations

This refers to buying and selling of government securities by RBI to regulate short-term money supply. If RBI wants to induce liquidity or more funds into the system, it will buy government securities and inject funds, and if it wants to curb the amount of money out there, it will sell these to banks, thereby reducing the amount of cash that banks have. RBI uses this tool actively even outside of its monetary policy review to manage liquidity on a regular basis.

Statutory Liquidity Ratio

This is the percentage of banks' total deposits that they are needed to invest in government approved securities. The lesser the amount of SLR, the more banks have to lend outside. The SLR has been brought down from 22% to 21.5% in this policy and the endeavour will be to reduce it by 0.25% every quarter till 31 March 2017.

COMMERCIAL BANKS

The modern commercial banking system started in India in the beginning of the 19th century. Bank of Hindustan (1770) was the first bank to be established (Alexander and Co.) at Calcutta under European management. Other banks set up were Bank of Bengal (1806), Bank of Bombay (1840), and the Bank of Madras (1843) — these were called Presidency Banks. The first purely Indian bank was the Punjab National Bank (1894) but in 1881 was formed the first bank with limited liability to be managed by an Indian board, viz., the Oudh Commercial Bank.

State Bank of India

The Imperial Bank, which was created in 1921 by amalgamating the Presidency Banks of Bengal, Bombay and Madras, was nationalised in 1955 and renamed as State Bank of India (SBI). The SBI had seven subsidiaries. But now it has only 5. Fourteen banks were nationalised in July 1969 and six more in April 1980. These nationalised banks together with regional rural banks (RRBs) come under the category of public sector commercial banks. The other kind of commercial banks are the private sector commercial banks.

REGIONAL RURAL BANKS (RRBs)

These are set up with the objective of developing the rural economy by providing credit and encouraging other productive activities in the rural areas.

Public sector banks sponsor RRBs, subscribing to the share capital. The RRBs meet the credit needs of the weaker sections—small and marginal farmers, artisans, small entrepreneurs, etc.

The RRBs accumulated huge losses and fared badly in their recovery of loans; the government allowed them to grant loans to non-priority sectors as well so as to improve their financial position.

BHARATIYA MAHILA BANK

India's first all-women bank, Bharatiya Mahila Bank was inaugurated in Mumbai on Nov. 19, 2013, on the birth anniversary of former Prime Minister Indira Gandhi. The main objective of the bank is to focus on the banking needs of women and to promote their economic empowerment. The bank commenced operations with an initial capital of ₹ 1000 crore.

The salient features of newly established Bharatiya Mahila Bank are:

(1) Bharatiya Mahila Bank aims to service women and women-run businesses, support women's self-help groups and their livelihoods and promote further financial inclusion.

(2) An only for women bank first time in India and to be fully operated by women.

(3) Bharatiya Mahila Bank will be a universal bank and will provide every banking service and facility that is provided by comparable Public and Private sector banks. It will establish branches all over the country and in due course, some branches in abroad.

(4) This is the only and first public sector bank incorporated through an Act of the Parliament.

(5) Higher interest rate on the saving banks deposits–4.5% for deposits upto ₹ 1.00 lakh and 5.0% for deposits above ₹ 1.00 lakh.

(6) 5 branches of RMB become operational–Mumbai, Kolkata, Chennai, Ahmedabad, Guwahati. Two branches, viz., Delhi

and Indore will be operational after the assembly elections respectively in NCR Delhi and M.P.

COOPERATIVE BANK

The cooperative banks are so called because they have been organised under the provisions of the cooperative societies law of the states. Till 1969, cooperative societies were practically the only institutional source of rural credit. Since then the government has adopted a 'multi-agency approach' under which the cooperative banks and commercial banks, supplemented by RRBs, are encouraged to serve the rural sector. The major beneficiary of cooperative banking is the agricultural sector in particular and the rural sector in general.

In terms of organisational set-up of the cooperative banking system, the apex is the state cooperative bank (SCB) in each state (cooperation being a state subject); at the district level are the central cooperative banks (CCBs); and at the village level, there are primary agricultural credit societies (PACS).

The mediun-term and long-term credit to agriculture is provided by the land development banks. Though they are registered as cooperative societies, they are limited liability organisations. They have a two-tier structure. At the state level are the state land development banks (SLDBs) and at the local level are the branches of SLDBs and primary land development banks (PLDBs).

DEVELOPMENT FINANCIAL INSTITUTIONS

Industrial Finance Corporation of India (IFCI)

The Government of India set up the Industrial Finance Corporation of India (IFCI) in July 1948 under a special Act. The Industrial Development Bank of India, scheduled banks, insurance companies, investment trusts and co-operative banks are the shareholders of I.F.C.I. The Union Government had guaranteed the repayment of capital and the payment of a minimum annual dividend. The Corporation was authorised to issue bonds and debentures in the open market, to borrow foreign currency from the World Bank and other organisations, accept deposits from the public and also borrow from the Reserve Bank.

The IFCI performed three important functions:

(a) It granted loans and advances to industrial concerns and subscribed to the debentures floated by them.

(b) It guaranteed loans raised by the industrial concerns in the capital market.

(c) It underwrote the issue of stocks, shares, bonds and debentures of industrial concerns. It also subscribed to the equity and preference shares and debentures of companies.

IFCI was authorised to give long and medium-term finance to companies engaged in manufacturing, mining, shipping and generation and distribution of electricity.

IFCI had played a pioneering role in financing private sector investment and had a big hand in the rapid industrial development of India.

State Financial Corporation

The scope of assistance provided by the Industrial Finance Corporation of India was limited since it dealt with large public limited companies and co-operative societies which were engaged in manufacturing, mining, shipping and generation and distribution of electricity. But there were both small-scale and medium-sized industries which require financial assistance and for this purpose the State Governments desired to set up State Financial Corporations. The Government of India passed the State Financial Corporations Act in 1951 and made it applicable to all states. The authorised capital of a State Financial Corporation is fixed by the State Government within the minimum and maximum limits of ₹ 50 lakh and ₹ 5 crore and is divided into shares of equal value which are taken by the respective State Governments, the Reserve Bank of India, scheduled banks, co-operative banks, other financial institutions such as insurance companies and investment trusts and private parties. The shares are guaranteed by the State Government. A State Financial Corporation can augment its funds through issue and sale of bonds and debentures.

Industrial Credit and Investment Corporation of India (ICICI)

The Industrial Credit and Investment Corporation was sponsored by a mission from the World Bank for the purpose of developing small and medium industries in the private sector. It was registered in January, 1955 under the Indian Companies Act. The aim of I.C.I.C.I. was to stimulate the promotion of new industries, to assist the expansion and modernisation of existing industries and to furnish technical and managerial aid so as to increase production and afford employment opportunities. The Corporation granted:

(a) long-term or medium-term loans, both rupee loans and foreign currency loans;

(b) participated in equity capital and in debentures and underwrote new issues of shares and debentures;

(c) guaranteed loans from other private investment sources;

(d) provided financial services such as deferred credit, leasing credit, instalment sale, asset credit and venture capital.

The Industrial Development Bank of India (IDBI)

IFCI, the SFCs ICICI, and the Refinance Corporation of India were functioning for several years. They provided direct plans, subscribed to shares and bonds and to guarantee loans and deferred payments. The volume of long-term finance provided by these institutions were substantial and were steadily increasing too, but it was found inadequate to meet the requirements of new and growing industrial enterprises. On the one side, the needs of rapid industrialisation necessitated the establishment of a new institution with large financial resource. On the other side, there was the need to co-ordinate the activities of all agencies which are concerned with the provision of finance for industrial development. It was to fulfil this two-fold objective that the Government established the Industrial Development Bank of India (IDBI) which formally came into existence in July 1964.

The main function of IDBI, as its name suggests, was to finance industrial enterprises such as manufacturing, mining, processing, shipping, and other transport industries and hotel industry. IDBI granted direct assistance by way of project loans, underwriting of and direct subscription of industrial securities, soft loans, technical refund loans and equipment finance loans. The Bank guaranted loans raised by industrial concerns in the open market from scheduled banks, the State cooperative banks, I.F.C.I. and other "notified" financial institutions. It could assist industrial concerns in an indirect manner also, *i.e.*, through other institutions. It could refinance term loans to industrial concerns given by the IFCI, the State Financial Corporations, scheduled banks or State co-operative banks.

Small Industries Development Banks of India (SIDBI)

The Small Industries Development Bank of India (SIDBI) was set up by the Government of India under a special Act of the Parliament in April 1990 as a wholly-owned subsidiary of IDBI. SIDBI took over the outstanding portfolio of IDBI relating to the small scale sector worth over ₹ 4,000 crore.

SIDBI is now the principal financial institution for promotion, financing and development of small scale industries in the country. It coordinates the functions of existing institutions engaged in similar activities. Accordingly, SIDBI has taken over the responsibility of administering Small Industries Development Fund and National Equity Fund which were earlier administered by IDBI.

The important functions of SIDBI are as follows:

   (i) SIDBI refinances loans and advances extended by the primary lending institutions to small scale industrial units, and also provides resources support to them;

  (ii) SIDBI discounts and rediscounts bills arising from sale of machinery to or manufactured by industrial units in the small scale sector;

 (iii) SIDBI extends seeds capital/soft loan assistance under National Equity Fund, Mahila Udyam Nidhi and Mahila Vikas Nidhi and seed capital schemes through specified lending agencies;

 (iv) SIDBI grants direct assistance as well as refinance loans extended by primary lending institutions for financing export of products manufactured by industrial concerns in the small scale sector;

  (v) SIDBI provides services like leasing, factoring, etc., to industrial concerns in the small scale sector;

 (vi) SIDBI extends financial support to State Small Industries Development Corporations for providing scarce raw materials to and marketing the end-products of industrial units in the small scale sector; and

(vii) SIDBI provides financial support to National Small Industries Corporation for providing, leasing, hire-purchase and marketing support to industrial units in the small scale sector.

Industrial Investment Bank of India Limited (IIBIL)

IRBI was established on March 20, 1985 under Indian Industrial Reconstruction Bank Act, 1984 as a result of reconstituting Indian Industrial Reconstruction Corporation Ltd. The basic aim of establishing IRBI was to revive sick and closed industrial units and to act as a prime loan and reconstruction agency. IRBI grants loans and advances to industrial institutions. It accepts stocks, shares, bonds and debentures and also provides guarantee on deferred payments. The Government is now planning to establish a new reconstituted company in place of IRBI. A bill for this purpose has already been passed by Lok Sabha on March 6, 1997. Under new arrangements IRBI will work with the new name **'Industrial Investment Bank of India Ltd.'** (IIBIL) and this IIBIL will be a registered company under Company Act 1956. IIBIL is fully owned by Govt. of India. IIBIL's range of products and services include loans of various tenures for different purposes like loan for working capital facilities, equity participation, asset credit, equipment finance and investments in capital market and money market instruments. The authorised capital of IIBIL will be ₹ 1000 crore and its head office will be at Kolkata. Now, IIBIL will act as an autonomous development finance institution like IDBI, IFCI and ICICI.

MUDRA BANK

The Micro Units Development and Refinance Agency (known as the MUDRA Bank) was launched on April 8, 2015 which would primarily be responsible for regulating micro and small enterprise financing business, and supporting them. The roles envisaged for MUDRA include laying down policy guidelines for micro enterprise financing business and registration of MFI entities as well as their accreditation and rating.

Prime Minister Narendra Modi launched the ₹ 20,000 crore (₹ 200 billion) MUDRA Bank that aims to provide refinancing to small and medium enterprises, particularly those belonging to members of scheduled castes and scheduled tribes. According to Narendra Modi, the bank would help over six crore families. The bank would also get an additional ₹ 3,000 crore (₹ 30 billion) in the budget to create a credit guarantee corpus for guaranteeing loans being provided to the micro enterprises.

MUDRA Bank will offer loans under three schemes-**Shishu**-upto ₹ 50,000 **Kishor** upto ₹ 5 lac and **Tarun** upto ₹ 10 lac-based on stage of micro business. MUDRA Bank will also register MFIs and be responsible for accreditation and rating of MFI. It will also lay down policies for proper last mile practices to be followed by MFI to prevent indebtedness and provide proper client protection.

BANDHAN BANK

Bandhan Financial Services, a Micro Financial Institution (MFI), on August 23, 2015 started operations as a Scheduled Commercial Bank (SCB). Henceforth it has been named as Bandhan Bank. The banking services were inaugurated by the Union Finance Minister Arun Jaitley in Kolkata. On the inaugural day, the bank started operations with 501 branches in 24 states across the country with 1.43 crore accounts.

With this, Bandhan became the first micro finance company in the country to start operations as a full-fledged commercial bank. It is also the first commercial bank from Eastern India to get RBI clearance since independence. Bandhan started as a Non-Banking Finance Company in 2001 and focused on the lower strata of the especially an organized sector workers.

NATIONAL BANK FOR AGRICULTURE AND RURAL DEVELOPMENT (NABARD)

It is the apex banking institution providing finance for agriculture and rural development. NABARD was established on July 12, 1982 with the paid-up capital of ₹ 100 crore having 50 : 50 contribution of Indian Government and RBI.

NABARD was established with the aim of providing credit for promotion of agriculture, small scale industries, cottage and village industries, handicrafts and other allied economic activities in rural areas with a view to promote integrated rural development and secure prosperity in rural areas.

As an apex institution in rural credit structure, NABARD provides refinance facilities to various such financial institutions which provide loans to promote productive activities in rural areas. To meet its loan requirements, NABARD obtains funds from Government of India, World Bank and other agencies. It also mobilises resources by issuing bonds and debentures guaranteed by Union Government. Besides, it also utilises the funds of National Rural Credit Fund.

In 2006-07, a separate window of Bharat Nirman for construction of Rural Roads under PMGSY was started. Total sanctions by NABARD to National Rural Road Development Agency (NRRDA) under RIDF as on March 31, 2010, aggregate to ₹ 18,500 crore and the entire amount has been released to NRRDA.

CHAPTER

19

Export-Import Policy

The import policy in the post-independence period was guided by considerations of a growth-oriented policy which should ultimately lead us to the objective of self-reliance:

Export-Import Policy during First Decade of Planning

The needs of massive programme of industrialisation contemplated in the Second Plan led to the adoption of a liberal import policy in mid-50's. Import went up sharply both in the private and public sectors. The schemes of modernisation, replacement and expansion undertaken in the private sector and the programmes of the building up of heavy and basic industries in the public sector led to an unprecedented rise in imports. Exports did not expand as planned. Accordingly, India lost all its accumulated sterling balances to pay off its adverse balance. The country also suffered from a serious shortage of foreign exchange—a veritable foreign exchange crisis. This necessitated a reversal of import policy and drastic restrictions were placed on imports.

230

During the Second Plan period, it was felt that export earnings could not be significantly increased unless industrialisation gathered momentum. This fact was given expressions in Second Plan in the following words: "India's export earnings are derived from a few commodities. Three of them, namely, tea, jute and cotton textile, account for nearly one-half of the quota. These major exports are meeting increasing competition from abroad. This limits the scope for any substantial increase in exports in the short run. While every effort has to be made to promote exports of new items and to develop and diversify the markets for country's major exports, it has to be recognised that it is only after industrialisation has proceeded some way that increased production at home will be reflected in large export earning."

Mudaliar Committee Recommendations

The Government appointed the Import and Export Policy Committee headed by Mr. Mudaliar in 1962 to review Government's trade policy. The Committee felt that developmental and maintenance imports were both essential for a growing economy and therefore, urged upon the government to provide facilities for the import of raw materials, components, etc., for all existing industries subject to higher priorities to new industries in (i) power and transport which had proved a serious bottleneck; (ii) 'export-oriented' industries; and (iii) industries producing raw materials and components now imported. Industries depending almost entirely on indigenous raw materials could arrange their own foreign exchange for the import of plant and machinery. The recommendations of the Committee were accepted by the Government.

The import policy of restriction of non-essential goods on the one side and liberalisation of imports on essential goods on the other was successful to a large extent—imports were controlled and exports were pushed up. This policy helped to reverse the persistent trade deficit.

Export-oriented Export-Import Policy

Since 1975-76, the Government of India has been following a liberalised import policy with the objective of increasing production, especially export production. There has been an increased emphasis on enhancing maintenance imports in order to promote capacity utilisation. Since the principal purpose of the import policy was to encourage exports, it is characterised as export-oriented import policy.

Export-Import (EXIM) Policy (1985)

Mr. Vishwanath Pratap Singh, the then Commerce Minister, announced the Export-import Policy on the 12th April 1985. For the first time, the Government announced the policy on a three-year basis. The basic aim of the new policy was to facilitate production through easier and quicker access to imported inputs, impart continuity and stability of Exim Policy, strengthen the export production base, facilitate technological upgradation and effect all possible savings in imports.

Import-Export Policy (1990)

The government announced on April 30, 1990 a new Import-Export Policy for a 3-year period. The Policy statement made it clear: "Improvement in our Balance of payments position can be achieved not so much through import curtailment as through promotion of exports." The new policy has, therefore, provide further momentum to the ongoing process of liberalisation with emphasis on strengthening the impulses of industrial and export growth. The salient features of the new policy were:

1. List of items imported under Open General Licence (OGL) were expanded to facilitate easy access to import of items that are not available within the country.

2. The number of capital goods items permitted under OGL was increased from 1,261 to 1,343. This has been the major thrust of liberalisation.

3. Imports of certain raw materials such as petroleum products, fertilizers, oils/oilseeds, feature/video films, newsprint, cereals, phosphoric acid, ammonia etc. were canalised through public sector agencies in view of essential character of these imports from the point of view of bulk consumption and the requirements of small Actual Users. However, trading houses/star trading houses were also permitted to import canalised items in order to promote exports.

4. A scheme of automatic licensing was introduced under which upto 10 per cent of the value of the previous year's licence can be imported.

5. For Registered Exporters, the concept of net foreign exchange earnings was made a guiding criterion for issue of licences thereunder.

   (a) REP (Replenishment) licensing scheme was expanded and simplified.

   (b) Export services like computer software, overseas management and consultancy service contracts as well as advertising jobs would qualify for import replenishments.

   (c) Under the scheme of registration of Export Houses and Trading Houses, for determining eligibility, the annual average of net foreign exchange earnings in the base period should not be less than ₹ 5 crores for an Export House and ₹ 20 crores for a Trading House. These houses would be eligible for additional licences for import of raw materials, components, consumables and tools and capital goods allowed under OGL, besides other limited permissible items and canalisd items.

(d) A scheme of Star Trading Houses was introduced for exporters with an average annual net foreign exchange earnings of ₹ 75 crores in the preceding three licensing years of the base period.

(e) Under the Duty Exemption Scheme, Blanket Advance Licensing was introduced for manufacturer-exporters having a minimum net foreign exchange earnings of ₹ 10 crores during the preceding 3 years.

(f) The Import-Export Passbook Scheme introduced in January 1986 was withdrawn.

Evaluation of India's Export-Import Policy

The 1985 import policy was broadly welcomed by various Chambers of Commerce and Industry, business and industrial houses and leading industrialists. The policy aimed at restricting unnecessary imports, but permitted imports for encouraging indigenous production and promoting exports. The policy also intended to pursue technological upgradation through imports. The policy was aware of the need to check dumping of goods by multinationals and, therefore, gave support to the indigenous industries by selective restrictions on imports. Another welcome feature of the import policy was the fillip it gave to the small-scale and cottage industries as well as to agricultural exports, all this would help to maximise utilisation of our manpower and agricultural resources. As regards promotion of exports, the import policy contained clear cut measures to expand India's exports. The various measures were direct and positive and a general feeling was that India's import policy was clearly export-oriented.

However, critics noted some developments of a serious nature which would adversely affect our economy. They are:

(i) Adverse effect on the growth of capital goods industry in India: The most serious liberalisation has been attempted in the Exim Policy 1985-86 in the Capital Goods List bringing 208 items under the OGL list. Among the additions was microprocessor based equipment, machine tools, spinning machines, jute machinery etc. The impact of this wave of liberalisation is bound to be adverse. Given the limited size of the market and the problems of technology transfer and the procedural bottlenecks created by licensing, the development of capital goods industry which was never a very lucrative proposition for Indian industrialists, was made much more frightening in the wake of liberal imports of customs duty concessions.

(ii) Import Policy likely to hit small-scale industries: Although the statement of objectives specifically mentioned encouragement of the small-scale sector, but the measures suggested do not match with the professed aims. Rather the Government in the name of modernisation was helping big business to import labour-saving machinery. *Economic and Political Weekly* exposing double talk of the Government mentioned: "the government's pretensions of encouraging the handloom sector by controlling the textile industry are exposed by the fact that the latest in the labour-saving textile machinery, air jet and water jet looms (including shuttle-less looms). have been placed under OGL on the plea of modernisation."

(iii) Adverse effect on indigenous industry: The new import policy was trying to over-reach its objectives of liberalisation and under pressure from multinationals opened areas in which indigenous industry had adequate capacity. There was certainly far reaching implications of such sweeping relaxations in imports. The Gujarat State Fertilizer Corporation (GSFC) and the Soda Ash Industry have been continuously pleading before the Government to restrict imports of caprolactum and soda ash since it would hit their interests adversely but the powerful multi-nationals forced the Government to dump these raw materials in India. This posed a problem of survival for the indigenous industry.

(iv) Technological dumping in the name of technology upgrading: According to RBI *Report on Currency and Finance (1989-90),* capital goods imports increased from ₹ 3,168 crores in 1984-85 to ₹ 8,831 crores in 1989-90 *i.e.,* they have grown at an annual growth rate of 22.8 per cent during the 5 year period. There is, therefore, a relentless drive for unfettered import of capital goods, design and drawings and technology. This is a dangerous trend from the country's point of view. Criticising this approach, the *Economic and Political Weekly* mentioned: "What is missed in this line of reasoning is that production capacities once built on imported technologies and imported capital goods have to be sustained by imported raw materials, spares and parts. The so-called "inflexible imports" are, therefore, destined to grow constantly and relentlessly." Secondly, experience has also shown that the multinationals are hardly interested in technology transfer. Rather they in the name of technological upgradation, carry on 'technological dumping' of such technologies which have been superseded in the developed countries. This, the critics argue, is far more deleterious than dumping of goods–including capital goods.

From the foregoing analysis, it becomes evident that opening the door of imports much wider would result in increasing the trade gap. Such indiscriminate liberalisation would create more dependence in terms of foreign exchange and widen the trade gap.

EXPORT-IMPORT POLICY (2002-2007)

Union Commerce and Industry Minister Mr. Murasoli Maran announced the EXIM policy for the 5 year period (2002-07) on March 31, 2002. The main thrust of the policy was to push India's exports aggressively by undertaking several measures aimed at augmenting exports of farm goods, the small scale sector, textiles, gems and jewellery, electronic hardware etc. Besides these, the policy aimed to reduce transaction cost to trade through a number of measures to bring about procedural simplifications.

The salient features of Exim policy were as under:

I. Special Economic Zones

Indian banks were allowed to set up offshore banking units (OBUs) in Special Economic zones. These units would act as magnets to attract foreign direct investments. These offshore banking units would be virtually foreign branches of Indian banks, but located in India. OBUs would be exempt from cash reserve ratio (CRR), statutory liquidity ratio (SLR) and would give access to SEZ units and SEZ developers to international finance at international rates. This measure was aimed to make special Economic Zones internationally competitive.

II. Employment Oriented Measures

EXIM (2002-07) policy initiated a number of measures which would help employment orientation. Among them were the following:

(a) **Agriculture:** Exim policy removed all quantitative restrictions on all agricultural products except a few sensitive items like jute and onions.

(b) **Cottage Sector and handicrafts:** (i) An amount of ₹ 5 crores under market access initiative (MAI) were earmarked for promoting cottage sector exports coming under KVIC. The units under handicrafts could also access funds under MAI. (ii) Under export promotion capital goods (EPCG) scheme, these units would not be required to maintain an average level of exports, while calculating export obligation. (iii) These units would be entitled to the benefit of Export House status on achieving lower average export performance of ₹ 5 crore as against ₹ 15 crores for others; and (iv) The units in handicraft sector would be entitled to duty-free imports of an enlarged list of items up to 3 per cent of f.o.b value of their exports.

(c) Small Scale Industry: With a view to encouraging further development of centres of economic and export excellence such as Tirpur for hosiery, woollen blankets in Panipat, woollen knitwear in Ludhiana, following benefits would be available to small-scale sector.

1. Common service providers in these areas would be entitled to the facility of Export Promotion Capital Goods (EPCG) Scheme.
2. Entitlement for Export House status at ₹ 5 crores instead of ₹ 15 crores for others.

(d) Textiles: Duty entitlement passbook (DEPB) rates for all kinds of blended fabrics permitted. Such blended fabrics were to have lower rate as applicable to different constituent fabrics.

(e) Gems and jewellery: Rough diamonds import allowed on zero custom duty basis.

III. Growth-Oriented

(a) Strategic package for status holders—The status holders would be eligible for the following facilities: (i) 100 per cent retention of foreign exchange in exchange earners foreign currency (EEFC) account.

(b) Neutralising high fuel cost—Fuel costs to be rebated for all export products. This would enhance the cost competitiveness of our export products.

(c) Diversification of markets—The following initiatives have been taken:

Focus LAC (Latin American Countries) was launched in November 1997 in order to accelerate trade with these countries. Our exports to these countries have increased by 40 per cent. To consolidate the gains of these programmes, this was extended upto March 2003.

Focus Africa was launched in April 2002. There is a tremendous potential for trade with sub-Saharan African region.

During 2000-01, Indian exports to this region accounted for US$I.8 billion and imports were $ 1.5 billion.

IV. Duty neutralisation instruments

(a) *Advance licence:* Duty Exemption Entitlement Certificate (DEEC) book was abolished. Redemption on the basis of shipping bills and bank realisation certificates.

Withdrawal of advance licence for annual requirement (AAL) as problems were encountered in closure of AAL. The exporters could avail of advance licence for any value.

(b) *Duty entitlement pass book* (DEPB): Value cap exemption granted on 429 items to continue.

(c) *Export promotion capital goods* (EPCG) licences of ₹ 100 crore or more to have 12 year export obligation period with 5 year moratorium period.

Assessment of EXIM Policy (2002-07)

Mr. Murasoli Maran, the then Minister for Commerce and Industry took a number of initiatives by providing tax concessions, streamlining certain procedures and removing quantitative restrictions.

Another positive feature of the policy was have 'Focus Africa' so that Indian exports to African countries can be developed. This initiative would help Indian exporters to explore this fast growing market which has been neglected earlier.

A big initiative to permit offshore banking units (OBUs) would help to develop foreign branches of Indian banks. The move was intended to provide international finance at international rates. This would lower the cost of credit to our exporters and thus make them more competitive. This initiative, specially directed at Special Economic Zones was another healthy feature of the Exim Policy.

However, critics raised several issues which need consideration. EXIM policy intended to boost the export of agriculture. In this effort, it intended to export wheat and thus reduce the mounting bufferstocks of foodgrains reaching the astonishingly high figure of 58 million tonnes in on January 1, 2002. There are two options before the government—(i) to export these foodgrains and earn foreign exchange and (ii) to use these foodgrains in 'food for work' programme and thus create employment in public works programme. It is really very disappointing that the Food Corporation of India is selling wheat in the international market as cattle feed at throwaway prices. The question arises: Why is the quality of wheat procured by FCI poor when the Government continues to raise the support price of wheat for the farmers year after year? It only speaks volumes about rampant corruption in FCI. The failure of the Central Government to persuade state governments to lift foodgrains from FCI is evident from the fact that as against an allocation of 28.55 million tonnes in 2000-01 in case of rice and wheat, the offtake was merely 11.72 million tonnes which is only 41 per cent of the allocation. This was mainly the consequence of an irrational policy fixing the issue price of foodgrains quite high. The result was that the public preferred to buy foodgrains from the open market. The Government, if it wants to increase the exports of agricultural products, should pay more attention toward improving the quality of rice and wheat procured so that it can fetch a good price in the international market.

EXIM Policy has laid great emphasis on Special Economic Zones (SEZs) which is a new incarnation of the Export Promotion Zones (EPZ) and Export-oriented Units (EOUs) promoted earlier. But the experience of the EPZ and EOUs has not been very happy. Together they account for only 12% of total exports. Too many procedural hurdles have prevented them from performing better. It would be very wise if the Special Economic Zones are not saddled with such excessive bureaucratic hurdles and not enabled to capture export markets. It may be noted the Special Economic Zones in China account for over 40 per cent of Chinese exports. India should learn to improve the performance of SEZs.

EXIM Policy made some concessions to help cottage and handicraft sector and small scale units which account for nearly 35 per cent of the country's exports. But ironically, the policy did not pay adequate attention to the most important aspect of increasing bank credit to this sector.

Foreign Trade Policy (FTP): 2009-14

In 2008-09, the world faced an unprecedented economic slow-down and witnessed one of the most severe global recessions in the post-war period that affected countries across the globe in varying degrees. All major economic activities like industrial production, trade capital flows, unemployment, investment and consumption took a hit.

India has not been affected to the same extent as other economies of the world during this phase. Yet our exports have suffered a decline since October 2008 significantly due to shrinkage of demand in the traditional markets of our exports due to global economic slowdown and the reduced international prices of commodities. India's exports in dollar terms showed a growth of about 48.1% from April to September, 2008 whereas from October, 2008, it started declining, bringing down the annual growth to 13.6% in 2008-09. After showing a negative growth for seven consecutive months in 2009-10, India's exports have entered the positive territory (growing at 18.2% during the month of November, 2009-10). Agriculture and industry has shown remarkable resilience and dynamism in contributing to a healthy growth in exports.

The short term objective of FTP (2009-14) is to arrest and reverse the declining trend of exports and to provide additional support especially to those sectors which have been hit badly by recession in the developed world. The long term policy objective for the Government is to double India's share in global trade by 2020.

In order to meet the objectives stated above, the major thrust areas of strategy spelt out in FTP (2009-14) comprise a mix of policy measures including fiscal incentives, institutional changes, procedural rationalization, enhanced market access across the world and diversification of export markets. The FTP envisages three basic pillars for supporting India's exports. These are (i) infrastructure related to exports, (ii) bringing down transaction costs, and (iii) providing full refund of all indirect taxes and levies. The prime importance here is on a stable policy environment conducive to foreign trade by way of continuation of exporter friendly and transparent schemes/ facilities. In addition, after the operationalisation of the Goods and Services Tax (GST) regime, the Government will make concerted attempts to see that the GST rebates are given on all indirect taxes and levies on exports. A special thrust would be provided to employment intensive sectors which have witnessed job losses in the wake of this recession, especially in the fields of textile, leather, handicrafts, etc.

Given the current economic climate, policy measures initiated in the FTP 2009-14 would basically be in force for a two year period after which mid-course corrections could be undertaken, if required. In the meantime, sectoral reviews to assess the impact of these measures on Indian exports would be carried out and accordingly appropriate initiatives would be taken.

Foreign Trade Policy 2009-14:

- To arrest and reverse declining trend of exports is the main aim of the policy. This aim will be reviewed after two years.

- To Double India's exports of goods and services by 2014.

- To double India's share in global merchandise trade by 2020 as a long term aim of this policy. *India's share in Global merchandise exports was 1.45% in 2008.*

- Simplification of the application procedure for availing various benefits.
- To set in motion the strategies and policy measures which catalyse the growth of exports.
- To encourage exports through a "mix of measures including fiscal incentives, institutional changes, procedural rationalisation and efforts for enhance market access across the world and diversification of export markets.

Foreign Trade Policy 2015-2020

On 1st April 2015, the new Foreign Trade Policy (FTP) for the period 2015-20 was announced which replaces the 2009-14 FTP which expired on 31st March 2014. With the announcement of new policy, exporters' one-year wait for new FTP has come to end.

Some **highlights** of the present Foreign Trade Policy 2015-2020

- India to be made a significant participant in world trade by 2020.
- Commerce Minister announced two new schemes in Foreign Trade Policy 2015-2020. Two New Schemes announced in FTP are namely "Merchandise Exports from India Scheme (MEIS)" and "Services Exports from India Scheme (SEIS)". These schemes (MEIS and SEIS) replace multiple schemes earlier in place, each with different conditions for eligibility and usage.
- Merchandize exports from India (MEIS) to promote specific services for specific Markets Foreign Trade Policy.
- For services, all schemes have been replaced by a 'Services Export from India Scheme'(SEIS), which will benefit all services exporters in India.
- FTP would reduce export obligations by 25% and give boost to domestic manufacturing.

- Incentives (MEIS & SEIS) to be available for SEZs also. FTP benefits from both MEIS & SEIS will be extended to units located in SEZs. − Both MEIS and SEIS firms and service providers can now get subsidized office spaces in SEZ (Special Economic Zones), along with other benefits. With a view to boost the Special Economic Zones, Government has decided to extend both the incentive schemes for export of goods and services to units in SEZs.

- e-Commerce of handicrafts, handlooms, books etc., eligible for benefits of MEIS. e-Commerce exports up to ₹ 25000 per consignment will get SEIS benefits.

- e-Commerce Exports Eligible For Services Exports From India Scheme. − As part of Digital India vision, mobile apps would be created to ease filing of taxes and stamp duty, automatic money transfer using Internet Banking have been proposed. > Online procedure to upload digitally signed document by Chartered Accountant/Company Secretary/Cost Accountant to be developed.

- Agricultural and village industry products to be supported across the globe at rates of 3% and 5% under MEIS. Higher level of support to be provided to processed and packaged agricultural and food items under MEIS.

- Industrial products to be supported in major markets at rates ranging from 2% to 3%.

- Branding campaigns planned to promote exports in sectors where India has traditional Strength.

- Business services, hotel and restaurants to get rewards scrips under SEIS at 3% and other specified services at 5%.

- Duty credit scrips to be freely transferable and usable for payment of customs duty, excise duty and service tax.

- Manufacturers who are also status holders will be enabled to self-certify their manufactured goods as originating from

India. – Tax and duty on Indian manufacturers have been reduced, to boost Make in India vision.

- Reduced Export Obligation (EO) (75%) for domestic procurement under EPCG scheme.
- Inter-ministerial consultations to be held online for issue of various licences.
- No need to repeatedly submit physical copies of documents available on Exporter Importer Profile.
- Validity period of SCOMET export authorisation extended from present 12 months to 24 months.

  Export obligation period for export items related to defence, military store, aerospace and nuclear energy to be 24 months instead of 18 months.

- Calicut Airport, Kerala and Arakonam ICDs (Inland Container Depots), Tamil Nadu notified as registered ports for import and export.
- Vishakhapatnam and Bhimavarm added as Towns of Export Excellence.
- Certificate from independent chartered engineer for redemption of EPCG authorisation no longer required.

Now let us understand how this achieves the desired objectives of the nation.

Impact on the Economy

According to some experts the focus in this FTP has been "Simplicity And Stability". Accordingly, the policy on the one hand seeks to realign the multiple schemes with the objective of reducing complexities. On the other had it want to promote the increased use of technology to reduce the transaction cost and manual compliances.

One significant announcement in the policy is that it will move away from relying largely on subsidies and sops. Critics however point out that, this is prompted by World Trade Organisation (WTO) requirements that export promotion subsidies should be phased out, but according to some experts there are ways of getting around it and other countries are doing it all the time.

There has been talk of boosting services exports for quite a few years now, but information technology and information technology-enabled services (IT/ITES) dominated the basket. The share of this segment in the overall export basket is 50 per cent and 90 per cent in the services export basket.

More importantly, this sector was overly dependent on western markets and, consequently, extremely vulnerable to even the smallest of developments there. The policy, fortunately, turns its attention to other sectors where India has inherent advantages – healthcare, education, R&D, logistics, professional services, entertainment, as well as services incidental to manufacturing.

To sum up, it may be mentioned that Commerce and Industry Ministry alone cannot create an environment to boost exports. For this purpose, it has to co-ordinate with the Ministry of Power and Transport so that the delays in handling of goods for export can be taken care of. Similarly, the Commerce Ministry has to pursuade the Ministry of Finance to allocate more resources for infrastructure development. Not only that, the Centre and State Governments must co-ordinate to fulfil the objective of increasing exports. This can be done by making our exports more competitive. This requires an improvement of technology in the export sector and the development of an efficient infrastructure.

Balance of Payments

The **balance of payments (B.O.P** or **BoP)**, of a country is the record of all economic transactions between the residents of the country and the rest of the world in a particular period (over a quarter of a year or more commonly over a year). These transactions are made by individuals, firms and government bodies. Thus the balance of payments includes all external visible and non-visible transactions of a country. It is an important issue to be studied, especially in international financial management field, for a few reasons.

First, the balance of payments provides detailed information concerning the demand and supply of a country's currency.

Second, a country's balance-of-payment data may signal its potential as a business partner for the rest of the world. If a country is grappling with a major balance-of-payment difficulty, it may not be able to expand imports from the outside world. Instead, the country may be tempted to impose measures to restrict imports and discourage capital outflows in order to improve the balance-of-payment situation. On the other hand, a country with a significant balance-of payment surplus would be more likely to expand imports, offering marketing opportunities for foreign enterprises, and less likely to impose foreign exchange restrictions.

Third, balance-of-payments data can be used to evaluate the performance of the country in international economic competition. Suppose a country is experiencing trade deficits year after year. This trade data may then signal that the country's domestic industries lack international competitiveness. To interpret balance-of-payments data properly, it is necessary to understand how the balance of payments account is constructed. These transactions include payments for the country's exports and imports of goods, services, financial capital, and financial transfers. It is prepared in a single currency, typically the domestic currency for the country concerned. Sources of funds for a nation, such as exports or the receipts of loans and investments, are recorded as positive or surplus items. Uses of funds, such as for imports or to invest in foreign countries, are recorded as negative or deficit items.

While the overall BoP accounts will always balance when all types of payments are included, imbalances are possible on individual elements of the BoP, such as the current account, the capital account excluding the central bank's reserve account, or the sum of the two. Imbalances in the latter sum can result in surplus countries accumulating wealth, while deficit nations become increasingly indebted. The term **'balance of payments'** often refers to this sum: a country's balance of payments is said to be in surplus (equivalently, the balance of payments is positive) by a specific amount if sources of funds (such as export goods sold and bonds sold) exceed uses of funds (such as paying for imported goods and paying for foreign bonds purchased) by that amount. There is said to be a balance of payments deficit (the balance of payments is said to be negative) if the former are less than the latter. A BoP surplus (or deficit) is accompanied by an accumulation (or decumulation) of foreign exchange reserves by the central bank.

INDIA'S BALANCE OF PAYMENTS ON CURRENT ACCOUNT

1951-52 to 1955-56—The First Plan Period

During the First Plan period, the balance of payments was affected by the Korean War boom, American recession of 1953 and favourable monsoon at home which helped to boost agricultural and industrial production.

While India had been experiencing persistent trade deficit, she had generally a surplus in net invisible; accordingly India's adverse balance of payment during the First Plan was only ₹ 42 crore. The overall picture during the First Plan was, however, quite satisfactory.

1956-57 to 1960-61—The Second Plan Period

An important feature of the Second Plan period was the heavy deficit in the balance of trade which aggregated to ₹ 2,339 crore. Earnings on account of invisibles and donations from friendly countries totalled ₹ 614 crore. Making an allowance for these, the unfavourableness in the balance of payments during the Second Plan period was of the order of ₹ 1,725 crore. The highly unfavourable balance of payments in the Second Plan was the result of (a) heavy imports of capital goods to develop heavy and basic industries, (b) the failure of agricultural production to rise to meet the growing demand for food and raw materials from a rapidly growing population and expanding industry; (c) the inability of the economy to increase exports; and (d) the necessity of making minium 'maintenance imports' for a developing economy. As a result, the foreign exchange reserves sharply declined and the country was left with no choice but to think of ways and means to restrict imports and expand exports.

Third Plan and Annual Plans and BOP

It is clear that the balance on current account was unfavourable during the Third Plan. This was mainly because (a) imports were expanding faster under the impact of defence and development and to overcome domestic shortages (import of foodgrain, for example) and (b) exports were extremely sluggish and failed to match imports. The imbalance in the current account of over ₹ 1,951 crore was financed by loans from foreign countries, PL 480 and PL 665 funds, loans from the World Bank and withdrawals from I.M.F. In spite of all these loans, assistance and withdrawals, there was also some depletion of foreign exchange reserves of the country.

The serious adverse balance of payments which started with the Second Plan continued relentlessly during the Third and the Annual Plans.

It will be observed that the trade deficit during the Annual Plans was quite large. It was because of the heavy imports of foodgrains to overcome famine conditions and internal shortage of foodgrains on the one side and inadequate exports due to economic recession on the other. Besides, devaluation of the rupee was a failure and instead of reducing the trade balance deficit, it further aggravated it. A very interesting development in this period was that net invisible which used to be positive and which used to reduce the trade deficit, either dwindled or even became negative (for the first time). During this period, heavy amount had to be paid by India in the form of interest payments on loans contracted earlier. This wiped out the surplus on invisible account. Consequently, the influence on net invisibles in reducing the balace of payments deficit was negligible.

1969-70 to 1973-74: The Fourth Plan Period

One of the objectives of the Fourth Plan was self-reliance—*i.e.,* import substitution of certain critical commodities (which are of key importance for the Indian economy) on the one side and export promotion so as to match the rising import bill, on the other. Accordingly, the Government managed to restrict imports and succeeded in expanding exports. On the import side, restriction of imports was made possible through good crops in 1968-69 and 1970-71, and consequent significant reduction of imports of foodgrains. On the export side, vigorous export promotion measures succeeded in boosting exports of traditional as well as non-traditional items.

The abnormal favourableness in the invisibles account in 1973-74 was due to the receipt of ₹ 1,680 crore from the U.S.A. on the disposition of PL 480 and other rupee funds. The trade deficit during the Fourth Plan was ₹ 1,564 crore and the surplus in net invisibles accounted for ₹ 1,664 crore. The net result was a surplus in the balance of payments, for the first time, though the surplus was only a nominal amount of ₹ 100 crore.

1975-76 to 1978-79: The Fifth Plan Period

During the Fifth Plan, trade balance was affected by two factors: (a) the value of imports was rapidly mounting due to the hike in oil prices, and (b) the value of exports was also rising under the impact of promotional measures. These two factors explained the gradual decline in the deficit in the trade balance and the appearance of a surplus in the trade balance in 1976-77. But the persistent upward rise in imports and the inadequate increase in exports due to the relative decline in export prices were responsible for the revival of deficit trade balance in the last two years of the Figth Plan period. Another outstanding feature of this period was the sharp increase in net invisibles receipts during 1975-76 to 1978-79. The main factors responsible for the increase in invisible receipts were: (i) stringent measures taken against smuggling and illegal payment transactions; (ii) the relative stability in the external value of the rupee at a time when major international currencies were experiencing sizeable fluctuations; (iii) increase in earnings from tourists; (iv) the growth of earnings from technical, consultancy and contracting services; and (v) increase in the number of Indian nationals going abroad for employment and larger remittances sent by them to India.

The Sixth and the Seventh Plan Period

There has been a sea change in the balance of payments position since 1979-80. As against the surplus balance of payments experienced by the country during the whole of the Fifth Plan, India started experiencing adverse balance of payments from 1979-80 onwards. For one thing, trade deficit began to widen from 1978-79. The disquieting picture was due to the tremendous rate of growth of imports on the one side and a much lower rate of growth of exports since 1979-80 on the other. The trade deficit which was more than offset by the flow of funds under net invisibles during the Fifth Plan period, could not be so offset since 1979-80. The current balance of payments bacame adverse to the tune of ₹ 11,384 crore during the Sixth Plan. Apart from net external assistance, India had to meet this colossal deficit in the current account through withdrawals of SDRs and borrowing from IMF under the extended facility arrangement. Besides, India used part of its accumulated foreign exchange reserves to meet its deficit in the balance of payments.

During 1985-86 and 1989-90, the total trade deficit amounted to ₹ 54,204 crore for the Seventh Plan. Making an adjustment for the positive balance on invisible account, the deficit in balance of payment on current account was ₹ 41,047 crore. The highly adverse balance of payments position was the cause for serious concern.

1990-91 and Thereafter

For the first time during the last 40 years, net invisibles became negative to the tune of ₹ 435 crore in 1990-91. This was largely the consequence of a net ouflow of investment income of the order of ₹ 6,732 crore in 1990-91 as against ₹ 4,875 crore in 1989-90 – as increase by 98 per cent. Thus, the cushion available through net invisibles to partly neutralise the trade deficit was removed.

During the Eighth Plan (1992-93 to 1996-97), trade deficit mounted, by 1996-97, it had reached a record level of ₹ 52,561 crore from that of ₹ 16,934 crore in 1990-91 – a theefold increase. For the Eighth Plan period, invisibles neutralised the trade deficit to the extent of about 58 per cent – a really commendable achievement. Despite this, the balance of payments has shown continuously a deficit in all the years.

During 1997-98, the current account deficit reached a record level of ₹ 20,883 crore and during 1998-99, it declined to ₹ 16,789 crore. In 1999-2000, it again increased to ₹ 20,331 crore. This was largely due to a much greater trade deficit of the order of ₹ 77,359 crore which could not be neutralised through net invisibles earned a surplus of ₹ 57,028 crore. The situation improved in 2000-01 and the current account deficit declined to ₹ 16,426 crore.

During 2001-02, although trade deficit was 54,955 crore, the heavy receipts on account of invisibles amounting to ₹ 71,381 crore not only wiped out the trade deficit, but also created a surplus in current account balance of the order of ₹ 16,926 crore. Taking the entire Ninth Plan period (1997-98 to 2001-02), trade deficit was wiped out to the extent of 82 per cent by invisible account surplus, Consequently, the total deficit in current account balance was of the order of the ₹ 53,175 crore for the Ninth Plan.

The external sector outcome in 2014-15 and the first half (H1) of 2015-16 indicate continued moderation in levels of trade and current account deficits with broadly adequate financing. This owed largely to the fall in global crude oil and commodity prices. The sluggish global growth not only adversely impacted merchandise exports but also caused the invisibles surplus to grow only marginally during this period. Under the capital/finance account of balance of payments (BoP), foreign investment reached a peak level of US $ 73.5 billion in 2014-15. Adjusting for the exceptional special swap facility offered by the government to finance the Current Account Deficit (CAD) in 2013-14, the level of net NRI deposits in 2014-15 is broadly comparable to the peak normal level of 2012-13. Capital/finance flows (net) were US $ 88.2 billion in 2014-15, driven largely by investment flows. Higher capital/ financial flows with low CAD resulted in large accretion to reserves (US $ 61.4 billion) in 2014-15.

During H1 of 2015-16, despite a decline in merchandise exports India's external sector situation remained comfortable. Some of the salient external sector developments were as follows: (i) lower trade deficit and modest growth in invisibles resulted in lower CAD; (ii) the increase in FDI inflows and NRI deposits continued; and (iii) there was net outflow of portfolio investment. Although there was a net outflow under portfolio investment, capital/financial flows were in excess of CAD and their absorption by the Reserve Bank of India (RBI) led to an accretion in reserves.

Current Account

The current account shows the net amount a country is earning if it is in surplus, or spending if it is in deficit. It is the sum of the balance of trade (net earnings on exports minus payments for imports), factor income (earnings on foreign investments minus payments made to foreign investors) and cash transfers. It is called the *current* account as it covers transactions in the "here and now" – those that don't give rise to future claims.

Despite moderation in India's exports, India's external sector position has been comfortable, with the current account deficit (CAD) progressively contracting from US$ 88.2 billion (4.8 per cent of GDP) in 2012-13 to US$ 22.2 billion (1.1 per cent of

GDP) in 2015-16. The CAD further narrowed in 2016-17 (H1) to 0.3 per cent of GDP. In 2016-17 (H1), sharp contraction in trade deficit outweighed the decline in net invisible earnings. The downward spiral in international crude oil prices resulted in a decline in oil import bill by around 18 per cent which together with a sharp decline in gold imports led to a reduction in India's overall imports (on BoP basis). Net services receipts declined by 10 per cent in H1 of 2016-17 despite increase in services receipts (4.0 per cent) as growth in services payments was higher (16 per cent). However, growth of receipts of software was marginal and financial services receipts declined. Subdued income conditions in source countries, particularly in the gulf region due to downward spiral in oil prices continued to weigh down on remittances by Indians employed overseas as private transfers moderated to US$ 28.2 billion in H1 of 2016-17 from US$ 32.7 billion in H1 of 2015-16.

Capital/finance Account

The capital account records the net change in ownership of foreign assets. It includes the reserve account (the foreign exchange market operations of a nation's central bank), along with loans and investments between the country and the rest of world (but not the future interest payments and dividends that the loans and investments yield; those are earnings and will be recorded in the current account). If a country purchases more foreign assets for cash than the assets it sells for cash to other countries, the capital account is said to be negative or in deficit.

Despite higher net repayments on overseas borrowings and fall in banking capital (net) with building up of foreign currency assets by banks & decline in NRI deposits (net), robust inflow of foreign direct investment (FDI) and net positive inflow of foreign portfolio investment (FPI) were sufficient to finance CAD leading to an accretion in foreign exchange reserves in H1 of

2016-17. The net FDI flows of US$ 21.3 billion recorded a growth of about 29 per cent over the corresponding period of last year. There was net inflow of portfolio investment amounting to US$ 8.2 billion in H1 of 2016-17 as against outflow of US$ 3.5 billion in H1 of 2015-16. Banking capital recorded net outflow of US$ 6.8 billion, primarily on account of acquisition of foreign currency assets by banks, while net repayment of external commercial borrowings resulted in an outflow of US$ 4.6 billion in H1 of 2016-17. With net capital flows remaining higher than the CAD, there was net accretion to India's foreign exchange reserves (on BoP Basis).

Industrial and Labour Policy

Industry refers to economic activities which are connected with raising, producing or processing of goods and services.

The industrial policy of any government seeks to formulate a philosophy for the pattern of industrialisation.

The concept of 'industrial policy' is comprehensive and it covers all those producers, principles, policies, rules and regulations which control the industrial undertakings of a country and shape the pattern of industrialisation. It incorporates fiscal and monetary policies, the tariff policy, labour policy and government's attitude not only towards external assistance but the public and private sector also.

The Industrial Policy Resolution, 1948

This policy divided the industries into four broad categories:

The first category included the manufacture of arms and ammunition, the production and control of atomic energy and the ownership of railways. This category would belong to the exclusive monopoly of the Central Government.

289 (S&E)—17

The second category included coal, iron, ship-building, aircraft and telephones. New plants in these industries would be taken only by the Government.

The third category included certain basic industries such as automobiles, tractors, heavy machinery, machine tools, cement, sugar, etc. The Government of India would regulate these industries because of the importance of these industries.

The last category included all the other industries except the above. These industries were open to private sector.

Industrial Licensing Act, 1951

Following the Industrial Policy Resolution of 1948, the Industrial (Development and Regulation) Act of 1951 was passed. This Act provided the framework for the licensing and regulation of industrial investment in India.

The Industrial (Development and Regulation) Act of 1951 has the following objectives:

 (i) The development and regulation of industrial investments and production according to plan priorities.

 (ii) The encouragement of 'small' industries;

(iii) The prevention of concentration of ownership of industries in India; and

(iv) Balanced regional development so as to reduce the inequalities.

Industrial Policy Resolution, 1956

This Resolution was passed in the Parliament in 1956. When this Resolution was passed, the slogan of "Socialistic Pattern of Society" was popular. This mixed economy approach was slightly changed giving more importance to public sector.

The following are the important features of the Industrial Policy Resolution of 1956:

(i) There is a new classification of industries in this Resolution. Industries are divided into three categories. First category includes 17 industries which are the exclusive responsibility of the state.

(ii) The second category includes 12 industries which are to be progressively state-owned. The state will start these industries. The private sector can also supplement them. Some of the important industries in this category are machine tools, the chemical industry, fertilizers, etc. They are open to the initiative and enterprise of private sector.

(iii) The remaining industry will be in private sector subjected to control and regulation of the Government.

New Industrial Policy, 1991

Making a sharp departure from the Industrial Policy Resolution, 1956, the Government announced a new industrial policy on July 24, 1991. The basic philosophy of the new policy has been summed up as: 'continuity with change'. The major mission of the policy was to correct the distortions or weaknesses that may have crept in the industrial structure as it has developed over the last four decades.

The new industrial policy seeks to achieve the following objectives:

(i) To maintain a sustained growth in the productivity and gainful employment.

(ii) To attain international competitiveness.

(iii) To correct the distortions or weaknesses that may have crept in the industrial structure as it has developed over the last four decades.

(iv) To consolidate the strength built up during the last four decades of economic planning and to build on the gain already made.

The pursuit of these objectives will be tempered by

(a) The need to preserve the environment, and

(b) The need to ensure the efficient use of available resources.

In pursuit of the above objectives, Government has decided to take a series of initiatives in respect of the policies relating to the following areas:

- Industrial licensing has been abolished for all projects except for a short list of industries related to security and strategic concerns, social reasons, hazardous chemicals and overriding environmental reasons, and items of luxurious consumption.

- Only six industries groups where security and strategic concerns predominate are under the purview of industrial licensing.

  These are : alcohol, cigarettes, hazardous chemicals, electronics, aerospace and defence-equipment, drugs and pharmaceuticals and industrial explosive. (Drugs and Pharmaceuticals are now exempt from the list)

- Approval will be given for direct foreign investment up to 51 per cent equity in high priority industries (34 such groups of industries have been identified). Such clearance will be available if foreign equity covers the foreign exchange requirement for imported capital goods.

National Manufacturing Policy, 2011

The Government of India notified a National Manufacturing Policy (NMP) on November 4, 2011 with the objective of enhancing the share of manufacturing in GDP to 25 per cent and creating 100 million jobs over a decade. It seeks to empower rural youth by imparting necessary skill sets to make them employable. Sustainable development is integral to the spirit of the policy and technological value addition in manufacturing has received special focus.

The policy is based on the principle of industrial growth in partnership with the states. The Central Government will create the enabling policy framework, provide incentives for infrastructure development on a Public Private Partnership (PPP) basis through appropriate financing instruments, and state governments will be encouraged to adopt the instrumentalities provided in the policy.

During 2014, a list of what constitutes defence equipment were notified, with the stipulation that any item not specifically included in the list, including those for dual use having military as well as civilian applications stand delicensed. Further, the initial validity of industrial licenses for all sectors (other than Defence Sector) has been extended to three years with a provision to grant two extensions of two years each. Thus, time to commence commercial production is now seven years (3 + 2 + 2 = 7). The initial validity of industrial licence for defence sector were revised to 15 years (Fifteen years), further extendable up to 18 years for existing as well as future licenses.

National Manufacturing Policy

The Department notified the National Manufacturing Policy (NMP) in 2011 with the objective of enhancing the share of manufacturing in GDP to 25 per cent and creating 100 million jobs by 2022. The policy is based on the principle of industrial growth in partnership with the states. The Central Government will create the enabling policy framework, provide incentives for infrastructure development on a Public Private Partnership (PPP) basis through appropriate financing instruments, and State Governments are encouraged to adopt the instrumentalities provided in the Policy. The proposals in the policy are sector neutral, location neutral and technology neutral except incentivisation of green technology. While the NIMZs are an important instrumentality, the proposals contained in the Policy apply to manufacturing industry throughout the country including wherever industry is able to organize itself into clusters and adopt a model of self-regulation as enunciated therein.

Important instruments/features of the policy are:- National Investment and Manufacturing Zones (NIMZs); rationalization and simplification of business regulations; simple and expeditious exit mechanism for manufacturing units; incentives for SMEs; industrial training and skill upgradation measures; financial and institutional mechanisms for technology development, including green technologies; government procurement; and special focus sectors.

Make in India

After the launch of 'Make in India' initiative in 2014, ministries/departments concerned with 22 thrust sectors identified under 'Make in India', announced their Action Plans for implementation over one year and three years. Quantifiable and measurable milestones in respect of each activity of the Action Plans have been identified by the ministries/departments concerned with a view to monitor the implementation of these Action Plans.

This Department has launched an online 'Make in India Dashboard' in April 2016, to enable ministries/departments to view and update the progress of their Action Plans on their own in a timely manner. This Dashboard is being monitored by this Department to evaluate the overall progress of the 'Make in India' related initiatives and address and resolve any issues.

To provide further impetus to 'Make in India' initiative, new Action Plans pertaining to the Ministry of Health & Family Welfare have been identified.

Under the 'Make in India' initiative, a 'Seven Year Strategy' has been adopted which involves redefining the sectors covered by the new initiative, adding new sectors like medical devices while removing sectors that lose relevance in an evolving economy, to maximize job creation potential with evolution of the economy. It should also expand its reach to include service sectors, which have the greatest employment potential. Sectors such as tourism and hospitality are important for their job creation potential. With the objective to generate awareness about the investment opportunities and prospects of the country, to promote India as a preferred investment destination in the markets overseas and to increase Indian share of Global FDI, an interactive portal http://www.makeinindia.com has been created for dissemination of information and interaction with the investors.

Startup India

The 'Startup India' initiative, aims at fostering entrepreneurship and promoting innovation by creating an ecosystem that is conducive to growth. The initiative strives for providing a long due impetus to the entrepreneurial set up in economic landscape of the country. An Action Plan of 19 action items spanning across areas such as simplification and handholding, funding support and incentives and industry-academia partnership and incubation was announced. It is established globally that Startups are driving the economic growth of nations, creating employment and fostering a culture of innovation. It is, therefore, incumbent on the Government to nurture emerging talent and entrepreneurship as part of the larger goal of nation building.

Since the launch of the initiative, a number of forward looking strategic amendments to the existing policy ecology have been introduced, like:

Startup Hub: A Startup India Hub has been set up to address queries of various startups and assist them through their life cycle. Additionally, a facility for interaction for entrepreneurs on Twitter known as 'Twitter Seva' has also been launched.

Rolling-out of Mobile App and Portal: The Startup India Portal and Mobile App have been made operational. The portal and the app provide functionalities such as making application for obtaining real-time Startup recognition, verification of recognition certificate, information availability such as list of incubators, Securities and Exchange Board of India (SEBI) registered funds, notifications issued by various departments, etc.

Fast-tracking Patent Registration and Legal Support: A scheme for Startups IPR Protection (SIPP) for facilitating fast track filing of patents, trademarks and designs by Startups has been introduced. The scheme thus provides for expedited examination of patents filed. This will reduce the time taken in getting patents. The fee for filing of patents has also been reduced up to 80 per cent.

Relaxed Norms in Public Procurement for Startups: Provisions have been introduced in the procurement policy to relax norms pertaining to prior experience/turnover for micro and small enterprises.

Tax Incentives: Tax incentives for Startup companies for a period of three years have been introduced in the Finance Act 2016.

Building Innovation Centres and Setting up of Seven Research Parks: Two Research Parks, 16 Technology Business Incubators (TBIs) and 10 Startup Centres have been approved and shall be made operational soon. 25-30 new Innovation Centres have been envisaged to be launched in the current financial year.

Promoting Startups in Biotechnology Sector: Scheme guidelines have been drawn by Department of Bio-Technology (DBT) to scale up existing 15 bio-incubators.

Launching of Innovation Focused Programme: Scheme guidelines for Innovation core and Ucchattar Avishkar Yojana (UAY) have been finalized by Ministry of Human Resource Development (MHRD). The guidelines for the National Initiative for Developing and Harnessing Innovations (NIDHI) has been formulated and notified.

LABOUR POLICY

Labour Policy in India has been evolving in response to specific needs of the situation to suit requirements of planned economic development and social justice and has two fold objectives, *viz.*, maintaining industrial peace and promoting the welfare of labour.

The law relating to labour and employment in India is primarily known under the broad category of "Industrial Law". Industrial law in this country is of recent vintage and has developed in respect to the vastly increased awakening of the workers of their rights, particularly after the advent of Independence. Industrial relations embrace a complex of relationships between the workers, employers and government, basically concerned with the determination of the terms of employment and conditions of labour.

Industrial labour in India has exhibited certain well-known features which have affected the trade union organisation. In the first instance, most industrial workers have their roots in villages. Quite a large number of them have left their traditional occupations and have migrated to the cities in search of permanent or temporary employment. Most of them still retain their attachment to land and the periodic migration from the town to the village is a common characteristic of our industrial labour. Only in recent years, a new class of industrial labour without roots in agriculture is emerging in our towns and cities.

Secondly, industrial labour is largely uneducated. As a result, they do not understand the problems which their industries confront and the problems which they themselves are facing. This is also one of the factors for weak trade union organisation.

Thirdly, industrial labour in India is not united but is divided and sub-divided on the basis of region, religion, language and caste. It is only in recent years that some of these differences are disappearing gradually and some degree of unity on the basis of economic consideration is taking place.

Finally, Indian workers do not remain in the same job for considerable amount of time. There is high labour turnover. Absenteeism, indiscipline etc., are quite common. This may be because the workers were originally from the rural areas where people were comparatively free; or it may be because of their lack of education and love of leisure.

Causes of Industrial Disputes

There are several causes of industrial disputes. The most important cause is the demand for more wages. It is generally known that the Indian industrialists have not been following an enlightened policy in the matter of paying wages. In recent years, particularly, wages have not been rising in proportion to the rise in prices. Most of the industrial disputes were the result of a demand for higher wages.

The demand for bonus or for the increase in bonus has been another major cause for industrial disputes. There is an increasing feeling among the workers that they should have a greater share in the profits of the industrial concerns. Non-acceptance of this fact by the employers has been a source of friction among the employers and employees.

The demand for improved working conditions—such as lesser working hours, better safety measures in the factory, canteen facilities, holidays and leave, etc.—are also considered to be responsible for many industrial disputes.

SOCIAL SECURITY

The social security schemes in India cover only a small segment of the organized work-force, which may be defined as workers who are having a direct regular employer–employee relationship within an organization. The social security legislations in India derive their strength and spirit from the Directive Principles of the State Policy as contained in the Constitution of India. These provide for mandatory social security benefits either solely at the cost of the employers or on the basis of joint contribution of the employers and the employees. While protective entitlements accrue to the employees, the responsibilities for compliance largely rest with the employers.

Social Security Laws

The principal social security laws enacted for the organised sector in India are:

- The Employees' State Insurance Act, 1948;
- The Employees' Provident Funds & Miscellaneous Provisions Act, 1952 (Separate provident fund legislations exist for workers employed in coal mines and tea plantations in the state of Assam and for seamen);
- The Employee's Compensation Act, 1923;
- The Maternity Benefit Act, 1961;
- The Payment of Gratuity Act, 1972.

Administration of Social Security Acts

The provisions of the Employees' Compensation Act, 1923 are being administered exclusively by the State Governments. Cash benefits under the Employees' State Insurance Act, 1948 are administered by the Central Government through the Employees' State Insurance Corporation (ESIC), whereas the State Governments and Union Territory Administrations are administering medical care alongwith ESIC under the Employees' State Insurance Act, 1948. The Employees' Provident Funds and Miscellaneous Provisions Act, 1952 is administered by the Government of India through the Employees' Provident Fund Organisation (EPFO). In mines and circus industry, the provisions of the Maternity Benefit Act, 1961 are being administered by the Central Government through the Chief Labour Commissioner (Central) and by the State Governments in factories, plantations and other establishments. The Payment of Gratuity Act, 1972 is administered by the Central Government in establishments under its control, establishments having branches in more than one State, major ports, mines, oil-fields and railway companies and by the State Governments and Union Territory Administrations in all other cases. This Act applies to factories and other establishments.

The Employees' Compensation Act, 1923

The main objective of the Act is to impose an obligation upon the employers to pay compensation to workers for accidents arising out of and in the course of employment.

The Act applies to the persons employed in factories, mines, plantations, mechanically propelled vehicles, construction works and certain other hazardous occupations. The Act provides for payment of compensation to the employees and their dependents in case of injury and accident (including certain occupational diseases) arising out of and in the course of employment and resulting in disablement or death.

Entitlement

In order to be an "employee" within the meaning of section 2(1) (dd) of the Employees' Compensation Act, first, a person should be employed for the proposes of the employer's trade or business; and lastly, the capacity in which he works should be one set out in the list in Schedule II of the Act.

Benefits

The rate of compensation in case of death is an amount equal to fifty per cent of the monthly wages of the deceased workman multiplied by the relevant factor or an amount of ₹ 1,20,000, whichever is more. Where permanent total disablement results from the injury, the compensation will be an amount equal to sixty per cent of the monthly wages of the injured workman multiplied by the relevant factor or an amount of ₹ 1,40,000, whichever is more.

The Employees State Insurance Act, 1948

Coverage

The Employees' State Insurance Act, 1948 applies to factories employing 10 or more persons. The provisions of the Act are being brought into force area-wise in stages. The Act contains an enabling provision under which the "appropriate government" is empowered to extend the provisions of the Act to other classes of establishments—industrial, commercial, agricultural or otherwise. Under these provisions, the State Governments have extended the provisions of the Act to shops, hotels, restaurants, cinemas including preview theatres, road motor transport undertakings, newspaper establishments, educational and medical institutions employing 10 or more employees. Employees of factories and establishments covered under the Act drawing monthly wages upto ₹ 21,000 per month and ₹ 25,000 per month for persons with disabilities are covered under the Scheme.

Funding and Operation of the Scheme

The ESI Scheme is mainly financed by contributions from the employers and employees. The rates of the employers' and the employees' share of contribution are 4.75% and 1.75%, respectively. The Corporation has prescribed a ceiling on reimbursement of Medical Care Expenditure to State Government. At present the prescribed ceiling is ₹ 3000 per Insured Person Family Unit per annum. The expenditure on Medical Care is shared between ESI Corporation and State Government in the ratio of 7:1 with the ceiling. All capital expenditure on construction of ESI Hospitals and other buildings including their maintenance is borne exclusively by the Corporation.

Health & Cash Benefits under ESI Scheme

Besides from medical care, the beneficiaries under ESI Scheme are also provided an array of cash benefits. It is payable in times of physical distress due to sickness, temporary or permanent disablement resulting in loss of earning capacity, confinement in respect of insured women, etc. Dependents of insured persons who die of employment injury caused by accident or occupational disease are entitled to monthly payments called the dependent benefits.

Employees' Provident Funds and Miscellaneous Provisions Act, 1952

The Employees' Provident Funds and Miscellaneous Provisions Act, 1952 is a welfare legislation enacted for the purpose of instituting provident funds, pension fund and deposit linked insurance fund for employees working in factories and other establishments. The Act aims at providing social security and timely monetary assistance to industrial employees and their families when they are in distress and/or unable to meet family and social obligations and to protect them in old age, disablement, early death of the bread winner and in some other contingencies.

Presently, the following three Schemes are in operation under the Act through the Employees' Provident Fund Organisation (EPFO):

- Employees' Provident Funds Scheme, 1952
- Employees' Deposit Linked Insurance Scheme, 1976
- Employees' Pension Scheme, 1995

Employees Deposit Linked Insurance Scheme, 1976

Employees Deposit-Linked Insurance Scheme, 1976 (EDLI) is applicable to all factories/establishments with effect from

1st August, 1976. All the employees, who are members of the Employees' Provident Fund Scheme, are required to become members of this Scheme. Employers are required to pay contributions to the Insurance Fund at the rate of 0.5 per cent of pay, *i.e.*, basic wages, dearness allowance including cash value of food concession and retaining allowance, if any. The benefit under para 22 of this Scheme on the death of an employee has been further increased by 20% in addition to the benefits already provided therein.

Employees' Pension Scheme, 1995

The Employees' Pension Scheme, 1995 has been introduced w.e.f. 16-11-1995. With the introduction of the Pension Scheme, the erstwhile Employees' Family Pension Scheme, 1971, has ceased to operate. However, the pensioners who were drawing benefits under the erstwhile Employees' Family Pension Scheme, 1971 will continue to draw Family Pension under the Employees' Pension Scheme, 1995.

Benefits Under the Scheme

The Employees' Pension Scheme, 1995 provides the following benefits to the members and their families:

- Monthly member pension
- Disablement pension
- Widow/ widower pension
- Children pension
- Orphan pension
- Disabled Children/Orphan Pension
- Nominee pension
- Pension to dependent parents
- Withdrawal benefit

The Maternity Benefit Act, 1961

The Act was passed in September, 1961 and received its assent on 12th December, 1961. The Act regulates the employment of women in factories, mines, the circus industry, plantation units and shops or establishments employing 10 or more persons except the employees covered under the Employees State Insurance (ESI) Act, 1948 for certain periods before and after birth and provides for maternity and other benefits. It extends to the whole of India, except the State of Sikkim. It also provides for maternity leave and payment of certain monetary benefits to women workers subject to fulfilment of certain conditions during the period when they are out of employment on account of pregnancy. The services of a woman worker cannot be terminated during the period of her absence on account of pregnancy except for gross misconduct. Maximum period for which a woman can get maternity benefit is twelve weeks. The Act had been amended in 2008. A medical bonus of ₹ 3,500 is being provided from 19.12.2011 under the Act.

A proposal for increasing the maternity benefit for working women from existing 12 weeks to 26 weeks up to two surviving children and 12 weeks for more than two children is under the consideration by amending the Maternity Benefit Act, 1961. The proposed amendment Bill has also provisions of maternity benefits for adopting and Commissioning mothers. It also seeks crèche and work from home facility. The Amendment Bill has been passed in the Rajya Sabha and is likely to be passed by the Lok Sabha.

The Payment of Gratuity Act, 1972

Objective

The Payment of Gratuity Act, 1972 provides for a scheme of compulsory payment of gratuity to employees engaged in factories, mines, oil-fields, plantations, ports, railway companies, motor transport undertakings, shops or other establishments on the termination of his employment after he has rendered continuous service for not less than five years on his superannuation, or on his retirement or resignation, or on his death or disablement due to accident or disease. Provided that the completion of continuous service of five years shall not be necessary where the termination of the employment of any employees is due to death or disablement. Payment of Gratuity is an employer's liability under the extant provisions of the PG Act.

Coverage

- Every factory, mine, oil-field, plantation, port and railway company.

- Every shop or establishment within the meaning of any law for the time being in force in relation to shops and establishments in a State, in which ten or more persons are employed or were employed on any day of the preceding twelve months.

- Every motor transport undertaking in which ten or more were employed on any day of the preceding twelve months.

- Such other establishments or class of establishments in which ten or more employees are employed or were employed on any day of the preceding twelve months as the Central government may, by notification, specify in this behalf.

A shop or establishment once covered shall continue to be covered notwithstanding that the number of persons employed therein at any time falls below ten.

Entitlement

Every employee, other than apprentice irrespective of his wages is entitled to receive gratuity after he has rendered continuous service for five years or more. Gratuity is payable at the time of termination of his service either (i) on superannuation or (ii) on retirement or resignation or (iii) on death or disablement due to accident or disease. Termination of services includes retrenchment. However, the condition of five years' continuous service is not necessary if services are terminated due to death or disablement. In case of death of the employee, the gratuity payable to him is to be paid to his nominee, and if no nomination has been made, then to his heirs.

Calculation of Benefits

For every completed year of service or part thereof in excess of six months, the employer pays gratuity to an employee at the rate of fifteen days' wages based on the rate of wages last drawn. As per section 4(3) of the Act, the amount of the gratuity payable to an employee shall not exceed ₹ 10,00,000.

Fiscal Policy

Fiscal policy is playing an important role on the economic and social front of a country. Traditionally, fiscal policy in concerned with the determination of state income and expenditure policy. But with the passage of time, the importance of fiscal policy has been increasing continuously for attaining rapid economic growth.

Accordingly, it has included public borrowing and deficit financing as a part of fiscal policy of the country. An effective fiscal policy is composed of policy decisions relating to entire financial structure of the government including tax revenue, public expenditures, loans, transfers, debt management, budgetary deficit, etc.

The policy also tries to attain proper balance between these aforesaid units so as to achieve the best possible results in terms of economic goals. Harvey and Joanson, M., defined fiscal policy as "changes in government expenditure and taxation designed to influence the pattern and level of activity".

OBJECTIVES OF FISCAL POLICY

In India, the fiscal policy is gaining its importance in recent years with the growing involvement of the government in developmental activities of the country.

Following are some of the important objectives of fiscal policy adopted by the Government of India:

1. To mobilise adequate resources for financing various programmes and projects adopted for economic development.
2. To remove poverty and unemployment.
3. To attain the growth of public sector for attaining the objective of socialistic pattern of society.
4. To reduce regional disparities.
5. To reduce the degree of inequality in the distribution of income and wealth.
6. To raise the rate of savings and investment for increasing the rate of capital formation.
7. To promote necessary development in the private sector through fiscal incentive.
8. To arrange an optimum utilisation of resources.
9. To control the inflationary pressures in economy in order to attain economic stability.

In order to attain all these aforesaid objectives, the Government of India has been formulating its fiscal policy incorporating the revenue, expenditure and public debt components in a comprehensive manner.

ROLE OF FISCAL POLICY IN ECONOMIC DEVELOPMENT

One of the important goals of fiscal policy formulated by the Government of India is to attain rapid economic development of the country.

To attain such economic development in the country, the fiscal policy of the country has adopted following two objectives:

1. To raise the rate of productive investment of both public and private sector of the country.

2. To enhance the marginal and average rates of savings for mobilising adequate financial resources for making investment in public and private sectors of the economy.

The fiscal policy of the country is trying to attain both these two objectives during the plan periods.

TECHNIQUES OF FISCAL POLICY

Following are the four important techniques of fiscal policy of India:

(i) Policy of Taxation of Government of India

One of the important sources of revenue of the Government of India is the tax revenue. Both direct and indirect taxes are being levied by the Government of India. Direct taxes are progressive by nature and most of indirect taxes are regressive in nature. Taxation plays an important role in mobilising resources for plan.

During the First, Second and Third Plan, additional taxation alone contributed nearly 12.7 per cent, 22.8 per cent and 34 per cent of public sector plan expenditure respectively. The shares during the Fourth, Fifth, Sixth and Seventh Plan were 27 per cent, 37 per cent, 22 per cent and 15 per cent respectively.

Total tax revenue collected by the Government of India stands at 72.13 per cent of the total revenue of the Government. Mobilisation of taxes by the Government stands around 15 to 16 per cent of the national income of the country during recent years.

Main objectives of taxation policy in India includes:

(a) Mobilisation of resources for financing economic development;

(b) Formation of capital by promoting saving and investment through time deposits, investment in government bonds, in units, insurance etc.;

(c) Attainment of equality in the distribution of income and wealth through the imposition of progressive direct taxes; and

(d) Attainment of price stability by adopting anti-inflationary taxation policy.

(ii) Public Expenditure Policy of Government of India

Public expenditure is playing an important role in the economic development of a country like India. With increase in responsibilities of the government and with the increasing participation of government in economic activities of the country, the volume of public expenditure in a highly populated country like India is increasing at a galloping rate. In 1992-93, the public expenditure as percentage of GDP was around 30 per cent.

Public expenditure is of two different types, *i.e.*, developmental and non-developmental expenditure. Developmental expenditure of the Government is mostly related to the developmental activities *viz.*, development of infrastructure, industry, health facilities, educational institutions, etc.

The non-developmental expenditure is mostly a maintenance type of expenditure, which is related to maintenance of law, order, defence, administrative services, etc. The public expenditure incurred by the Government of India has been creating a serious impact on the production and distribution pattern of the economy.

Following are some of the important features of the policy of public expenditure formulated by the Government of India:

(a) **Development of infrastructure:** Development of infrastructural facilities which includes development of power projects, railways, road, transportation system, bridges, dams, irrigation projects, hospitals, educational institutions, etc., involves huge expenditure by the Government as private investors are very much reluctant to invest in these areas considering the low rate of profitability and high risk involved in it.

(b) **Development of public enterprises:** Development of heavy and basic industries is very important for the development of underdeveloped country. But the establishment of these industries involves huge investment and a considerable proportion of risk. Naturally private sector cannot take the responsibility to develop these industries.

Development of these industries has become a responsibility of the Government of India particularly since the introduction of Industrial Policy, 1956. A significant portion of public expenditure has been utilised for the establishment and improvement of these public enterprises.

(c) **Support to Private Sector:** Providing necessary support to the private sector for the establishment of industry and other projects is another important objective of public expenditure policy formulated by the Government of India.

(d) **Social Welfare and Employment Programmes:** Another important feature of public expenditure policy pursued by the Government of India is its growing involvement in attaining various social welfare programmes and also on employment generation programmes.

(iii) Policy of Deficit Financing of Government of India

Following the policy of deficit financing as introduced by J.M. Keynes, the Government of India has been adopting the policy for financing its developmental plans since its inception. The deficit financing in India indicates taking loan by the Government from the Reserve Bank of India in the form of issuing fresh dose of currency.

Considering the low level of income, low rate of savings and capital formation, the Government is taking recourse to deficit financing in increasing proportion. Deficit financing is a kind of forced savings.

During the First, Second, Third and Fourth Plan deficit financing as percentage of total plan resources was to the extent of 17 per cent, 20 per cent, 13 per cent and 13.5 per cent respectively. But due to adverse consequence of deficit financing through inflationary rise in price level, the extent of deficit financing was reduced to only 3 per cent during the Fifth Plan.

But due to resource constraint, the extent of deficit financing again rose to 14 per cent and 16 per cent of total plan resources respectively.

(iv) Public Debt Policy of the Government of India

As the taxation has got its limit in a poor country like India due to poor taxable capacity of the people, thus the Government is taking recourse to public debt for financing its developmental expenditure. In the post-independence period, the Central Government has been raising a good amount of public debt regularly in order to mobilise a huge amount of resources for meeting its developmental expenditure. Total public debt of the Central Government includes internal debt and external debt.

Internal Debt

Internal debt indicates the amount of loan raised, by the Government from within the country. The Government raises internal public debt from the open market by issuing bonds and cash certificates and 15 years annuity certificates. The Government also borrows for a temporary period from RBI (treasury bills issued by RBI) and also from commercial banks.

External Debt

As the internal debt is insufficient thus the Government is also collecting loan from external sources, *i.e.*, from abroad, in the form of foreign capital, technical knowhow and capital goods. Accordingly, the Central Government is also borrowing from international financing agencies for financing various developmental projects.

These agencies include World Bank, IMF, IDA, IFC, etc. Moreover, the Government is also collecting inter-governmental loans from various developed countries of the world for financing its various infrastructural projects.

ADVANTAGES OF FISCAL POLICY OF INDIA

Following are some of the important merits or advantages of fiscal policy of Government of India:

Incentives to Savings

The fiscal policy of the country has been providing various incentives to raise the savings rate both in household and corporate sector through various budgetary policy changes, viz., tax exemption, tax concession, etc. The savings rate increased from a mere 8.6 per cent in 1950-51 to 37.7 per cent in 2007-08.

Inducement to Private Sector

Private sector of the country has been getting necessary inducement from the fiscal policy of the country to expand its activities. Tax concessions, tax exemptions, subsidies, etc., incorporated in the budgets have been providing adequate incentives to the private sector units engaged in industry, infrastructure and export sector of the country.

Capital Formation

Fiscal policy of the country has been playing an important role in raising the rate of capital formation in the country both in its public and private sectors. The gross domestic capital formation as per cent of GDP in India increased from 8.4 per cent in 1950-51 to 19.9 per cent in 1980-81 and then to 39.1 per cent in 2007-08. Therefore, it has created a favourable impact on the public and private sector investment of the country.

Mobilisation of Resources

Fiscal policy of the country has been helping to mobilise considerable amount of resources through taxation, public debt, etc., for financing its various developmental projects. The extent of internal resource mobilisation for financing plan increased considerably from 70 per cent in 1965-66 to around 90 per cent in 1997-98.

Reduction of Inequality

Fiscal policy of the country has been making constant endeavour to reduce the inequality in the distribution of income and wealth. Progressive taxes on income and wealth tax exemption, subsidies, grant, etc., are making a consolidated effort to reduce such inequality. Moreover, the fiscal policy is also trying to reduce the regional disparities through its various budgetary policies.

Alleviation of Poverty and Unemployment

Another important merit of Indian fiscal policy is that it is making constant effort to alleviate poverty and unemployment problem through its various poverty eradication and employment generation programmes, like, IRDP, JRY, PMRY, SJSRY, EAS, NREGA, etc.

SHORTCOMINGS OF FISCAL POLICY IN INDIA

Following are the major shortcomings of the fiscal policy of the country:

Inflation

Fiscal policy of the country has failed to contain the inflationary rise in price level. Increasing volume of public expenditure on non-developmental heads and deficit financing has resulted in demand-pull inflation. Higher rate of indirect taxation has also resulted in cost-push inflation. Moreover, the direct taxes have failed to check the growth of black money which is again aggravating the inflationary spiral in the level of prices.

Negative Return of the Public Sector

The negative return on capital invested in the public sector units has become a serious problem for the Government of India. Inspite of having a huge total investment to the extent of ₹ 4,21,089 crore in 2007 on PSUs the return on investment has remained mostly negative or lower. In order to maintain those PSUs, the Government has to keep huge amount of budgetary provisions, thereby creating a huge drainage of scarce resources of the country.

Instability

Fiscal policy of the country has failed to attain stability on various fronts. Growing volume of deficit financing has created the problem of inflationary rise in price level. Disequilibrium in its balance of payments has also affected the external stability of the country.

Defective Tax Structure

Fiscal policy has also failed to provide a suitable tax structure for the country. Tax structure has failed to raise the productivity of direct taxes and the country has been relying much on indirect taxes. Therefore, the tax structure has become burdensome to the poor.

Growing Inequality

Fiscal policy of the country has failed to contain the growing inequality in the distribution of income and wealth throughout the country. Growing trend of tax evasion has made the tax machinery ineffective for the purpose. Growing reliance on indirect taxes has made the tax structure regressive.

SUGGESTIONS FOR NECESSARY REFORMS IN FISCAL POLICY

Following are some of the important measures suggested for necessary reforms of the fiscal policy of the country:

Progressive Taxes

The tax structure of the country should try to infuse more progressive elements so that it can put heavy burden on the rich and less burden on the poor. Necessary amendments should be made in respect of irrigation tax, sales tax, excise duty, land revenue, property taxes, etc.

Agricultural Taxation

The tax net of the country should be extended to the agricultural sector for rapping a huge amount of revenue from the rich agriculturists.

Broad-based Tax Net

Tax net of the country should be broad-based so that it can cover increasing number of population having the taxable capacity.

Checking Tax Evasion

Adequate measures be taken to check the problem of tax evasion in the country. Tax laws should be made stricter for prosecuting the tax evaders. Tax machinery should be made more efficient and honest to gear up its operations. Tax rate should be reduced to encourage the growing trend of tax compliance.

Increasing Reliance on Direct Taxes

Tax machinery of the country should attach much more reliance on direct taxes instead of indirect taxes. Accordingly, the tax machinery should try to introduce wealth tax, estate duty, gift tax, expenditure tax etc.

Simplified Tax Structure

Tax structure and rules of the country should be simplified so that it can encourage tax compliance among the people and it can remove the unnecessary harassment of the tax payers.

Reduction of Non-Development Expenditure

The fiscal policy of the country should try to reduce the non-developmental expenditure of the country. This would reduce the volume of unproductive expenditure and can reduce the inflationary impact of such expenditure.

Raising the Profitability of PSUs

The Government should try to restructure its policy on public sector enterprises so that its efficiency and rate of return on capital invested can be raised effectively. PSUs should be managed in rational manner with least government interference and on commercial lines. Accordingly, the policy of budgetary provisions for maintaining the PSUs should gradually be eliminated.

MEASURES OF FISCAL POLICY REFORMS

The Government of India has introduced several fiscal policy reforms which constitute the main basis of the stabilisation policy of the country.

Following are some of the important measures of fiscal policy reforms adopted by the Government of India in recent years:

Reduction of Rates of Direct Taxes

The peak rate of income tax was reduced to 30 per cent in 1997-98 budget. This has resulted in an increase in the share of direct taxes in total revenue of the country from 19 per cent in 1990-91 to around 61 per cent in 2008-09.

Fall in the volume of Government Expenditure

Several measures were undertaken recently by the government. Accordingly, total expenditure of the Government under various heads has been reduced. As a result, total public expenditure as per cent of GDP has declined from 19.7 per cent of GDP in 1990-91 to 16.9 per cent in 2008-09.

Reduction in the Volume of Subsidies

Central Government has been making huge payments in the form of subsidies, *i.e.*, food subsidies, fertiliser subsidies, export subsidies etc. Steps have been taken to reduce these subsidies in a phased manner.

Reduction in Fiscal Deficit

The Central Government has been trying seriously to contain the fiscal deficit in its annual budget. Accordingly, it has reduced the extent of fiscal deficit from 7.7 per cent of GDP in 1990-91 to 6.1 per cent in 2008-09. But fiscal stabilisation necessitates containing the fiscal deficit at least to 3 per cent of GDP.

Disinvestment in Public Sector

Another important fiscal policy reforms introduced by the Government of India is to disinvest the shares of the public sector enterprises. The government has disinvested as part of its stake in 39 selected PSUs since the disinvestment process began in 1992. Till 2006-07, it has raised around ₹ 51,608 crore through disinvestment of share of PSUs.

In the mean time, the Government has constituted a Disinvestment Commission to advise it on how to go about disinvesting the shares of PSUs. The Commission, in its first three reports has given its recommendations on 15 PSUs out of 50 referred to it.

The Commission submitted at least eight reports covering 43 PSUs and also undertook diagnostic studies in 1998-99 in respect of these undertakings for giving recommendations.

23

International Economic Institutions

An International Economic Institution is a Financial Institution that has been established by more than one country, and hence are subjects of international law. Its owners or shareholders are generally national governments, although other international and other organisations occasionally figure as shareholders. Almost every country exports and imports products to benefit from the growing international trade. The growth of international trade can be increased, if the countries follow a common set of rules, regulations, and standards related to import and export.

These common rules and regulations are set by various international economic institutions. These institutions aim to provide a level playing field for all the countries and develop economic cooperation. These institutions also help in solving the currency issues among countries related to stabilizing the exchange rates.

IMF

The International Monetary Fund (IMF) is an international organization created for the purpose of standardizing global financial relations and exchange rates. The IMF generally monitors the global economy, and its core goal is to economically strengthen its member countries. Specifically, the IMF was created with the intention of:

- Promoting global monetary and exchange stability.
- Facilitating the expansion and balanced growth of international trade.
- Assisting in the establishment of a multilateral system of payments for current transactions.

Fixed exchange rates, also known as the Bretton Woods system (named after the original UN conference at which the IMF was conceived), refer to the value of a currency being tied to the value of another currency, or to gold. The system of fixed exchange rates was established by the IMF as a way to bolster the global economy after the Great Depression and World War II. This system was abolished in 1971, and ever since, the IMF has promoted the system of floating exchange rates, which means that the value of a currency can change in relation to the value of another. This is the familiar system today.

Countries must apply to be a part of the IMF, although any country can apply. Over time, the stipulations of being a member have changed, with membership requirements being more relaxed when the Fund was in its early stages. Countries are required to make membership payments, or quotas, which are assigned to individual countries based on their economic size and stipulate how much they contribute. These quotas are larger for more powerful economies, and they form a pool from which countries in need can take loans. Member countries are also required to adhere to the Code of Conduct, and stricter regulations may be imposed on those countries who apply in hopes of financial aid.

Members not only have access to the broad range of services provided by the IMF, but also to the economic records of other member countries.

The IMF has completely reshaped the global economy and redefined the ways in which countries trade with and take loans from other countries. The IMF was first conceived at a UN conference in 1944, among the 44 attending countries, before it was officially created in 1945. These countries wanted to globally stabilize exchange rates and financial communication between countries, especially following the disastrous Great Depression and World War II. Goals included international cooperation and trade, the reduction of poverty and financial crises, and economic growth. Although the Fund has evolved over the years to become what it is today and adapt to changing times, it still operates around the same guiding principles.

The IMF played a large role in the economic restructurization of the post-World War II world. After the war, some countries were in economic distress, and others were reluctant to trade with certain countries after the fighting. The Fund helped smooth over the economic post-war transition period and restabilize the global economy so it could move toward prosperity, using systems such as fixed exchange rates.

Currently, there are 189 member countries in the IMF, which is based out of Washington, D.C. Each country or region is represented by a member on the Fund's Executive Board and numerous staff members. The ratio of board members from each country is based on the country's global financial position, so that the most powerful countries in the global economy have the heaviest representation. The United States has the highest voting power, followed by Asian countries such as Japan and China and Western European countries such as Britain, Germany, France, and Italy.

While the IMF sets standards for the global economy and monitors the financial communications between countries, it also helps those countries in need by lending them the money necessary to turn their economy around and rebuild their financial structure. Countries contribute to a pool from which countries in need can borrow as a short-term loan. The IMF also assists countries in developing sustainable financial policies, provides economic advice, helps countries maximize their financial effectiveness, and works to help developing countries stabilize and sustain themselves in the global economy.

The IMF plays three major roles in the global monetary system. The Fund surveys and monitors economic and financial developments, lends funds to countries with balance-of-payment difficulties, and provides technical assistance and training for countries requesting it.

WORLD BANK

The World Bank is an international organization dedicated to providing financing, advice and research to developing nations to aid their economic advancement. The World Bank was created out of the Bretton Woods agreement as a result of many European and Asian countries needing financing to fund reconstruction efforts. As of 2016, the Bank predominantly acts as an organization that attempts to fight poverty by offering developmental assistance to middle- and poor-income countries.

The World Bank is a provider of financial and technical assistance to developing countries around the globe. The bank considers itself a unique financial institution that provides partnerships to reduce poverty and support economic development by giving loans and offering advice and training to both the private and public sectors. The World Bank was established in 1944, is headquartered in Washington D.C.

The World Bank has expanded from the single institution that was created in 1944 to a group of five unique and cooperative institutional organizations. The first organization is the International Bank for Reconstruction and Development (IBRD), an institution that provides debt financing to governments that are considered middle income. The second organization within The World Bank is the International Development Association (IDA), a group that gives interest-free loans to governments of poor countries.

The International Finance Corporation (IFC), the third organization, focuses on the private sector and provides developing countries with investment financing and financial advisory services. The fourth part of The World Bank is the Multilateral Investment Guarantee Agency (MIGA), an organization that promotes foreign direct investments in developing countries. The fifth and final organization is the International Centre for Settlement of Investment Disputes (ICSID), an entity that provides arbitration on international investment disputes.

The World Bank has two stated goals that it aims to achieve by 2030. The first is to end extreme poverty by decreasing the amount of people living on less than $1.90 a day to below 3% of the world population. The second is to increase overall prosperity by increasing the income growth in the bottom 40% of the world's population.

Beyond its specific goals, the World Bank provides qualifying individuals and governments with low-interest loans, zero-interest credits and grants. These debt borrowings and cash infusions help with global education, health care, public administration, infrastructure and private sector development. The World Bank also shares information with world governments through policy advice, research and analysis and technical assistance.

WTO

The WTO was created on January 1, 1995, and is headquartered in Geneva, Switzerland. It was born out of the General Agreement on Tariffs and Trade (GATT), which was established in 1947. A series of trade negotiations, GATT rounds began at the end of World War II and were aimed at reducing tariffs for the facilitation of global trade on goods. The rationale for GATT was based on the Most Favoured Nation (MFN) clause, which, when assigned to one country by another, gives the selected country privileged trading rights. As such, GATT aimed to help, all countries obtain MFN-like status so that no single country would be at a trading advantage over others.

The WTO replaced GATT as the world's global trading body in 1995, and the current set of governing rules stems from the Uruguay Round of GATT negotiations, which took place throughout 1986-1994. GATT trading regulations established between 1947 and 1994 (and in particular those negotiated during the Uruguay Round) remain the primary rule book for multilateral trade in goods. Specific sectors such as agriculture have been addressed, as well as issues dealing with anti-dumping.

The purpose of the WTO is to ensure that global trade commences smoothly, freely and predictably. The WTO creates and embodies the legal ground rules for global trade among member nations and thus offers a system for international commerce. The WTO aims to create economic peace and stability in the world through a multilateral system based on consenting member states (currently there are 164 members) that have ratified the rules of the WTO in their individual countries as well. This means that WTO rules become a part of a country's domestic legal system. The rules, therefore, apply to local companies and nationals in the conduct of business in the international arena. If a company decides to invest in a foreign country, by, for example, setting up an office in that country, the rules of the WTO (and hence, a country's local laws) will govern how that can be done. Theoretically, if a country is a member of the WTO, its local laws cannot contradict WTO rules and regulations, which currently govern approximately 97% of all world trade.

WTO members negotiate World Trade Agreements, which are later ratified by the participating nations' parliaments or congresses. WTO agreements involve five principles:

- With some exceptions, members must provide equal trade-agreement terms to all fellow WTO countries. This equal treatment is known as most-favoured-nation status. Members also must offer "national treatment," meaning a WTO member may not discriminate against products from other WTO countries once the products have entered the member's market.

- WTO agreements must work to lower trade barriers such as customs duties, tariffs, import bans and quotas.

- WTO agreements must help provide a stable and predictable business environment by including commitments about future trade policies.

- WTO agreements must define fair and unfair trade practices.

- WTO agreements must consider the special needs developing countries may have in implementing WTO requirements.

Dispute settlement processes are written into WTO agreements, which are legally binding. WTO members enforce agreements according to predetermined procedures, but there is some concern that economically strong countries may be able to ignore complaints brought by poorer countries, whose sanctions or other penalties may not hurt the offending country enough to stimulate compliance.

The WTO is one of the most powerful and controversial legislative bodies in the world. Ideally, the purpose of the WTO is to facilitate free trade while helping governments meet social and environmental goals.

Whether free trade and the WTO accomplish these goals is the subject of considerable debate. Some question whether free trade benefits wealthy nations and multinational corporations rather than communities and the environment. Further, approximately two thirds of WTO members are developing countries, and some of these countries are concerned that poor domestic infrastructure, political instability, and certain tariff arrangements disproportionately inhibit their abilities to engage in profitable trade. Critics also point out that a country's choice not to join the WTO may effectively place an embargo on the goods and services of that country.

United Nations Conference on Trade and Development

UNCTAD, established in 1964, is the principal organ of United Nations General Assembly. It provides a forum where the developing countries can discuss the problems related to economic development. UNCTAD is headquartered in Geneva, Switzerland and has 193 member countries.

The conference of these member countries is held after every four years. UNCTAD was created because the existing institutions, such as GATT, IMF, and World Bank were not concerned with the problem of developing countries. UNCTAD's main objective is to formulate the policies related to areas of development, such as trade, finance, transport, and technology.

The main objectives of UNCTAD are as follows:

(a) Eliminating trade barriers that act as constraints for developing countries.
(b) Promoting international trade for speeding up the economic development.
(c) Formulating principles and policies related to international trade.
(d) Negotiating the multinational trade agreements.
(e) Providing technical assistance to developing countries specially low developed countries.

It is important to note that UNCTAD is a strategic partner of WTO. Both the organizations ensure that international trade helps the low developed and developing countries in accelerating their pace of growth. On 16th April, 2003, WTO and UNCTAD also signed a Memorandum of Understanding (MoU), which identifies the fields for cooperation to facilitate the joint activities between them.

New Development Bank (NDB)

The New Development Bank (NDB), formerly referred to as the BRICS Development Bank, is a multilateral development bank established by the BRICS states (Brazil, Russia, India, China and South Africa). According to the Agreement on the NDB, "the Bank shall support public or private projects through loans, guarantees, equity participation and other financial instruments." Moreover, the NDB "shall cooperate with international organizations and other financial entities, and provide technical assistance for projects to be supported by the Bank."

The initial authorized capital of the bank is $100 bln divided into 1 mln shares having a par value of $100,000 each. The initial subscribed capital of the NDB is $50 bln divided into paid-in shares ($10 bln) and callable shares ($40 bln). The initial subscribed capital of the bank was equally distributed among the founding members. The Agreement on the NDB specifies that the voting power of each member will be equal to the number of its subscribed shares in the capital stock of the bank.

The bank is headquartered in Shanghai, China. The first regional office of the NDB will be opened in Fortaleza Declaration, South Africa.

Asian Development Bank (ADB)

Headquarters : Manila, the Philippines.

Membership: Regional Members Afghanistan, Australia, Bangladesh, Bhutan, Cambodia, China, Cook Islands, Fiji Islands, Hong Kong, India, Indonesia, Japan, Kazakhstan, Kiribati, Republic of Korea, Kyrgyzstan, Laos, Malaysia, Maldives, Marshall Islands, Micronesia, Mongolia, Myanmar, Nauru, Nepal, New Zealand, Pakistan, Papua New Guinea, the Philippines, Samoa, Singapore, Solomon Islands, Sri Lanka, Taiwan, Thailand, Tonga, Tuvalu, Uzbekistan, Vanuatu and Vietnam.

Non-Regional Members: Austria, Belgium, Canada, Denmark, Finland, France, Germany, Italy, the Netherlands, Norway, Spain, Sweden, Switzerland, Turkey, the UK, and the USA.

Origin: The Asian Development Bank (ADB) is a regional development bank established on 19 December 1966, which is headquartered in the Ortigas Center located in Mandaluyong, Metro Manila, Philippines. The company also maintains 31 field offices around the world to promote social and economic development in Asia. The bank admits the members of the United Nations Economic and Social Commission for Asia and the Pacific (UNESCAP, formerly the Economic Commission for Asia and the Far East or ECAFE) and non-regional developed countries. From 31 members at its establishment, ADB now has 67 members, of which 48 are from within Asia and the Pacific and 19 outside. The ADB was modeled closely on the World Bank, and has a similar weighted voting system where votes are distributed in proportion with members' capital subscriptions. ADB releases an annual report that summarizes its operations, budget and other materials for review by the public. The ADB-Japan Scholarship Program (ADB-JSP) enrolls about 150 students annually in academic institutions located in 10 countries within the Region. Upon completion of their study programs, scholars are expected to contribute to the economic and social development of their home countries. ADB is an official United Nations Observer.

Objectives: The ADB aims at fostering economic growth, reducing poverty, improving the status of women, supporting human development and protecting the environment.

Structure: The Board of Governors is ADB's highest policy making body—it meets annually. The Board of Directors is its executive body and consists of 12 directors (8 from regional and 4 from non-regional members).

Asia-Pacific Economic Cooperation (APEC)

Headquarters : Singapore.

Membership : The APEC has 21 member economies as its membership consists of economies rather than countries- Australia, Brunei, Canada, Chile, China, Hong Kong, Indonesia, Japan, Korea (Republic of), Malaysia, Mexico, New

Aisa Pacific Economic Cooperation

Zealand, Papua New Guinea, Peru, the Philippines, Russia, Singapore, Taipei (Taiwan), Thailand, the USA and Vietnam.

Origin: APEC was founded in 1989 to assist the growing inter-dependence among Asia-Pacific economies.

Objective: The main objective of APEC is to promote free and open trade in the Asia-Pacific region through trade and investment, liberalisation and facilitation.

Economic Cooperation Organisation (ECO)

Headquarters : Teheran, Iran.

Membership : Iran, Pakistan, Turkey, Afghanistan, Azerbaijan, Kazakhstan, Kyrgyzstan, Tajikistan, Turkmenistan and Uzbekistan.

Economic Cooperation Organisation

Origin: The ECO is an inter governmental organisation established in 1985 by Iran, Pakistan and Turkey.

Objectives: The main aims are to promote regional economic cooperation among member-states; promote conditions for sustainable economic development; and raise the standard and quality of living in the member-states. The main areas of cooperation are trade, industry, agriculture, environment, drug control, energy, communications and cultural, social, technical and scientific fields.

Organisation for Economic Cooperation and Development (OECD)

Headquarters: Paris, France.

Membership: Australia, Austria, Belgium, Canada, Czech Republic, Denmark, Estonia, Finland, France, Germany, Greece,

Hungary, Iceland, Israel, Ireland, Italy, Japan, Republic of Korea, Luxembourg, Mexico, the Netherlands, New Zealand, Norway, Poland, Portugal, Spain, Slovakia, Slovenia, Sweden, Switzerland, Turkey, the United Kingdom and the United States.

Origin: The OECD was founded in 1961 to replace the Organisation for European Economic Cooperation (OEEC) which was established in 1948. Initially it was a pure European body but with the accession of Canada and the USA as full members its status was altered.

Objectives: The main objectives of the OECD are to promote policies designed to achieve the highest sustainable economic growth and employment and a rising standard of living in the member countries, while maintaining financial stability, and thus contributing to the world economy; to contribute to the second economic expansion in member as well as non-member countries in the process of economic development; and to contribute to the expansion of the world trade on a multilateral, non-discriminatory basis in accordance with international obligations.

The greater part of the Work of the OECD is carried out by 200 specialised bodies. There are three other bodies that form— a part of the OECD system-the International Energy Agency (IEA), the Nuclear Energy Agency (NEA) and the Centre for Educational Research and Innovation (CERI).

Shanghai Cooperation Organisation (SCO)

Secretariat : Beijing, People's Republic of China

Membership: China, Kazakhstan, Kyrgyzstan, Russia, Tajikistan and Uzbekistan

Origin: The SCO came into being as the Shanghai Five in 1996 when a Treaty establishing the grouping was signed in Shanghai, China, by China and four former Soviet Republics -

Kazakhstan, Kyrgyzstan, Russia and Tajikistan–to resolve border issues. The China-(erstwhile) Soviet frontier runs some 4,000 miles. Uzbekistan joined the grouping in 2000 as an observer member. In June 2001, the SCO was launched as the updated version of the Shanghai Five to combat Islamic terrorism and ensure regional security in Central Asia. Uzbekistan was automatically admitted to the SCO.

South Asian Association for Regional Cooperation (SAARC)

Headquarters : Kathmandu, Nepal.

Membership: Bangladesh, Bhutan, India, Maldives, Nepal, Pakistan, Sri Lanka and Afghanistan.

Origin: The Declaration on South Asian Regional Cooperation was adopted in 1983 and an Integrated Programme of Action (IPA) was launched. The Charter establishing SAARC was adopted at the first summit meeting in Dhaka in December 1985.

Objectives: The objectives of SAARC are–(i) to promote and strengthen collective self-reliance among members; (ii) to promote the welfare of the people of South Asia; (iii) to facilitate active collaboration and mutual assistance in the economic, social, cultural, technical and scientific fields; (iv) to strengthen cooperation with other developing countries, and among themselves through international forum on matters of common interest.

The 20th SAARC Summit is the 20th meeting of the heads of state of the eight SAARC countries after their previous meeting in Pakistan was boycotted by all SAARC members. The Summit will take place in 2018.

International Finance Corporation (IFC)

World Bank established IFC in July 1956. This corporation provides loan to private industries of developing nations without any government guarantee and also promotes the additional capital investment in these countries. Thus, the main work of IFC is to ensure the financial support to private sector in developing countries. In the end of March 2016, its membership was 184. On June 30, 2015 it was having total authorised capital of $ 2.58 billion.

Objectives :

1. To provide loans to private sector.

2. To co-ordinate capital and management.

3. To induce capitalist countries to invest in developing countries.

International Development Association (IDA)

IDA is an associate institution of World Bank known as soft loan window of World Bank. IDA was established on September 24, 1960. It kept its membership open to all members of World Bank. At present 173 countries are its member. IDA provides loan to its member countries and no interest is charged on these long-term loans. These soft loans are provided to the poor countries of the World. During 1995-96 (July-June) India ranked first among the nations getting assistance from IDA. Vietnam and China stood second and third respectively in this list. The resources of IDA include subscribed capital by member countries, general replenishments by developed countries, net income transferred by IBRD etc.

IDAs is administered by the same group which manages the working of World Bank.

Multilateral Investment Guarantee Agency

MIGA is a member of the World Bank Group. It came into existence on April 1988. Its mission is to promote Foreign Direct Investment (FDI) into developing countries to help support economic growth, reduce poverty and improve people's lives. MIGA's operational strategy plays to its foremost strength in the market place—attracting investors and private insurers into difficult operating environments. MIGA's strategies focus on insuring investments in the areas where it can make the greatest difference.

- Countries eligible for assistance from the International Development Association (the world's poorest countries).
- Conflict-affected environments.
- Complex deals in infrastructure and extractive industries, especially those involving project finance and environmental and social considerations.
- South-South investments (from one developing country to another).

MIGA offers comparative advantages in all of these areas – from its unique package of products and ability to restore the business community's confidence, to its ongoing collaboration with the public and private insurance market to increase the amount of insurance available to investors. As a multilateral development agency, MIGA only supports investments that are developmentally sound and meet high social and environmental standards. MIGA applies a comprehensive set of social and environmental performance standards to all projects and offers extensive expertise in working with investors to ensure compliance to these standards.

MIGA's membership is 181. Bhutan was the last member to join MIGA.

International Centre for Settlement of Investment Disputes

ICSID is an autonomous international institution established under the Convention on the Settlement of Investment Disputes between States and Nationals of Other States (the ICSID or the Washington Convention) with over one hundred and forty member States. The Convention sets forth ICSID's mandate, organization and core functions. The primary purpose of ICSID is to provide facilities for conciliation and arbitration of international investment disputes.

The ICSID Convention is a multilateral treaty formulated by the Executive Directors of the International Bank for Reconstruction and Development (the World Bank). It was opened for signature on March 18, 1965 and entered into force on October 14, 1966.

There are currently 159 signatory States to the ICSID Convention. Of these, 148 States have also deposited their instruments of ratification, acceptance or approval of the Convention. However, India is not a member of this organisation.

General Agreement on Tariffs and Trade (GATT)

During great depression of 1930s the international trade was badly affected and various countries imposed import restrictions for safe-guarding their economies. This resulted in a sharp decline in the world trade. In 1945, USA put forward many proposals for extending international trade and employment. On October 30, 1947, 23 countries at Geneva, signed an agreement related to tariffs imposed on trade. This agreement is known as General Agreement on Tariffs and Trade (GATT). It came into force on January 1, 1948. Initially GATT was established in the form of a temporary arrangement but later on it took the shape of a permanent agreement. GATT's headquarter was in Geneva.

On December 12, 1995, GATT was abolished and replaced by World Trade Organisation (WTO) which came into existence on January 1, 1995.

South Asian Free Trade Area (SAFTA)

At the 12th summit of the SAARC in Islamabad in January 2004, the member-countries signed the SAFTA agreement. Under the agreements, the developing countries within SAARC– or the less developed countries– will reduce their tariffs to

0-5 per cent in seven years from the date of entry into force of the agreement. The less developed countries (LDC) member-states will reduce their tariffs to 0-5 per cent in 10 years. The SAFTA accord came into force in July 2006.

Indian Ocean Rim Association for Regional Co-operation (IORARC)

The formal establishment of IORARC was declared on March 5, 1997 at Port Louis of Mauritius for promoting economic co-operation among the countries in coastal regions of Indian Ocean. India, South Africa and Australia had been making all efforts for this co-operation for the last 2 years. This association will work as a bridge between 3 continents—Asia, Africa and Australia.

The charter of this newly formed union was accepted unanimously by Foreign Ministers of 14 member nations in Port Louis Summit held on March 5-7, 1997. Pakistan tried its best to join this union but India and Mauritius proposed to postpone any further induction till the union becomes strong. It was accepted by the union. The charter of the union keeps the entry open for all the nations situated in the Rim area of Indian Ocean.

Membership : India, Australia, Malaysia, Indonesia, Sri Lanka, Singapore, Oman, Yaman, Tanzania, Kenya, Mozambique, Madagascar, South Africa and Mauritius.

www.ingramcontent.com/pod-product-compliance
Lightning Source LLC
Chambersburg PA
CBHW050741180726
48003CB00018B/73